Specters of Belonging

Studies in Subaltern Latina/o Politics
Series editors: Raymond Rocco, University of California, Los Angeles,
and Alfonso Gonzales, University of California, Riverside

The Fight for Time: Migrant Day Laborers and the Politics of Precarity
Paul Apostolidis

Specters of Belonging: The Political Life Cycle of Mexican Migrants
Adrián Félix

Specters of Belonging

The Political Life Cycle of Mexican Migrants

ADRIÁN FÉLIX

OXFORD
UNIVERSITY PRESS

OXFORD
UNIVERSITY PRESS

Oxford University Press is a department of the University of Oxford. It furthers
the University's objective of excellence in research, scholarship, and education
by publishing worldwide. Oxford is a registered trade mark of Oxford University
Press in the UK and certain other countries.

Published in the United States of America by Oxford University Press
198 Madison Avenue, New York, NY 10016, United States of America.

Library of Congress Cataloging-in-Publication Data
Names: Félix, Adrián, 1983– author.
Title: Specters of belonging : the political life cycle of Mexican migrants / Adrián Félix.
Description: New York, NY, United States of America : Oxford University Press, [2019] |
Series: Studies in subaltern Latina/o politics |
Includes bibliographical references and index.
Identifiers: LCCN 2018023202 (print) | LCCN 2018039044 (ebook) |
ISBN 9780190879389 (Updf) | ISBN 9780190879396 (Epub) |
ISBN 9780190879372 (pbk. : acid-free paper) | ISBN 9780190879365 (hardcover : acid-free paper)
Subjects: LCSH: Mexicans—United States—Politics and government. |
Mexican Americans—Politics and government. | Mexican Americans—Attitudes. |
Naturalization—United States. | Citizenship—United States. | Return migration—México |
United States—Emigration and immigration—Social aspects. |
México—Emigration and immigration—Social aspects.
Classification: LCC E184.M5 (ebook) | LCC E184.M5 F45 2019 (print) |
DDC 973/.046872—dc23
LC record available at https://lccn.loc.gov/2018023202

9 8 7 6 5 4 3 2 1

Paperback printed by Sheridan Books, Inc., United States of America
Hardback printed by Bridgeport National Bindery, Inc., United States of America

Con todo mi amor para mi mamá Lilia Domínguez y mi abuelita Isabel Martínez de Domínguez.
Mis matriarcas migrantes.

"Me han puesto cercas,
corrales y fronteras.
Y no hay alguna
que yo no haya brincado..."
                    -El Solitario

Contents

Foreword: Ghosts across Borders

Adrián Félix is what a young, emerging scholar should be. He knows that the best stories aren't found in esoteric academic papers or weekend conferences but in the streets, at community free-for-alls, within rallies, and dusty roads. His dives into the hoi polloi (or, as we Mexicans like to call them, *el pueblo*) unearth the anecdotes and data that journalists dream of, but which he uses as the fuel for theoretical frameworks out of Herbert Gans and Mario T. García. And Félix writes not in the ivory tower gobbledygook, which dooms too many fine tomes to dusty, ignored stacks, but in a language that can cross over to the mainstream—the opening pages of this book are alone worth the price of admission.

But, more importantly, *el compa* Adrián knows the power of food.

Félix and I come from the city he focuses on for this book: Jerez, Zacatecas. It turned out he and my sister were classmates as undergrads at UCLA, but I had no clue who he was until he introduced himself to me when I once lectured at USC, where he was finishing his doctorate. We hit it off quickly, not just because of our shared background, but also because he was as obsessed with the food of our homeland as I was.

Cheese so ripe that its smell could penetrate through concrete. Toasted pumpkin seeds. Vats of quince paste. Fervi, the best Mexican chocolate on the planet thanks to its judicious use of almonds. *Birria de res*—beef prepared goat stew-style. And tiny black seeds called *acualaistas* that come from a fist-sized black squash considered a weed across the Southwest United States and most of México—but snacked on by *jerezanos* as if we were riding the bench at a baseball game.

I always gave him money on his many visits to Jerez for this book so he could return with these treats. It allowed us a chance to catch up and talk about his research while we munched on lunch. But, more importantly, we were doing in our own little way what the subjects in *Specters of Belonging* tried to do on a macro-scale: rage, rage, against the dying of our *jerezano* light.

I KNOW THE stories, themes, conclusions, and theories examined in *Specters of Belonging* well, because I lived it all.

Around the 1990s, when I was a teen, I remember my uncles and their friends organizing *clubes sociales*—hometown associations. They held dances in labor halls across Southern California to raise funds and transform their villages from places with no potable water and maybe one telephone line into humble suburbs. The *pachangas* went on for about fifteen years, until the men and women who collected millions of dollars for their countrymen realized it was all a ruse. Money would improve a road, but it wouldn't save their villages from the eternal stasis of the Mexican elites.

So some brave ones decided to enter politics. The pioneer was Andrés Bermúdez, whose roots are in my mother's village of El Cargadero and who once courted one of my aunts. The architect was Lupe Gómez, whose tax service is right next to one of my favorite Mexican beer bars. Félix talks about both men in this book, and I covered many of their stories in my days as a reporter. But I always ultimately wondered: Why were these migrants helping a country that forced them to a foreign land? Why spend so much time and money on efforts whose fruits they would never truly enjoy because their life was now in the United States? And why couldn't the Mexican government treat these *hombres* as returning heroes instead of sketchy enemies?

In other words, why fight for a ghost?

I refuse to romanticize what too many academics and activists do. And that's why *Specters of Belonging* is so important. Félix remains remarkably clear-eyed about a subject and people in which he has an admitted vested interest. He details the Pyrrhic victories won by the likes of Bermúdez and Gómez. He literally sees the idea of Mexican transnationalism to the graves of *jerezanos* buried back in the motherland even as they died in a country where most ended up spending the majority of their lives.

And although he unfortunately doesn't indulge readers in the *comida* the two of us have shared over the years, Félix introduces a new meal to the diet of transnational studies: the political campaign trail. Instead of obsessing over culture like too many scholars do, he instead focuses on the bureaucratic, the realpolitik, the glad-handlers, and godfathers. This is a mestizo version of *The Making of the President 1968*, with an ending as unfortunate as that classic but with a glimmer of hope brought on by the pluck of immigrants who gambled it all yet kept their honor—and ultimately kept the light of the past alive for others to seek it.

Félix joins a long list of *Zacatecanos/as* in American letters: historian Matt Garcia (whose pioneering research into Southern California Mexican citrus workers gave them a face and story long neglected by academic and mainstream writers), novelist Helena Maria Viramontes, anthropologist Martha Menchaca, and legendary Chicano cartoonist Lalo Alcaraz, with myself as a pretender to their greatness. We all, in our own way, deal with the visage of a past we can never return to, but which we can't help but to keep alive. Félix takes it to the next step by capturing the efforts of our courageous, damned *paisanos*. It's an honor to write this foreword, and watch out for Félix as his ideas permeate immigrant literature in academia.

And Adrián? I think I need another wheel of cheese . . . but I'll settle for *asado de boda*.

Gustavo Arellano

Acknowledgments

Where does a migrant ghost belong? In many ways, this book is about restless phantoms and how these migrant specters haunt the projects of nationalism, democracy, citizenship, political membership, and belonging of the U.S. and Mexican states. By these restless ghosts I am referring, of course, to Mexican migrants and their specters of belonging across the transnational space spanning the México-U.S. borderlands. As such, there are many spirits that inhabit these pages. But before I pay my respect and profess my gratitude to the souls who have nurtured this project, I am going to call out some enemy names. To someone writing and teaching on the political root causes of Mexican migration over the last decade, Donald Trump embodies the principal nemesis, and his nefarious rise to power is an affirmation of everything I've said about the United States in relation to ethnic Mexicans and people of color and aggrieved communities more broadly (Asian, Arab, Muslim, Black, Indigenous, Queer, Gender Nonconforming . . .)—it is a settler colonial, white supremacist, antimigrant, xenophobic, hetero-patriarchal, racist, nativist nation-state predicated on imperial citizenship. On the other end of the double-edged blade of transnationalism, I would be remiss if I didn't call out México's elite political class, but I will save my full scorn for and disdain of their corrupt regime for later. For now, suffice it to say that for a first-generation son of formerly undocumented, working-class migrants with limited formal schooling to be writing the acknowledgments to this book from the "internal exile" of his ancestral rural hometown deep in the heart of north-central México (the quintessential "spectral village" that so inspired López Velarde over a century ago) is the most fitting and poetic repudiation of Trump and everything he represents. This book is devoted to Mexican migrants' political struggles, and their specters of belonging will transcend and outlive the imperial citizenship regime of the U.S. state and the clientelistic citizenship regime of the Mexican state that seek to co-opt, domesticate, and/or exclude them altogether on both sides of the border.

Now, allow me to show my love for the many Mexican migrants, comrades, and colleagues who have inspired and supported this project in one way or another. For a book that's all about roving specters of belonging, there is one enduring phantom that continues to haunt my thinking on Mexican migration: the looming ghost of Don Andrés Bermúdez Viramontes. From the moment of Don Andrés' wake, the Bermúdez extended household has lovingly made me part of the family. I've attended baptisms, birthdays, and burials with the Bermúdez family, honoring the different stages of the migrant political life cycle that frame the chapters of this book. *Gracias* to Andrés Jr. for opening his home to me and for making a tradition out of his annual trek to Santa Cruz to speak with my students about his father's transnational legacy. I hope to one day be able to write a definitive political biography of Don Andrés and the many contradictions of this larger-than-life figure who continues to bedevil my musings on Mexican migration.

In my time in Northern California, I have been fortunate to work with the transnational political activists of Proyecto Migrante *Zacatecano* (PMZ)—a cross-border organization that builds on the legacy of Bermúdez and others but has broken away from the clientelistic grip of the Mexican state and its subnational political institutions and party apparatuses. In Northern California and North Texas, I would like to thank the following *Zacatecano/ a* political activists (not all PMZ members): Juan Castro, Don Herminio Rodríguez, Andrés Quintero, Silvia Ramírez, and Sergio Ortega.

The *Zacatecano* imprint on this book is evident from beginning to end, including the foreword and the cover, for which I have to thank an ever-polemical pair of *paisanos*—the irrepressible journalist Gustavo Arellano and legendary political cartoonist Lalo Alcaraz. While I am much more of an agrarian communist than a "rancho libertarian," there is no question that those two have been, and will, continue to be important voices in the raging debates around race and migration in the United States.

In my time in Santa Cruz, I had the honor of working with the following community organizations, whose indigenous organic intellectuals and epistemologies helped influence a book on mestizo Mexican migrants: Senderos, the Santa Cruz County Day Worker Center, and MILPA of East Salinas. Also, much love to the participants and volunteers at my citizenship and political education class, which is now entirely run by students.

Now, on to my amazing mentors, colleagues, and students. As an undergraduate student at UCLA, I am fortunate to have met Zachariah Mampilly, who saw potential in a first-generation kid from the northeast San Fernando Valley and introduced me to key mentors who would put me on the activist research path. As the first person in my family to go to college, it's very likely I would have fallen through the cracks if it weren't for mentors like Zach, whose work on armed nonstate actors and third world social movements continues to inspire me. Much love, also, to my UCLA partners in crime— Romeo Guzmán, Miguel Sauceda, Alberto Pereda, and my *compadre* Andrés Haro—and a shout out to the *profe* Ray Rocco, who has trained generations of scholar activists.

Once in graduate school at USC, I had the best advisor a PhD student could ask for—Ricardo Ramírez. Ricardo not only allowed me to spread my intellectual wings beyond the methodological confines of Latino politics, he also went above and beyond by making sure I was well nourished— intellectually, spiritually, physically. Ricardo has become a role model and a lifelong personal friend. The rest of my mentors and committee members at USC were just as wonderful. They include Janelle Wong, Nora Hamilton, Pierrette Hondagneu-Sotelo, Carol Wise, Laurie Brand, and Apichai Shipper. Other scholars of borders, migration, memory, and displacement who were deeply influential include George Sánchez, Michael Dear, Josh Kun, Manuel Pastor, and Macarena Gómez-Barris. A very special shout out to Robin D. G. Kelley for the most transformative graduate seminar experience ever and for being such a remarkable scholar and human being.

I wouldn't have survived graduate school without the moral and intellectual support of fellow graduate students, many of whom have launched their own successful careers as academics and continue to inspire me. From my years at USC I want to thank Abigail Rosas, Ana Elizabeth Rosas, Gerardo Licón, Gustavo Licón, Lisa Ybarra, Denise González, Jillian Medeiros, Glenda Flores, Hernán Ramírez, Jerry González, Ed Flores, and Emir Estrada. A special *saludo* to the *compa* Alex Aviña, whose beautiful and powerful book inspired the title for this manuscript. As an early career, interdisciplinary scholar in political science, I wouldn't have survived the often-hostile field without the support and camaraderie of friends like Arely Zimmerman, Raul Moreno, Chris Zepeda, Osman Balkan, and George Ciccariello-Maher. From the political and migration sociology crowd, thanks to Matt Bakker, Rocio Rosales, Melissa Abad, Lorena Castro, and Danny Olmos. From anthropology, many thanks to the homie Héctor Beltrán.

I am also indebted to colleagues at the Universidad Autónoma de Zacatecas, especially Rodolfo García Zamora, for insightful conversations and useful materials on my multiple field research trips. Thanks also to local archivists Leonardo de la Torre y Berúmen and Nico Rodríguez for granting me access to vital primary sources and sharing their vast local knowledge of Jerez with me.

Straight out of grad school, I had two amazing post-doc mentors who continue to play supportive roles at different junctures in my career: Phil Williams at the University of Florida (UF) and Jonathan Fox at UC Santa Cruz (now at American University). UF was a great place for me to teach Latino politics/studies and turned out to be an unlikely site for my first apprenticeship in Marxism (*¡ahí estamos compa Beto!*). Jonathan Fox's vast knowledge of Mexican politics and migration never ceases to amaze me, and he always keeps me sharp with his impossible devil's advocate questions.

UC Santa Cruz's department of Latin American and Latino Studies (LALS) was the most amazing intellectual community a young scholar activist could call home and it feels bittersweet to offer this as my *despedida*. In the LALS family and beyond I want to thank Sylvanna Falcón, Shannon Gleeson, Pat Zavella, Cat Ramírez, Gabi Arredondo, Rosa-Linda Fregoso, Cecilia Rivas, Jessica Taft, Fernando Leiva, Patricia Pinho, and Peggy Estrada. A special thanks to Alessandra Alvares, LALS's undergrad advisor. I am going to miss you all! Beyond LALS I want to thank Norma Klahn, Felicity Amaya-Schaeffer, Marcia Ochoa, Olga Nájera-Ramírez, Juan Poblete, Mark Massoud, Kent Eaton, Verónica Terríquez, Steve McKay, Eric Porter, Grace Peña Delgado, Kristina Lyons, and Nick Mitchell. I also want to thank the following folks who I met as grad students/post-docs at UCSC, several of whom have now launched successful careers in academia and beyond: Tania Cruz Salazar, Xóchitl Chávez, Claudia López, Ruben Espinoza, Chava Contreras, and, especially, Alicia Romero, for offering me a home away from home in our memorable years in exile in San José.

Last but not least, I want to thank my undergraduate students at UCSC and beyond—too many to name here but special mention is in order for Adi Reséndez (for her ongoing work with Latin American artisan communities); Andrés Arias, Lili Romero, and Adriana Garcia (for accompanying me on different occasions to immigration court as I served as an expert witness); Miriam Campos (for carrying the torch of the citizenship class in Santa Cruz); Angel Álvarez (for being a trusted liaison with community organizations); Juan Quiñones (for being my entrée into local San José politics, even when I didn't want him to be!); Christy Sandoval (for her phenomenal work as choreographer/director at Teatro Campesino); Citlally Figueroa (for being such a gracious empress of all things East San José); and Jocelyn Aguirre (for sharing with me the intimate ruptures of Mexican migration in her personal and family life). It is for you and the future generations of students to come that I write. I look forward to the next phase of my career in the Department of Ethnic Studies at UC Riverside, where I get the honor of working with my *colega*, Alfonso Gonzales.

Throughout my career, I've had the financial support of several institutions and programs including the McNair Scholars Program, the American Political Science Association Minority Fellows Program, the Ford Foundation Predoctoral Fellowship Program, the UC President's Postdoctoral Fellowship Program, the Institute for Latino Studies Young Scholars Symposium at Notre Dame, and the Woodrow Wilson Early Career Enhancement Fellowship for Junior Faculty, among others. This last award allowed me to take a (much-needed) sabbatical in the Department of Ethnic Studies at Santa Clara University. I want to thank my colleagues Anna Sampaio, James Lai, Clarisa Pérez-Armendáriz, and Patrick Lopez-Aguado for my short but productive stay at SCU. During this award period, I had the honor of working with Alicia Schmidt Camacho. Alicia and Lisa García Bedolla are two of my greatest academic role models for their deep sense of community, solidarity, social justice, and family.

Speaking of *familia*, I want to end by thanking my closest friends, family, and loved ones. In my time in Santa Cruz/San José, a couple of *jalisciense/Zacatecano* families lovingly opened their homes to me: the González and Santillán-Castro clans. Of course, my greatest source of love, support, and inspiration is my immediate family. I thank my father Rosendo Félix—in many ways the quintessential *Zacatecano* migrant (for better and for worse!) who has worked incessantly since arriving to the United States in the late 1970s—for those nights when he was especially generous with his memories of life back in the *rancho*. I listened intently. I also want to thank my four brothers and their partners—Iván, Esteban, Jonathan, and Ernesto and my lovely *primas*, Diana, Jackie, Stephanie, and Mónica. I hope this book makes you proud, the way each one of you makes me proud in your own unique way. I can't wait to share this book with my *sobrinos/as*! Special thanks to my *tío* Carlos, for being a constant research companion in Zacatecas and for sharing his uniquely mad view of the world with me.

I have always been *bendito entre las mujeres* and, as such, the greatest source of moral and spiritual support has been the women in my family—my migrant matriarchs—the loving legion of *tías* (my *tía* Lupe, Chela, and Toña especially), *abuelita* (my sweet *abue* Chabela), and above all, my dear mother, Lilia. Upon migrating to the United States, my loving mother selflessly endured countless sacrifices with the interest of her children always in mind. *La amo con todo mi corazón mamá y le dedico esta obra con todo mi cariño.*

Last, I thank Claudia Judith González and her family—my eternal *mestiza* muse.

Adrián Félix
Jerez, Zacatecas
January 1, 2018

Specters of Belonging

1

Introduction

THE POLITICAL LIFE CYCLE OF
MEXICAN MIGRANTS

The Thickening of Transnational Citizenship

It was the closing day of Guadalupe Gómez's campaign for a seat in México's federal congress in the midterm elections of summer 2009. A longtime resident of Orange County, California, Gómez was the only contender to run as a "migrant candidate," doing so with the right-wing Partido Acción Nacional (National Action Party, or PAN) in his home state of Zacatecas. Like Gómez, I traveled from Southern California to Zacatecas to shadow the migrant-turned-politician as he took to the campaign trail. It had been an intense summer of campaigning in the migrant-sending *municipios* of Zacatecas and its remote *ranchos* (villages)—the state that, like the candidate, my parents had left for the United States in search of work decades earlier.[1] On the final day of the campaign, I traveled to the charming municipality of Genaro Codina to attend Gómez's last speech before driving back two hours to the district seat for the official closing rally that evening.[2] As Gómez delivered his speech and subsequently shook hands and listened to the grievances of the gathered crowd—mostly local *campesinos* who supplement their livelihood with remittances from relatives in the United States—I reached over to the candidate with the familiarity of a campaign operative and uttered that I would get a head start back to the district seat to await his final rally later that night. By that point, I had become such a fixture at Gómez's campaign

All personal names in this study were changed for purposes of anonymity except in the case of political officials and activists who consented to being interviewed for this project.

events that he began publicly acknowledging the presence of a "U.S. academic" in his speeches.[3]

I took to the road with the sense of satisfaction that came on the closing day of what turned out to be a competitive campaign for the migrant candidate. Little did I know that further up the highway, I would find myself, quite literally, in the wrong place, at the wrong time. Unbeknownst to me, as we wrapped up Gómez's closing campaign event, a gun battle had unfolded between members of the Mexican military and cartel henchmen in a community not far from Genaro Codina. As luck would have it, I approached that community precisely as one of the cartel gunmen was trying to make an escape. I slowed my vehicle as I neared the speed bumps, the only barrier that allows local villagers to cross the narrow two-lane highway. A man stood by the side of the road and slowly began to cross. I made nothing of it at first, until the man stopped in the middle of the lane, reached for his waistband, pulled out a handgun, assumed the shooting position and aimed directly at me, unflinchingly. As my truck was coming to a halt (with nowhere to turn), I realized that the gunman was in urgent need of a getaway vehicle, his face covered in blood. Well aware of the modus operandi of these roving armed bands, my immediate reaction was to not surrender my vehicle and instead swerve out of his line of fire and speed away, hoping for the best. I put my truck in gear, turned the wheel and ducked, expecting to hear the blast from the gun and glass shattering as I sped past him, flying over the speed bumps. Yet, there was nothing. As I looked up and into the rearview mirror, adrenaline rushing through my body, I realized that the subject was out of ammunition, effectively having emptied his rounds in the gun battle with the soldiers. My immediate thought was of the candidate who was coming up the highway. For a split second, I considered turning around and confronting the injured suspect. Seeing a Federal Police patrol car racing down the highway, instead I continued driving, phoning Gómez directly to alert him of the scene up the road.

What exactly were Gómez and I—two residents of Southern California—doing in rural México in the midst of a raging "Drug War"?[4] To the cynics, Gómez was there for the spoils of office and I, the "academic," was there to document and "study" Mexican migrants' incursion into the increasingly troubled politics of their homeland. Yet, despite some political and ideological differences between the two of us (I am no PANista), I believe that Gómez and I were there for the same reason. As Gómez put it on a separate occasion, we were both there because *"tenemos nuestro corazón allá"* (we left our heart over there). Indeed, Gómez's—and to some degree my own—return was akin to our (post)revolutionary poet Ramón López Velarde's fateful arrival to a "subverted Eden," a "spectral village" ensnared in violence where the "prodigal son" found his "hope shattered" but not defeated.[5] It was our deliberate diasporic return to the homeland's "maize-covered surface" and its "mutilated territory," to cite López Velarde's more celebrated post-revolutionary poetics.[6]

Over the course of the last thirty years, Lupe Gómez has lived, established and operated a successful business, and raised a family in Orange County, California.[7] He is a naturalized U.S. citizen and a registered Democrat. As a successful business owner, Gómez says he has the "mind of a Republican" when it comes to cutting taxes but is a "Democrat at heart," because of his commitment to social justice and the welfare state. This degree of migrant social, economic, and political "integration" in the United States notwithstanding, Gómez has clearly maintained strong ties with his community and country of origin. Notably, Lupe Gómez has been an active leader in California-based Mexican hometown associations (HTAs) from the state of Zacatecas. He's a past president of the famed Federación de Clubes *Zacatecanos* del Sur de California.[8] Despite the risks, and his full-time obligations in Orange County, Gómez was the only person to run for a single-member-district seat in México's 2009 congressional elections as a U.S.-based "migrant candidate," an option that has been made available to *paisanos* since the early 2000s (see chapter 3 for a full discussion). Nearly ten years after his initial bid for office, Gómez was recruited as a proportional representation candidate for México's federal congress in the 2018 election cycle, this time by Movimiento Ciudadano. In short, Lupe Gómez is a paradigmatic example of the *thickening of transnational citizenship*—the political process by which Mexican migrants simultaneously cultivate cross-border citizenship claims in México and the United States over the course of their "civic lives" (see Wals 2010).[9] To borrow from Levitt's classic ethnography, "The more diverse and thick a transnational social field is, the more numerous the ways it offers migrants to remain active in their homelands" and in the United States (2001: 9).

As the U.S. state has "thickened" its border with México over the last decades (see Andreas 2009), escalating the racialized policing of migrant bodies, so too have Mexican migrants "thickened" their cross-border claims of transnational political membership and belonging (Smith and Bakker 2008).[10] Since September 11, 2001, the "homeland security state" has deepened its migration-control apparatus in Latino communities throughout the United States (Gonzales 2013) in a process akin to what political geographers have called "internal bordering" (see Dear 2013).[11] As De Genova puts it, "in the everyday life of Mexican migrants in innumerable places throughout the US, 'illegality' reproduces the practical repercussions of the physical border between the US and México" (2004: 161). While the "borderlands condition no longer necessarily remains geographically fixed" states Gilberto Rosas, the "thickening of the borderlands condition" opens up "new political imaginaries" in the form of "the transnational articulation" of migrant struggles and subjectivities (2006: 344; see also Schmidt Camacho on these "migrant imaginaries" whereby migrants "create new imaginative worlds out of their trajectories of loss and displacement," 2008: 6). Indeed, Marxian anthropologists noted the thickening of Mexican migrant civil society as a condition of the restructuring of global capitalism early on. "Just as capitalists have responded to the new forms of economic internationalism by establishing transnational corporations, so workers have responded by creating transnational circuits" wrote Roger Rouse about the migrant network spanning Aguililla, Michoacán, and Redwood City, California, in the early 1990s (1991: 14).[12] Migrants' experiences of discrimination in the United States, as "proletarian servants in the paragon of 'postindustrial' society" (Rouse 1991: 12), reinforce transnational connections to their communities of origin. As Levitt reminds us in her cross-border Dominican case study, experiences of racial exclusion in the United States reinforced migrants' transnational attachments. Migrants "wanted to continue to belong" to their hometown, "because they realized they would never be allowed to achieve full membership in the United States. Enduring sending-community membership was like an insurance policy that guaranteed belonging in" a place they could call home (Levitt 2001: 111).

In the context of research on the "thickening" of borders, this book raises the concomitant question: How does transnational citizenship thicken across the political life cycle of Mexican migrants? In addressing this question, this book attempts to do what any good Mexican migration *corrido* does—narrate the thickening of transnational citizenship from beginning, middle, to end.[13] Specifically, it traces Mexican migrant transnationalism across the span of the migrant political life cycle, beginning with the "political baptism" (i.e., naturalization in the United States) and ending with repatriation to México after death. Even among Mexican migrants who have become permanently and politically engaged in the United States, cross-border connections to their country of origin live on, indicative of migrants' transnational potential to impact citizenship and democracy in both countries.[14] To be clear, this introduction is not an attempt to provide a "theory" chapter dictating the narrative flow of the thickening of transnational citizenship that animates the rest of this book. Rather, "cascading" throughout each chapter are ethnographic accounts of transnationalism across the various "step changes" of the migrant political life cycle.[15] Crucially, as a "political ethnography of transnational citizenship" (Smith and Bakker 2008), this book also critically reflects on my ethnographic accompaniment of Mexican migrants as they interface with state power on both sides of the border and contend with both states' restrictive membership regimes and their "internal boundaries of differential citizenship" (see Cabrera 2010: 73).

"*Él es Adrián, nos va a estudiar*": On Methods and Mexican Migration

El Día del Nochistlense (the Day of the Nochistlense Migrant)—a day to commemorate the cross-border lives of migrants from Nochistlán, Zacatecas, in Southern California—had become a full-blown multiday annual celebration. After a family-friendly gathering at Whittier Narrows Park, which brought out everyone from migration researchers of the University of Zacatecas to Labor Party opposition candidates for the mayoralty of Nochistlán, it was time to really get the party started. We relocated to the iconic Rancho El Farallón, where *nochistlenses* celebrate *charreadas* (Mexican rodeos) and, on this year, a *baile* (dance) with a *banda* from my hometown, La Chacaloza de Jerez, which would surely blast my favorite *ranchera* ballads and *corridos*.[16] Upon arriving at the familiar venue, a place where I had attended many *coleaderos* with my *charro* friends and family, I saw the usual suspects congregated in the unpaved parking lot. Lupe Gómez pulled up in his unmistakable BMW, and Efraín Jiménez, one of the prominent migrant leaders from Nochistlán who has gained some notoriety in the world of Mexican transnational organizing, arrived immediately after (see Burgess 2016 for a study on the work of these cross-border activists). Efraín, always on some new transnational venture, was promoting the Zacatecas-produced *mezcal* Don Antonio Aguilar and was pouring it generously among the group of several men gathered at the entrance to the *lienzo charro* (rodeo arena). Lupe and Efraín knew me and my academic pursuits well by this point, but the other *paisanos* had not met me, so Efraín proceeded to introduce me with that uniquely Mexican mix of menacing mockery: "*él es Adrián, nos va a estudiar*." "This is Adrián, he is going to study us," said Efraín with a wide grin and a chuckle. For the remainder of the night, Efraín humored himself by introducing me in this way. As the *mezcal* continued to flow, the mockery intensified. My introduction line became: "*Él es Adrián, nos va a estudiar pero al último lo vamos a estudiar a él*." "This is Adrián, he is going to study us" Efraín sarcastically repeated, "but in the end we are going to study him."

The teasing about the contradictions of my identity and positionality as the son of Mexican migrants turned "academic researcher" was well taken. After all, I—the son of Zacatecas migrants—was one of them (albeit with the privileges of being born into U.S. [imperial] citizenship). The mere thought that I was seeking to "study" Mexican migrants was laughable in their eyes, insofar as there was no degree of separation between "researcher" and "subjects" in terms of identity politics or our involvement in the migrant struggle. Any attempt at a political ethnography of migration would necessarily be an auto-ethnography, or, perhaps more accurately, it is what Anzaldúa called "autohistoria"—a "genre of writing about one's personal and collective history" (1987).[17] That Efraín inverted the epistemic power dynamic between ethnographer and interlocutor by saying that "my subjects" would study me was a reminder that these *Zacatecano* migrants would hold me and "my research" accountable. There was no better lesson of this activist-academic accountability than when I relocated to Northern California for what would become my first academic job as an assistant professor of Latin American and Latina/o Studies at UC Santa Cruz. In my effort to expand this study, I knew I had to reach out to *Zacatecano* migrant activists in Northern California to add another "case" to my book. Up to that point, most of my work had been with transnational migrant leaders based in greater Los Angeles, but I knew there was a cadre of *Zacatecano* cross-border organizers in San José, California. My plan was to reach out to these *paisanos*, with my newly acquired UC Santa Cruz credentials, and ask if I could interview them about their cross-border activism and organizations for my manuscript. Before I could do this, however, Juan Castro, a longtime San José-based *Zacatecano* activist, reached out to enlist me as part of their fledgling cross-border organization Proyecto Migrante *Zacatecano* (PMZ)—a breakaway offshoot of the migrant, hometown federations that was highly critical of these associations for being politically loyal to the government in our home state. Before I knew it, I was helping organize PMZ's second annual convention in Phoenix, Arizona, where I aided them in booking the keynote speaker. Before I could "interview" these migrant leaders, I had been anointed as a member of Proyecto Migrante's political committee and was collaboratively crafting some of the organization's founding documents, including the following transnational treatise.

Diasporic Direct Democracy: A Mexican Migrant Manifesto

Collaboratively crafting a cross-border "Mexican Migrant Manifesto" required these migrants to conjure their collective historical memory and reassert their transnational political subjectivity. "Both in the economic and political life of México," the manifesto proclaims, "migrants have been a centripetal force: a source of political change that revolves and comes from the outside in."[18] The document recalls the transnational travails of Mexican migrants and the cross-border character of Mexican politics at major turning points since the nineteenth century. In the 1860s, exiled President Benito Juárez found support among *Mexicanos* and the Juárez clubs they formed in the United States (FitzGerald 2010; see also Acuña 2008; Paredes 1958). In the lead up to the Mexican Revolution, the Flores Magón brothers organized Mexican migrant workers and continued to launch their campaign against dictator Porfirio Díaz while living in exile in the United States.[19] In the 1920s, Mexican presidential hopeful José Vasconcelos—the architect of the "cosmic race" national mythology—campaigned in Mexican communities in Chicago (Arredondo 2008). In the following decades, Mexican unionists in Texas were engaged in cross-border labor organizing with the Confederación de Trabajadores Mexicanos (CTM) (Schmidt Camacho 2008: 123). By the mid-twentieth century, Octavio Paz would immortalize his reflections on his time living in the United States and his return to "internal exile" back in México (Paz 1997; for a critical reading of Paz see De Genova 2008). In the political aftermath of the 1988 presidential election, Mexican migrants in the United States protested against electoral fraud outside Mexican consulates evincing an incipient cross-border *cardenismo* (Smith and Bakker 2008; Délano 2011). Today, Mexican migrants continue to engage in the politics of their communities of origin via their hometown associations (Bada 2014) and through a wide array of social movements and the building of an antisystem political party in Morena (Movimiento Regeneración Nacional).

The lives of the migrants who penned this manifesto offer a window into the political process that this book seeks to trace: the thickening of transnational citizenship in the context of antimigrant politics and an increasingly militarized North America (see Gonzales 2016). In the United States, these *Zacatecano* migrants are "electorally armed" naturalized U.S. citizens (see Zepeda-Millán 2017: 17); they are active participants in local politics, and they are involved in their children's schools.[20] On the Mexican side, they have leveled a scathing critique of the corruption, control, and cartelization that characterizes Mexican political parties and their clientelistic approach to migrants in the United States. In their manifesto, they call on their *paisanos* to be actively engaged not only in the United States but also in the politics of their home state. "Once again *Zacatecano* migrants will prove to be the vanguard in the representation of our people, both in Zacatecas and in the United States," the manifesto emphatically concludes.[21] This book is devoted to ethnographically tracing the simultaneous cross-border political ties that Mexican migrants cultivate across the span of their civic lives, from the "political baptism" to repatriation to México after death.[22] To foreshadow the narrative arc and structuring metaphor of the book, below I provide ethnographic episodes of the thickening of transnational citizenship across the different stages of the migrant political life cycle—from beginning, middle, to end.[23] But first, a brief reflection on the comparative implications of the central argument of this book for global migration and diaspora studies is in order. Throughout the book, I deploy the concept of *diasporic dialectics*—the iterative process by which migrants are in constant political struggle and negotiation with the state and its institutions of citizenship on both sides of the border, a dynamic not unique to the Mexican diaspora.[24]

Diasporic Dialectics: Transnational Citizenship as a Double-edged Political Weapon

Migrants throughout the world engage in what the late Benedict Anderson dubbed "long-distance nationalism" (1998) across a variety of regime types and in support of varying transnational social movements, all with their own unique diasporic dialectics. Borrowing from political theorist George Ciccariello-Maher, dialectics are "the dynamic movement of conflictive oppositions" and can constitute decolonial (revolutionary) and/or conservative (reactionary) power relations (2017: 2).[25] During the 1970s and 1980s, for example, revolutionaries in the Central American diaspora in the United States launched a transnational social movement in support of radical insurrections in their home countries, managing to curb U.S. coercion toward the region (see García Bedolla 2009). As Waldinger states, migrants have pursued "regime-changing nationalism, trying to replace the old regime, whether from left to right, as with the anticommunist Cuban exiles in Miami, or from right to left, as with Salvadorans who flocked to the United States in the 1970s and 1980s" (2015: 52). Elsewhere, members of the Tamil diaspora in the United States and beyond provided financial support for the Liberation Tigers of Tamil Eelam, drawing on proceeds from businesses in the ethnic economy in the host country (Mampilly 2011). As Apichai Shipper documents, North

Koreans in Japan operated as informants for the home regime and, in some cases, engaged in acts of violence in the host society (Shipper 2008). While not all diasporic politics are as contentious, these and other cases remind us to critically question presumptively normative processes of migrant "integration" into host societies and diasporic "incorporation" into the home country.

With regard to Latin American migration to the United States, Gonzales reminds us that Latino migrants are not clamoring for "integration" into U.S. imperial citizenship. One indigenous Mexican woman cited in his study memorably stated: "We don't want [citizenship] papers if they are stained with blood!" (2013: 142). Rogers reminds us that the so-called "political baptism" of English-speaking Afro-Caribbean migrants leaves open questions of whether they will be racialized as Latinos, African Americans, or pursue their "exit" option back to their home countries (2006). When it comes to diasporic "incorporation" into the home state, just as transnationally engaged Mexican migrants can be brought back into the clientelistic embrace of the Mexican state, Haitian migrants have been ensnared within the transnational tentacles of the Haitian state at different points in time, which has sought to implement the "transnational model into its practice of governmentality" (Laguerre 1999: 641). Beyond the Américas, when it comes to the end of the migrant political life cycle, Osman Balkan argues that for Muslim migrants in Europe, repatriation for burial after death serves as a powerful means to assert political belonging in the context of diaspora (2015a). Lastly, Sohail Daulatzai documents how the Black and Muslim diasporas have historically built communities of belonging in and across national and imperial spaces (2012). Drawing on the legacy of Malcolm X, Daulatzai reminds us of the urgent task of drawing connections "between domestic struggles for racial justice and . . . challenges to U.S. militarism and imperial power" abroad (2012: 193) and of the imperative need for migrants to resist "the domestication of their politics within a national framework" (2012: 194).

In the cultural and historical specificity of the Mexican case, I argue that Mexican migrants must resist "integration" into imperial citizenship in the United States and "incorporation" into clientelistic citizenship in México. In her critique of "Americanization" and assimilation, Alicia Schmidt Camacho helps us understand the two faces of U.S. imperial citizenship, which historically has "reinforced white supremacy in the domestic United States and furthered U.S. political hegemony through the Americas" and the world (2008: 39). Schmidt Camacho also warns about the danger of "domestication," which she sees not only as demarcating a "territorial boundary between the interior space occupied by citizens and the exterior domain of the foreign" but fundamentally as "the domestication of the transnational [migrant] class struggle" (2008: 121). "Immigrant rights activists go even further," writes Chris Zepeda-Millán, "contending that America's current 'incorporation' of foreign-born people of color should be understood as a system of 'immigrant apartheid'" (quoted in Zepeda-Millán 2017: 209). Indeed, even for Mexican migrants who have obtained citizenship rights in both countries, theirs is an "exclusionary inclusion" marked by "racialized alterity" or othering (Rocco 2014), with subalternity casting its long shadow over the arch of their political lives (Zepeda-Millán refers to "electorally armed" migrant citizens as political "brokers" for the undocumented, 2017). Yet, as this book shows, these migrants—with their iterative "dialectical motion"—continue to evince their "transcendent desires" from the margins of both citizenship regimes (Ciccariello-Maher 2017: 115). As Schmidt Camacho puts it, "The fortunes of Greater México . . . continue to depend on the ephemeral movements of migrant subaltern classes" (2008: 56). To understand the political potentialities and pitfalls of these diasporic dialectics in the Mexican case, I turn to how transnational citizenship is enunciated, enacted, and embodied across the different stages of the political life cycle of Mexican migrants with the following ethnographic episodes that will anchor the remaining chapters of the book.

Becoming a (Transnational) Citizen: The "Political Baptism" of Mexican Migrants

Antonio García, a migrant from Los Altos de Jalisco, is a *taquería* owner in Santa Cruz, California, and he is full of stories of anti-Mexican racism.[26] His fellow *taqueros* in nearby Felton have it slightly worse he says: they *regularly* endure racial slurs when walking down the streets. "You fucking Mexicans," they are told by some local whites, Antonio shared with me on a drive through the Santa Cruz Mountains. But mostly, white people in this area have come to love their food.[27]

Despite serving his "apprenticeship" in "illegality" (De Genova 2004: 174), I first met Antonio in a free citizenship class I taught for migrants at a local school in Santa Cruz, offered through the Mexican consulate-sponsored Plaza Comunitaria adult education program (see Délano 2010). He was a law-abiding, legal, permanent resident of the United States, and a proud *jalisciense*, who studied religiously for his naturalization exam, the first phase in the migrant political life cycle insofar as this is migrants' first direct encounter with the U.S. state script of singular political loyalties. However, his reasons for naturalizing had everything to do with racial politics and the exclusionary side of U.S. citizenship.[28] As Antonio told one of my undergraduate student volunteers and I during a focus group interview with the class, his reason for naturalizing was "because I no longer want to be a voice in the shadows."[29]

Like most Mexican migrants I have worked with in citizenship classrooms and workshops from California to Florida, Antonio's mythology of naturalization was infused by stories of fellow *paisanos* who have experienced the interview process. In particular, he had a staunch belief that *"paisa"* (as he refers to fellow Mexicans and Latinos) and Asian immigration officers who deliver the exam were the hardest. The bureaucratic arbitrariness and institutional inconsistency of the citizenship process notwithstanding, Antonio was ready for his naturalization interview, with complete command of the 100 civics questions and the working conversational English of a *taquero* from Jalisco.[30]

Thus we set out "over the hill" for his much anticipated citizenship exam at the U.S. Citizenship and Immigration Services (USCIS) regional office in San José. Antonio was well dressed for the occasion, the way he does for Catholic Mass every Sunday, and calmly took some last-minute civics coaching from me, as he reminisced about his circuitous journey as a migrant in this country at this momentous occasion in his civic life. We arrived to a busy but orderly waiting room, where migrants from México, Central America, India, and Ethiopia awaited their turn with a U.S. immigration official. We sat next to a group of Latina women who listened intently every time an officer emerged into the waiting room calling out a name. "Guadalupe Treviño," a disembodied voice called and the women instantly sat up in their seats and cheered on the soon to be U.S. citizen. Shortly thereafter, "An-tooonio Garcia" a male immigration officer called out and escorted Antonio into the entrails of the immigration bureaucracy. Sure enough, the officer was Asian.

Left eagerly waiting, I turned to the woman next to me and asked if she was related to Ms. Treviño. *"Es mi amiga"* (she is my friend), the woman from Nicaragua replied and then asked about my relationship to Antonio. I explained that I was his citizenship class instructor, and she blessed me saying: *"Es un don que Dios le ha dado de ayudar a la gente"* (It's a God-given gift of mine to help my people). Only a few minutes later, an unassuming Antonio emerged, fighting back a grin. I immediately stood and asked how it went. *"Todo bien"* Antonio replied, "all is good," as he shook my hand firmly, breaking out into a big smile. The woman next to me enthusiastically congratulated him as well.

It turned out that the immigration officer recognized Antonio from the *taquería* he previously owned in San José, Taquería Chapala. Antonio had named it after the iconic lake in Jalisco state where he used to fish as a child. The immigration officer was a regular at Chapala and was sad to see the business close when they relocated to Santa Cruz. Oh, how he missed their *burritos de lengua*. As Antonio briefly retold his interview to me, another working-class *paisano* anxiously walked over from one side of the waiting room and asked, "*¿Verdad que no es muy difícil oiga? Es que mi esposa está nerviosa*" (It isn't that hard is it?), looking for some added reassurance for his wife who was waiting for her turn at the citizenship interview. "*No, dígale que no se ponga nerviosa y todo va estar bien.*" Antonio advised to not allow her nerves to get the better of her, and she would do just fine. Then Guadalupe Treviño emerged from her citizenship exam, also glowing, to many congratulatory hugs from her friends and family. Guadalupe, Antonio, and other successful migrants waited to receive the date for their citizenship ceremony, where their naturalization would become official.

The soon to be U.S. citizens were handed a government form with the place and time for their citizenship ceremony and a list of questions that they were to fill out on the day of. Consistent with the "securitization of citizenship" (De Genova 2007; Sampaio 2015), among the questions were if they had committed any crime between the time of their citizenship interview and their ceremony; whether they had joined the Communist Party; and whether their willingness to bear allegiance to the U.S. had changed. On the day of the ceremony, I picked up Antonio from his *taquería*, took him home where he quickly changed into his Sunday best, and we trekked over the hill once again to his much-awaited citizenship ceremony. We arrived at the venue, where some of the migrants we encountered at the USCIS field office, looking much more relaxed, were being ushered into lines by some of the same immigration officers. I took my place in the guest line and told Antonio I would see him inside. As I took my seat, I once again was struck by the diversity of migrants and their families and supporters: Mexican, Filipino, and Indian migrants all eagerly awaiting the ceremony. The Mexican family sitting in front of me planned a house party in the East Bay with live *norteña* music. Antonio would later tell me that the newly naturalized sitting behind him were from Tepatitlán, Jalisco, the municipal seat nearby his hometown. "So-and-so is in Tepa," he overheard them say as they navigated Facebook on their smartphones before the ceremony started.

The citizenship ceremony began with a presentation by the Santa Clara County Registrar of Voters office in several languages including Vietnamese, Chinese, and Spanish.[31] The immigration officer facilitating the ceremony then explained that he would go through an alphabetical roll call of countries, asking migrants to stand and remain standing when their home nation was called out. This being Silicon Valley, among the 400-plus migrants being naturalized that day there were notable contingents from China and India as the roll call started. When the officer called out México, a roaring cheer came from the crowd, starting a trend emulated by several of the remaining Latin American and Asian countries, with notable cheers coming from Filipino and Vietnamese attendees.

When the rest of the political formalities were over, which can be understood as the "legal rituals of American nationalism" (Kun 2005: 7) meant to "infuse patriotism and nationalism into the ceremony" (Plascencia 2012: 170), Antonio was ready to celebrate. For this momentous occasion, the so-called "political baptism" of migrants in the United States (see Rogers 2006) where they are presumably imbued with the U.S. civic creed (Plascencia 2012), Antonio knew just the right place to celebrate: a nearby *taquería* in Campbell. We arrived at the hole-in-the-wall in the *paisa*, barrio part of town, where Antonio's first cousin was working the kitchen, grilling seasoned and spiced meats on the *plancha*. We ordered our share of *al pastor* and *asada* tacos, and he had a Mexican soda to cool down on this warm San José summer afternoon. A painting of a quaint Mexican plaza hung from the wall immediately next to where Antonio sat; the same one that adorns several of the *taquerías* in Santa Cruz. I asked Antonio if that was his hometown, a place he visits several times a year. "Yes," he nodded, beaming with pride. I couldn't think of a better way to celebrate Antonio's initiation into transnational citizenship.

The Consummation of Transnational Citizenship: The Civic Binationality of Juan Castro

If naturalization is the first stage of the migrant political life cycle, the "political baptism" of Mexican migrants, it is important to examine what transnational citizenship looks like within the orbit of the Mexican state and analyze diasporic dialectics and the danger of domestication in the context of its clientelistic embrace. Juan Castro, a San José-based migrant from Zacatecas who we met earlier, is an ideal embodiment of this political duality. On a trip to the state capitol in Sacramento in February 2014, Juan and I witnessed the swearing in of California's first undocumented attorney, Sergio García. The son of migrant *campesinos* from the Mexican state of Michoacán, Sergio successfully passed his bar examination despite the hardships of growing up undocumented in California. Needless to say, his historic swearing in ceremony was a momentous occasion, backed, of course, by a *mariachi.* "This is the stuff of migrant leaders," said Juan, of the young man who is professionally trained and has strong roots in the community, at an event that drew media, activists, friends and family, but where Latino state legislators were notably absent.

Sometime later, upon learning about Governor Jerry Brown's nomination of the México-born Stanford Law Professor Mariano Florentino Cuéllar to the California Supreme Court, Juan sent a congratulatory e-mail to a group of *Zacatecano* migrant leaders in California, Texas, and Nevada. "This is what Mexican migrants and their children in the U.S. should aspire to," wrote Juan of Cuéllar's notable transnational trajectory, not the "cross-border cronyism of those who trip over themselves for a photo with the corrupt politicians of our home state." The latter was one of Juan's usual jabs at *Zacatecano* leaders from migrant hometown associations in the United States who he sees as coopted by Mexican political parties and elites.[32]

A longtime resident of Northern California, Juan likes to introduce himself by saying that he was "*criado en Zacatecas y malcriado en California*" (raised in Zacatecas and spoiled in California). I've seen him use this line when addressing visiting politicos from México in California as an admonition to them that he will not be treated as a second-class citizen, with the usual clientelism and political paternalism with which Mexican parties and elites treat their *paisanos* at home and abroad. Juan's critical migrant subjectivity partly stems from his political experience living for thirty years in San José. Arriving at a young age, Juan graduated from high school, attended community college, and transferred to San José State University. While he has remained transnationally engaged in the political affairs of his home state and country—he was co-founder of El Congreso del Pueblo, is an active member of Proyecto Migrante *Zacatecano*, and was an adviser to the Institute of Mexicans Abroad—he has also been remarkably active in California local and state politics.[33] Not only has he worked in public administration for over two decades in Northern California, he has also served as a political strategist for candidates of mayoral and County Board of Supervisor positions in Santa Clara County. His civic volunteerism in the Latino community in San José has ranged from tutoring at a local community college to voter registration drives to participating in the planning of the unprecedented migrant rights marches of 2006.[34] Most recently, Juan joined me in campaign precinct walking for a young *Zacatecano* running for California State Assembly on the eastside of San José, single-handedly taking on the task of mobilizing migrant voters at local churches. Juan has also held U.S. and Mexican elected and appointed officials accountable. In the mid-2000s, he was part of back-to-back campaigns to remove a San José City Council member and the consul general at the Mexican consulate in the same city.

Juan's cynicism toward the Mexican government has not deterred him from attempting to fully exercise his transnational citizenship (in fact, these diasporic dialectics propel cross-border activists like Juan). In the 2013 elections to renew the Zacatecas state congress, with myself as part-time political consultant, Juan decided to vie for a party nomination for a "migrant deputy" seat in the state legislature. In Zacatecas' mixed-member political system, the two parties taking the largest share of votes in the election must advance a migrant deputy as part of their proportional representation seats, in order to meet the state's mandatory migrant quota (see Smith and Bakker 2008).[35] However, each political party has complete control over its internal migrant-candidate selection process. Knowing full well that they would be shut out by the ruling PRI—which has close corporatist ties with U.S.-based migrants loyal to the party—Juan and another *Zacatecano* migrant from Texas pursued their candidacies with the PAN and PRD, respectively. In the internal PAN elections, Juan was up against two nominally migrant candidates, who were clearly the inside favorites over the bona fide transnational citizen. One was a young, middle-class *Zacatecana* who had studied in New York and presumably was therefore a migrant. The other was a career PAN politician in Zacatecas who holds a U.S. visa and does little more than visit family in the United States from time to time. As coordinator of the political affairs committee of Proyecto Migrante *Zacatecano*, which officially endorsed Juan's candidacy, I wrote a letter to the PAN state leaders denouncing their "token transnationalism" and the "utter usurpation" of the migrant deputy category and called on the party to democratize their internal migrant-candidate selection process. After all, this was an egregious affront to the political subjectivity that *Zacatecano* migrants had fought so hard to enshrine in their home-state's constitution.[36] As Juan later put it in an e-mail to Mexican federal congressional representatives before they voted on a series of electoral reforms, the legal personhood of migrants was established to secure representation by bona fide U.S.-based migrant transnational citizens, not to reward elite politicians who hold U.S. tourist visas. While this chapter will trace the ongoing struggles of migrant leaders for full cross-border political membership and belonging (i.e., diasporic dialectics), it also highlights the challenges, contradictions, and limitations of transnational citizenship within a clientelistic citizenship regime.[37]

Transnational (After)life: The Political Last
Rites of Transnational Citizens

If these returned migrant politicians embody transnational citizenship to its fullest extent (with all of its contradictions), allow us to turn to the final stage of the migrant political life cycle with what is perhaps the ultimate testament of this transnationality: the cross-border practice of repatriating the bodies of deceased Mexican migrants from the United States to their communities of origin in rural México. In December 2013, my father informed me that a friend of his, Leonel Herrera, a migrant from the state of Durango, had unexpectedly passed. Knowing that I had been following the issue of posthumous repatriations for some years, my father shared that Leonel's widow had decided to repatriate his remains to his native *rancho* in Durango. Immediately, I paid a visit to the grieving Herreras in Los Angeles' working-class (but rapidly gentrifying) Mexican barrio of Cypress Park to inform them about the Mexican consulate's policy on subsidizing posthumous repatriations. Leonel's widow graciously invited me into their home, where I met the deceased's surviving young children. The home was like so many other working-class Mexican migrant Catholic households: framed images of patron saints and family portraits hung from the walls. Leonel was just as I had imagined him: a rail-thin Mexican migrant who had worked as a gardener in Los Angeles, always donning a *tejana* (cowboy hat).[38] His prized *charro* items also adorned the home: Leonel's sombrero and rope sat behind a glass case in the dining room. I knew that Leonel and my uncle José Manuel had been *charro* comrades; *charrería* "was his passion in life" his widow explained. After sharing that her decision to return her deceased husband to Durango was so that he could be buried in his community of origin where his aging parents still lived, I asked if she was familiar with the Mexican consulate's assistance with these posthumous repatriations. She was unaware that such a policy existed. I asked her if they had internet access so that I could look up the information on the consulate's web page. "Yes," she said and instructed her preteen daughter to bring me their laptop. The girl quickly handed me a MacBook, with a sweet smile on her face, still innocently unaware that her father was gone, and she returned to playing with her siblings. I looked up the telephone number, we listened to the prerecorded menu of consular services, selected *traslado de cadáveres* (repatriation of human remains) and took note of the instructions. She thanked me and said she would visit the consulate first thing in the morning. I told her I would accompany the family at Leonel's Mass at the end of the week and respectfully left the home.

When Friday came around, my brothers and I gathered at my father's upholstery shop where we waited to be picked up by my uncle José Manuel to pay our respects to the late Leonel. My uncle arrived a few minutes before the Mass was to start, and we jumped into his truck and headed to the Catholic Church down the street. He handed me a small, framed photograph: "*Este era mi amigo Adrián*" (This was my friend), my uncle told me in his usual brusque manner, although this time with a hint of sadness. There was Leonel in all of his *charro* glory, riding my uncle's horse, bringing down a bull by its tail.

When we arrived and gave our condolences to Leonel's brothers, all dressed in black, I didn't anticipate being overcome by emotion. After all, I had been to many a *misa de cuerpo presente* in my day. But the sight of Leonel's coffin being escorted into church with his young children following in tears was too much to bear. I told my father that I would have to be excused for the remainder of the evening and that I couldn't bring myself to attend the viewing at the Herrera home following the Mass. My father did attend and would later describe the gathering to me. The Herrera home in Cypress Park was packed with friends and family of the late Leonel. His coffin arrived from the Mass and was placed in the home's backyard. Then entered the *tamborazo*, the six-piece brass band common at *charrería* events, performing Leonel's favorite songs. The coffin was finally opened, overwhelming the immediate family members with grief. There was Leonel, his *tejana* resting gently atop his chest, ready to be returned to the *rancho* of his birth.

The migrant ethnic economy of mourning that has arisen around this practice has made these repatriations part of an emerging posthumous transnational tradition; one that has been among the policy priorities of returned migrant politicians, and one that the Mexican state has attempted to institutionalize at multiple levels of government.[39] The cross-border cultural politics behind posthumous repatriations are not entirely lost on the Mexican bureaucrats and state actors who interact with this diasporic demand. When I asked the bureaucrats of the Protection and Legal Affairs department at the Mexican consulate in San Francisco what the motives behind this posthumous migrant nostalgia market were, they agreed the reasons were profoundly cultural. "Tradition" the consular staff person stated summarily, "a family tradition." When a migrant dies in the United States, "families say 'we always decide to return to our land,'" she emphasized. Her supervisor, the consul in charge of this department, which administers these repatriations, added that the matter is not merely cultural but that this is also part of the cultural *politics* of migrant mourning. "This all relates back to the migration [policy] issue . . . if they [the family] decide that they will not remain here permanently, they prefer to have the body back with the family, in the community of origin." To this the consular staff person tellingly remarked, "Lest the body remain lost," unrecovered, suspended indefinitely in transnational space.

Like her counterparts in San Francisco, the consul in charge of the Protection and Legal Affairs department at the Mexican consulate in San José understood the cultural politics that undergird posthumous repatriations. When I asked her about the motives behind this transnational practice, she explained it was important for the "parents to see them, to bury them there," underscoring the ethno-territorial nature of this practice. To illustrate this point, she turned to the case of indigenous Mexican migrants from Oaxaca and their transnational moral communities.[40] "This is especially true in Oaxaca, where they pay so much homage to their dead. For them it is very important to pay homage to their dead. The *fiestas* they offer their dead are very important."[41] Speaking to the transnational afterlife of these deceased repatriated migrants, she stated: "It is important for loved ones to visit them in the cemetery . . . to have their dead there . . . and on Day of the Dead take flowers . . . take food on the Day of the Dead." For when the body is returned to the community of origin and to these posthumous cultural practices, the consul concluded, "the dead come back to life."

The remainder of this book theorizes the thickening of transnational citizenship across the different stages of the migrant political life cycle, from "political baptism" to repatriation to México after death. Building on earlier studies on the significant role of place (i.e., community of origin, community of settlement) and peoplehood (i.e. migrant social and family networks) in transnational ties, I focus on a political process that is arguably familiar to the Mexican diaspora writ large: the thickening of transnational citizenship across the migrant political life cycle. In that sense, this is not a classic case study of a transnational community (Nichols 2006; Levitt 2001) or a cross-border coalition (Smith and Bakker 2008). Instead, this book attempts to assemble the different phases of migrants' interface with the double-edged sword of transnational citizenship, on both sides of the border, drawing primarily on transnational ethnography among *mestizo* migrants from north-central rural México.[42] As a political ethnography of transnational citizenship, this book also critically captures my accompaniment of Mexican migrants as they navigate and negotiate transnationalism in life and death.[43]

2

Enunciations of Transnational Citizenship

MEXICAN MIGRANTS' ENCOUNTERS WITH
NATURALIZATION

Las Huellas de Don Juan/Don Juan's Imprints

To corroborate his identity before the state, Don Juan—a migrant from the
state of Zacatecas, México—had to have his fingerprints taken as part of
the requirements for petitioning to become a U.S. citizen. This bureaucratic
procedure is well known to citizenship applicants, seen as a routine part of
the naturalization process.[1] Unlike most migrants, however, Don Juan had
trouble with his biometrics, having to get his fingerprints taken multiple
times. As it turns out, Don Juan's fingerprints were illegible, such was the
damage sustained to his hands from the chemicals he handles at his factory
workplace, his identity essentially eroded from his toiling anonymously for
decades in the United States—an experience not uncommon to migrants in
other labor sectors, such as farmworkers.[2] Don Juan's experience of naturalization is ironically indicative of Mexican migrants' political condition in the
United States—alienated laborers, unrecognizable as potential citizens. By
bringing together Mexican migrants' narratives of naturalization and their
collective understanding of it—what I call their *mythology of citizenship*—
this chapter shows how perceived discrimination throughout the citizenship
process impacts migrants' sense of political belonging and allegiance to the
United States and to their country of origin, México. In order to understand
the staying power of Mexican migrant transnationality, we have to turn to the

*An earlier version of this chapter was published as "New Americans or Diasporic
Nationalists? Mexican Migrant Responses to Naturalization and Implications for Political
Participation."* American Quarterly *60 (3): 601–624.*

discrimination that citizen-eligible migrants perceive at a crucial moment in their civic lives: naturalization.

The Political Nexus between Naturalization, Discrimination, and Transnational Citizenship

In his ethnographic study of Mexican migrants' pursuit of U.S. citizenship, the political anthropologist Luis Plascencia describes the naturalization process and its attendant civic education as part of a "biopolitical project of incubating good citizens" with the ultimate goal of "producing governable subjects loyal to the United States" with the "proper fidelities" toward the state, "its institutions and its leaders" (2012: 113, 114). However, Plascencia explains that negative experiences throughout the naturalization process may ultimately have the effect of "disenchanting citizenship" for Mexican migrants. This chapter expands on Plascencia's research to explain how experiences like those of Don Juan relate to migrants' sense of *transnational* political belonging and identity. Stated succinctly, I discuss how the so-called "political baptism" of Mexican migrants in the United States relates to their cross-border affiliations, allegiances, and attachments.[3]

Seen as their formal initiation into the polity, naturalization has been described as migrants' "political baptism" in the United States (see, e.g., Rogers 2006). In this book, I treat naturalization as migrants' most direct encounter with the state's "civic creed" of singular political loyalties.[4] In the case of contemporary Mexican naturalization however, migrants have been mobilized to seek U.S. citizenship not out of a desire for assimilation or newfound patriotism to their country of settlement but rather in response to political threat and discrimination therein, fears that have come back to haunt migrants in the xenophobic Trump era (see Pantoja, Ramírez, and Segura 2001; Michelson and Pallares 2001; Ramírez 2013; Zepeda-Millán 2017). Described as a strategy of "political self-defense" (Pantoja and Segura 2003: 282), naturalization in antimigrant times can be seen as "a survival tactic against xenophobic terror, in which Mexicans pledge allegiance to their adopted country" in response to a direct political threat against their livelihoods (Kun 2005: 9). Under these political circumstances, naturalization does not represent migrants' uncritical allegiance to the United States or much less an abjuring of their *Mexicanidad*. As Josh Kun reminds us in his theorization of Mexican migrants' cultural enunciation of this citizenship contradiction, under antimigrant conditions the so-called "political baptism" does not signal "assimilation into American culture or a betrayal of . . . Mexican identity" (2005: 9). When citizenship is pursued in response to an antimigrant political assault, and when the naturalization process itself is fraught with discrimination, Mexican migrants refuse to accept "singular national allegiance, singular national pride, and singular public participation in American national culture" (2005: 10). Instead, these naturalizing Mexican migrants are the embodiment of transnational citizens, "whose identities and lives move in and out of this [bounded national] territory" and who enunciate a cultural production that "works necessarily *sin fronteras*, without borders" (2005: 11).

In the immediate political aftermath of the historic 2006 migrant rights marches, there was an increase in the number of legal permanent residents seeking naturalization (Zepeda-Millán 2017), in a pattern consistent with previous periods of antimigrant politics (Pantoja, Ramírez, and Segura 2001). Between January and October 2007, the United States Citizenship and Immigration Services (USCIS) saw a 59 percent increase in citizenship petitions from the same period in 2006, receiving 1,029,951 naturalization applications (Félix, González, and Ramírez 2008). From 2006 to 2007 and 2010 to the present, I conducted political ethnographies of citizenship classrooms in Southern and Northern California to understand the relationship between an antimigrant political context, migrants' decision to naturalize, and what this implies for their transnational identities and subjectivities. This period has been marked by the political resurgence of the antimigrant Right and the attendant surge in anti-Mexican sentiment, hate crimes, and record-breaking deportations—what Alfonso Gonzales calls the "anti-migrant hegemony" of the "homeland security state" (2013)— conditions that have intensified under Trump.[5] I argue that under migrant-hostile conditions, the "political baptism" does not signify a severing of ties with the community and country of origin but rather an opportunity for Mexican migrants to enunciate, enact, and embody new forms of transnational citizenship and subjectivities on both sides of the border.

Proto-Transnational Citizens: Mexican Naturalization in Historical Context

Citizenship acquisition is conventionally understood as a landmark in the process of "immigrant incorporation" (see Bloemraad 2006; Gordon 2007). In his study of immigrant adaptation in early twentieth-century Los Angeles, George J. Sánchez interprets Mexican migrants' decision to naturalize as a sign of permanent resettlement in the United States—which he equates with a permanent cutting of ties with the country of origin—and suggests that their mobilization in U.S. politics came at the expense of participation in Mexican politics (Sánchez 1993). The violence of the Mexican Revolution, the creation of the U.S. Border Patrol, and the repatriation of hundreds of thousands of Mexican nationals during the Great Depression were some of the political and economic forces that led to a second-generation dominance in Mexican communities in Los Angeles.[6] U.S.-born Mexicans and their political organizations broke with the earlier view against naturalization and called upon Mexican migrants to become U.S. citizens involved in U.S. elections, making for a generation decidedly focused on events north of the border. Yet, just as the "migrant presence . . . impelled Mexican Americans to demand their citizenship rights and social inclusion in the United States," it also "gave rise to new articulations of cross-border nationalism" as Alicia Schmidt Camacho reminds us (2008: 25). Naturalization, as it turns out, played a direct role in these transnational enunciations.

A closer examination of naturalization history reveals the connection between racial exclusion and transnational forms of belonging. Martha Menchaca's exhaustive history of Mexican naturalization shows that the Naturalization Treaty of 1868 was followed by a sustained period of anti-Mexican backlash. The legal battle for Mexican migrant naturalization was epitomized in the 1870 *People v. Pablo De La Guerra* California Supreme Court ruling, which determined that treaty law was vague on race and that the Fourteenth Amendment did not apply to Mexicans. As Menchaca states, the "California legislature refused to enforce the Naturalization Treaty of 1868 because it was the opinion of the legislators that unless Mexicans were white they were not citizens and thus ineligible to apply for citizenship" (2011: 67). Not surprisingly, such rulings precipitated a dramatic decline in naturalization petitions granted in the ensuing decade. "The percentage of petitions granted fell from 89 percent in 1869," Menchaca writes, "to .75 percent in 1879" (2011: 67).[7]

This racialized exclusion from U.S. citizenship was commonplace throughout the incipient Mexican diaspora in the early twentieth century, from California to Texas to Illinois, and seemingly infused Mexican migrants' mythology of naturalization early on. Natalia Molina, for example, documents how officers at the Bureau of Immigration and Naturalization sought to render Mexicans ineligible for citizenship. "Particularly when Mexican applicants 'looked Indian,'" she writes, "naturalization officers found it difficult to characterize their color as white, and as a result they leaned toward denying them citizenship" (2010: 172). In her groundbreaking history of Mexican migrants in Chicago during the interwar years, Gabriela Arredondo finds that a mere "1 percent of the Mexican population in Chicago actually applied for U.S. citizenship" (2008: 72–73). Among the reasons for this pronounced disinclination to naturalize was the widespread belief that ethnic Mexicans would continuously be racialized as "illegal aliens," irrespective of their formal citizenship status. Their "illegality," to borrow from legal scholar Devon Carbado, was "[v]isually inscribed" (2005: 633), almost literally "lacerated onto the body" (2005: 655).

For these early twentieth-century migrants, like Mexican migrants today, this process of racialization had a direct effect on their feelings of political attachment and allegiance. "[H]ow are [we] to become identified with th[is] country when a barrier of prejudice is opposed to it" said one Mexican migrant in a statement recovered in Arredondo's archival research (2008: 93). In a comment strikingly reminiscent of the narratives discussed later in this chapter, another early twentieth-century migrant questioned, "What advantages do you get by becoming naturalized? We are going to be subjected to the same difficulties that we are now suffering, in spite of our citizenship, because our looks cannot be changed by our nationality" (2008: 101). For Mexican migrants then and now, naturalization was no guarantee of racial belonging or first-class citizenship in the United States: "if you carry naturalization papers in your pocket . . . you may hold your head up and say to yourself, 'Now I am as good as anybody.' But that won't prevent an American person kicking you and saying 'Get out of here, you damned Mexican!'" (2008: 157). With this archival research, Arredondo helps us see the historical link between naturalization, discrimination, and an incipient transnational citizenship, undergirded by a "Mexicanism rooted in the revolutionary context from which many of Chicago's Mexicans emerged" (2008: 143). As such, Arredondo helps us envision these historical migrant actors as proto-transnational citizens, a pattern that, as this chapter will show, endures to this day.

The Political Birth of Transnational Citizens: Mexican Naturalization in the Twenty-First Century

In the age of the "transnational turn," expressions of migrant cross-border identities, activities, and loyalties abound. In the twenty-first century, scholars point to transformations in communication and travel technologies, putative tolerance of ethnic pluralism in the United States (Waldinger 2007b), and home-state rapprochement with their diasporas as some of the factors that facilitate cross-border interactions and identities (Iskander 2010; Délano 2011). The transnational character of Mexican migration has stirred debates regarding political allegiance and the nature and degree of contemporary Mexican migrant political "incorporation" in the United States, emphasizing failed "assimilation" on one end and a traditional pattern of political "assimilation" on the other (see Citrin et al. 2007). Consistent with the first view, Mexican migrants' ostensible failure to "assimilate" is attributed to proximity to the homeland, cross-border activities, institutions of dual nationality, and other factors inherent to "Mexican exceptionalism."[8] Researchers in the second camp have argued that Mexicans are indeed "assimilating" along traditional lines, citing migrant adherence to values such as economic individualism and U.S. patriotism. Under this view, migrants who become naturalized citizens are believed to be as, if not more, patriotic to their new country than white Anglo-Americans, controlling for background and other factors (de la Garza, Falcon, and Garcia 1996). However, both perspectives assume that national identities are mutually exclusive and that migrants cannot sustain simultaneous loyalties to their countries of origin and settlement. In this chapter, I advance an alternative perspective that challenges these citizenship conventions. As the ethnographic data will illustrate, cross-border loyalties and identities persist upon naturalization largely as a result of migrant self-identification in response to the institutional discrimination they face throughout the process of political enfranchisement. The political space where Mexican migrants expose the contradictions of U.S. citizenship and constitutionalism, as this chapter will show, is the citizenship classroom itself, which emerges as an important public sphere for the negotiation of transnational political belonging and membership.

What mobilizes Mexican migrants to pursue U.S. citizenship? How do Mexican migrants experience the naturalization process and what does it mean in the context of their transnational lives and identities? Drawing on extensive ethnographic fieldwork and in-depth interviews with Mexican migrants who were preparing for the naturalization interview (or had already completed it) in citizenship classrooms in Southern and Northern California, this chapter sheds light on these questions, focusing on the persistent political link between naturalization, discrimination, and transnational belonging.

Regarding the incentives to naturalize, Ong and Lee note that securing tangible benefits in an anti-immigrant context leads to "defensive naturalization" (2007). This chapter presents evidence of an added community empowerment motive driving a reactive naturalization, which is more politically purposeful and is more proactive than defensive.[9] As Michelson and Pallares find in their study of naturalization, Mexican migrants' "experience of being the targets of exclusionary policy led them to portray their experience in this country as discriminatory, even while they were becoming citizens" (2001: 66). In such cases, when ethnic identity is perceived as the basis of shared discrimination, the resulting salience of ethnicity encourages naturalization as a means for furthering community interests via collective political action in ways that are not reducible to notions of assimilation. As Zepeda-Millán notes, "racially charged legislative threats against undocumented immigrants also impact and will be contested by U.S.-born and naturalized members of their communities" (2017: 210).

In contrast to previous studies that attribute "failed assimilation" to forms of "Mexican exceptionalism," I argue that enduring cross-border loyalties postnaturalization are a product of the antimigrant context of reception sustained and reproduced by U.S. society and politics. Moreover, while the anxiety, intimidation, and other negative factors that account for low naturalization rates among Mexican migrants today are well known, I find that such experiences are countered by the collective emotions, rapport, and solidarity of the citizenship classroom. As such, the citizenship classroom emerges as a potentially empowering public space for the migrant rights movement. Rather than operating as a conduit for "Americanization," understood in terms of traditional assimilation, the citizenship classroom can be a space where migrants make the naturalization experience intelligible on their own cultural and political terms. Given the discrimination they perceive throughout the naturalization process, the citizenship classroom is also a site for migrants to discuss alternative forms of transnational membership and belonging. As my interviews show, Mexican migrants view the naturalization process as arbitrary, owing largely to the discretionary powers of immigration officials. In response to such bureaucratic inconsistency, the citizenship class functions as an alternative public space where migrants develop a counternarrative that exposes the arbitrariness of the naturalization process, creating a transnational, rather than assimilative, relationship to citizenship and national identity. Of course not all citizenship classes operate in this manner—they must actively be produced and defended as spaces of transnational belonging. Therefore, the citizenship classrooms discussed in this chapter serve as models to be replicated under the antimigrant Trump era.

Unlike in the early twentieth century, Mexican naturalization in the twenty-first century cannot be viewed as a sign of severed ties to the community and country of origin. As Sánchez notes, migrants who secure legalization no longer face institutional barriers to visit their home communities and reenter the United States legally. To this we add the Mexican government's dual nationality law and local policies like "La ley migrante" in Zacatecas, which allow migrants to participate in the civic life of their communities of origin (Smith and Bakker 2008). As Michael Jones-Correa demonstrates, migrants from countries recognizing dual nationality average higher naturalization rates in the United States than their counterparts from countries that do not (2001). Far from being an impediment to political participation, ethnic identification and attachment to the homeland postnaturalization may drive migrant political participation across borders. In an antimigrant climate, the so-called "political baptism" of migrants may, in effect, signal the political birth of transnational citizens.

"Political baptism" by Fire: Antimigrant Political Context and Mexican Naturalization

As research in Latino politics shows, naturalization rates among Mexican migrants (and Latinos more broadly) have been low relative to other national-origin groups. Citizen-eligible Latinos have been "characterized by their sluggishness between when they have been eligible to naturalize and when they actually undergo the process" (Barreto, Ramírez, and Woods 2005: 797; see also Ayón 2012). The 1990s momentarily disrupted these naturalization patterns, setting an important precedent for the argument presented here. Consider, for example, that in 1990, more than 270,000 migrants became U.S. citizens. Six years later, this figure soared to over a million, "with the proportion due to Mexican immigrants tripling from 6.5 percent to 20.8 percent" (Stamper Balistreri and Van Hook 2004: 113). By fiscal year 1999, this percentage had increased to 30 percent. The reasons for this change included a racially charged political climate and increased mobilization by ethnic and civic organizations, which were key in stimulating migrant naturalization and political participation (Pantoja, Ramírez, and Segura 2001). In their study on the impact of Immigration Reform and Control Act (IRCA) citizens on Latino voting, Barreto, Ramírez, and Woods summarize the literature on naturalization under threat as follows: "Latinos who naturalized between 1992 and 1996 in California were more likely to vote than their newly naturalized counterparts in Florida and Texas, which had no corresponding salient and divisive state ballot measures in the same period" (2005: 796). Their findings confirm that it is contentious antimigrant politics that drives foreign-born Latinos to naturalize and to vote: "These results show in a convincing manner that the IRCA reform, by itself, was not ultimately responsible for producing additional Latino votes in 1996 or 2000, or the growth in Latino votes over that timespan . . . most of the increase in Latino voting is associated with the increase in Latinos who registered between 1994 and 1996—a particularly divisive time for Latinos in California" (2005: 807). Clearly, an antimigrant context during key stages in the civic lives of migrants (i.e., naturalization, voter registration, etc.) can mark their sense of political identity and, as this chapter will argue, their cross-border allegiances as well.

Mexican migrants' historical disinclination to naturalize is not entirely surprising. Mexican migrants describe the naturalization process as one rife with patronizing officials, unreasonable criminalization, humiliation, fear, and anxiety. An egregious example of immigration institutional intimidation was shared by a male Mexican migrant during an informal conversation we sustained shortly before one of our citizenship classes. This person reported encountering intimidation tactics at a federal immigration building, where he was singled out, placed in a solitary room, and was repeatedly interrogated by immigration authorities in an aggressive fashion about his legal past. Migrants who encounter such hostile bureaucratic treatment are understandably fearful about the naturalization process and their encounters inform the broader mythology of citizenship. Such encounters suggest that even as they embark on the "political baptism", Mexican migrants are serving their "apprenticeship" in "illegality" (De Genova 2004: 174).[10] Throughout the formal citizenship acquisition process, Mexican migrants are reminded that naturalization does not necessarily denaturalize their "illegality." Here, what is being policed is not only their "behavior" but also their very identity, which is seen as a "de facto status crime," to borrow from Lisa Cacho (2012: 43).

In addition, Mexican migrants have long been discouraged by feelings of disloyalty to the home country and misinformation about losing rights and privileges therein upon naturalizing (Waslin 2005: 3). However, this chapter suggests a shift in the popular conception of citizenship, signaling an emerging consensus in favor of naturalizing among noncitizens. The federal government's effort to make naturalization more demanding (e.g., increased fees, greater English-language knowledge requirements) may be the impetus for migrants to seek full de jure political membership in the United States.[11] From a migrant's perspective, the pragmatic reasons to naturalize include the continuous hiking of fees, increased ability to obtain dual nationality, and the debunking of long-held myths about naturalization. On top of this, however, a hostile political climate and subsequent migrant rights protests promoted by the ethnic media may account for the decision to "seek enfranchisement as an act of political expression" (Pantoja, Ramírez, and Segura 2001: 729).

As mentioned, the current migrant-hostile political climate is not without precedent. The mid-1990s temporarily disrupted stagnant naturalization patterns when citizen-eligible Latinos reacted to the confluence of an antimigrant political context and attendant political protests advertised by the ethnic media (see Zepeda-Millán 2017). Like recent antimigrant legislation, Proposition 187, the 1994 California initiative, was punitive in nature in that it sought to deny public services to undocumented migrants and required public officials to report suspected undocumented persons to the Immigration and Naturalization Service (Pantoja and Segura 2003: 266). In this context, citizen-eligible migrants became more aware of immigration and ethnicity as salient issues. Additionally, "because Proposition 187 was seen as a move against Latino immigrants, a large number of Latino non-citizens, perhaps out of fear of losing certain services or status, made the decision to begin the naturalization process" (Pantoja, Ramírez and Segura 2001: 731). An antimigrant political context resulted in "defensive naturalization." A similarly contentious political environment has resurfaced today as evidenced by continued migrant-focused policy debates and hostile public rhetoric from elected officials and pundits, albeit this time triggering a more politically purposeful reactive naturalization, a pattern that seems to be repeating itself under Trump.[12]

However, this push to naturalize should not be mistaken for uncritical patriotism to the United States. In their study of Anglo and Mexican support for "core American values," Rodolfo de la Garza and his associates find that Mexican respondents were often more individually oriented and more patriotic than Anglos. When explaining why this is so, the authors state, "as the joyous tears shed at citizenship ceremonies indicate, immigrants who become naturalized citizens have undergone a major transition with intense emotional overtones" (1996: 347). The presumption is that legal migrants who make the decision to naturalize do so out of patriotism to their new country. The ethnographic findings in this chapter complicate this picture. This study's ethnographic narratives suggest that, citizenship oath notwithstanding, these patriotic "new Americans" do not necessarily cut-off ties or allegiance to their communities and country of origin. In other words, ethnic attachment and identification with the homeland do not necessarily cease or diminish upon naturalization, and this is consistent with other studies (see Itzigsohn and Saucedo 2002; Ramírez and Félix 2011). Unlike the "failed assimilation" and "traditional assimilation" camps that focus solely on factors endogenous to

"Mexican exceptionalism" or the naturalization process exclusively, this analysis also considers the recurrent external factor of an antimigrant political context of reception. Additionally, the interviews and ethnographic material presented here have implications for earlier research that found that new citizens are not always civically minded (see DeSipio 1996). Although they face a dearth of political information common to many migrants, my respondents suggest that newly enfranchised Mexican migrants are naturalizing with the political interests of their undocumented brothers, sisters, and children in mind.[13]

Inside the Classroom: Political Ethnographies of Citizenship Classes

The data for this chapter come from ethnographic fieldwork, in-depth interviews, and focus groups in citizenship classes gathered primarily between 2006 and 2011 in Southern and Northern California. Conducting participant observation in these civic spaces allowed me to volunteer, coordinate, and teach citizenship classes; interview individual migrants who were pursuing U.S. citizenship; and facilitate focus groups with class participants. I will begin by discussing in detail the dynamics of the first of the citizenship classes I gained access to in 2006-2007 in Southern California, in the immediate aftermath of the unprecedented wave of migrant rights mobilizations (Robinson 2006; Zepeda-Millán 2017). At this site, citizenship instruction was offered Monday through Thursday, from 6 p.m. to 8 p.m. The venue was a small classroom that accommodated about twenty-five students. However, attendance was usually around thirty-five and sometimes as high as fifty. Although by a narrow margin, women often outnumbered men. This particular citizenship course was based on continuous enrollment, with no firm beginning or end date. The instructor was Benjamín, a naturalized Mexican migrant for more than ten years, in his late forties, who was interviewed for this study.[14] The *cinto piteado* wearing, cowboy boot-clad instructor, with heavily accented English, created a welcoming and vibrant cultural and learning environment for all students. Class participants were mostly migrants from México, but there were a few students from El Salvador, Guatemala, and Honduras, as well as one from Perú and one from Argentina.

Twelve respondents were interviewed, six men and six women. With the exception of Benjamín and Felipe (who was interviewed the day of his citizenship interview), all participants were in the process of naturalizing. The duration of the interviews averaged around sixty minutes and followed a semistructured guide. Six interviews were conducted on-site, during, but separate from, class instruction. The remaining six were conducted at the home of Doroteo and Adela, the only married couple interviewed for this chapter. All interviews were conducted in Spanish.

Respondents, ranging in age from thirty to sixty-four, represented different migrant cohorts (i.e., different time of arrival to the United States, and hence different experiences amid shifting political contexts). All participants were working class: occupations included housekeeping, maintenance, carpentry, construction, welding, and factory assembly work. One respondent was retired. Ten respondents came from rural regions in México (in the states of Guanajuato, Michoacán, Jalisco, Zacatecas, Nayarit), while two came from large urban centers: Guadalajara and México City. Education levels were generally low (elementary school) among the older respondents but slightly higher for the younger migrants, reflecting the educational variance among migrant cohorts. English proficiency was mostly low but ranged to intermediate. All respondents were married (one was widowed) with children born or raised in the United States.

What Mobilizes Mexican Migrants to Become U.S. Citizens?

Before discussing the catalysts of citizenship acquisition, it is important to identify the impediments to naturalization among Mexican migrants. As Waslin points out, several of the factors historically involved in low Latino naturalization include

> lack of outreach to eligible immigrants, confusion about the naturalization process, fear of mistreatment by the U.S. immigration service, feelings of disloyalty to the home country, the loss of property rights and other rights and privileges in the home country, and a continuing desire to eventually return to the home country. (2005: 3)

All of these factors were echoed in the citizenship classrooms I visited and are part and parcel of the Mexican mythology around naturalization. Regarding future outlook and return ideology upon arrival to the United States, Don Felipe (age forty-six), remarked,

> I think that a lot of people who come, all of us who come, arrive and never think that we will stay in this country. Usually, we all think that

we will stay for some time and then we will return. But we don't have a deadline, a specific date to return. We always think that one day we will return and in the end, we don't go back.

"I thought I was coming for five years and I have been here for fifteen," said Beatriz (age fifty-four). On top of this apparent "myth of return," many Mexican migrants eschewed naturalization out of fear of losing rights in the home country. "In the past I have heard that a lot of people thought they would lose their Mexican nationality by becoming U.S. citizens. Therefore, they did not want to become U.S. citizens. But today I don't hear much about that," recalled Rosaura (age thirty). Don Juan (age fifty-two) provided further insight:

> When I became a resident, a lot of people would say that persons who became citizens would lose their rights in México. I am not sure if that is true. Now the rhetoric has changed. Now they say that you don't lose any rights in México. I think you can now have dual citizenship.

When asked whether he knew individuals who do not want to naturalize, Jose Alfredo (age fifty-five) replied, "Yes, there are a lot of people because they fear losing who knows what. But that is not so. Now, you no longer lose your Mexican citizenship." Don Juan remembered popular conceptions of legal residence and naturalization among his *paisanos* as follows:

> People used to say that if you went to México, you could not be there for more than six months. After that, you had to return to the U.S. I am not sure if that was true. In any case, most of us ended up living here in the U.S., and we only return to México to visit and for vacation.

Yet another reason that dampened prospects for naturalization among Mexicanos was the belief that "if you became a U.S. citizen, you could not own property in México." However, Don Juan dismissed this and other myths:

> But that is not true. It is in México's interest for people to invest in property, homes. A lot of people refused to become U.S. citizens in the past because they thought that meant rejecting their rights as Mexicans. But, fortunately, México has facilitated dual citizenship. So, this is no longer a problem.

Likewise, Jose Alfredo, who plans to return to Guanajuato once he retires, stated: "Previously, an American citizen could not own property in México. They could not own a house. They could not be an *ejidatario* and now you can . . . have land." While prior to the amendments to Mexican nationality law in the 1990s it was not a myth that becoming a U.S. citizen meant restrictions on owning property in México (along the coast and borders), fear of losing rights in the home country is part of the contested and changing knowledge production that comprises the Mexican *mythology* of citizenship.[15] Whereas previously an ideology of return discouraged naturalization, México's dual nationality law seems to free up migrants who desire an eventual return to seek citizenship in the United States (DeSipio 2006: 110; see also Jones-Correa 2001).

When asked why they were seeking citizenship, most class respondents immediately listed the need to legalize relatives, secure tangible benefits (employment, health care), and/or the right to vote. Don Felipe and Benjamín, the only two respondents in the sample who were already citizens, replied respectively: "The motive is the right to vote, but I have another reason that compelled me further, that is to legalize my wife." Similarly, Benjamín, the citizenship class instructor, stated, "that was one of the reasons why I became a citizen, because [my family was] here undocumented. So in order to fix their papers, that was the reason why I became a citizen sooner." Indeed, family reunification is a major component of the transnational migrant experience. To put it in Don Ignacio's (age sixty-four) words, "we are here but we are never complete. We are here and our people are over there."

Among the tangible benefits listed by respondents were health care, better employment, and a pension. Dolores (age forty-two) said she sought citizenship for benefits, a better salary, and perhaps a "government job one day." She also associated citizenship with access to health care, which can otherwise be "taken away from you, but if you are a citizen, they continue to help you." Dolores lamented that her brother "can't get Medi-Cal for his children because they don't have papers, except for his daughter who was born here [in the United States]."[16] She was grateful that her children, who are U.S.-born, have basic health care. About her nine-year-old son's speech impediment she stated, "the therapists say they will help him as long as he needs it. And it is all because he is a U.S. citizen." Lastly, Dolores recalled an anecdote about a friend who took her elderly mother to the doctor and was denied treatment because she was not a citizen. "I don't want that to happen to me," Dolores said solemnly. "I have to think ahead. I don't want to be a burden for my children." Notably, female migrants seemed to think about the social reproductive costs throughout the course of their life spans and the strains this could create on the family unit.

Finally, many migrants also thought ahead to their retirement. "Once I retire, I am going back to my homeland," Doroteo (age forty-six) exclaimed. "But I want to make sure they send my check over there, to La Barca [his hometown]." When calculating the benefits of being a permanent resident versus a citizen, Jose Alfredo stated: "If you retire one day, and you want your money sent to México, a sum will be deducted. On the other hand, if you are a citizen, you get the entire sum with nothing deducted." These statements and desires are emblematic of migrants' mythologies of citizenship (in some instances part truth, part myth) that are shared and circulated through conversations in diasporic circuits and networks.

When citizenship is sought to secure essential benefits and services, the process can be described as *instrumental naturalization*. This is related but different from Ong and Lee's concept of *defensive naturalization* in that the latter is sought for protection in an antimigrant context. Lastly, my interviews posit a *reactive naturalization* that is more politically purposeful and perhaps more offensive than defensive, producing a "proactive reaction leading to more activity" (Michelson and Pallares 2001: 70). The legal scholar Devon Carbado's term *racial naturalization*, an extremely important concept for how we think about political membership and belonging beyond formal, legalistic categories, will be discussed subsequently.

Reactive Naturalization: "One more vote es la fuerza"

While Latino politics researchers have consistently found a statistical correlation between an antimigrant political climate and increased naturalization rates, the political ethnography of citizenship classrooms presented here captures the stories behind the statistics and the narratives behind the naturalization numbers. The ethnographic data I collected overwhelmingly supports the claim that Mexican naturalizers "seek enfranchisement as an act of political expression" (Pantoja, Ramírez, and Segura 2001: 729). While it is not surprising that most respondents listed voting as a top motive, and while self-reported intent to vote should be viewed cautiously as such claims do not always materialize, this was a recurring theme that received ample justification without much probing. Some interviewees were outright enthusiastic about voting. When asked whether she planned to register, Beatriz exclaimed, "Yes, I have received voter registration forms and I say, 'when will I be able to fill you out!'" On top of naturalizing in order to regularize his wife's status,

Felipe stated he is also doing it "for the right to vote because we do witness a whole lot of injustices and we need to become a majority so that they can take us into consideration." Felipe had unsuccessfully attempted to naturalize in the mid-1990s. When asked why he waited ten years to give it a second attempt, he replied: "Now is when things are getting hot, with the whole driver license issue," referring to the much debated bill proposed by then California Senator Gil Cedillo that would have allowed undocumented migrants to drive legally, and alluding to the racial backlash that followed and the resurfacing of a contentious political climate.[17] When asked why she felt voting was important, Doña María (age sixty-one) replied, "Well, because these are things that we have to do. That is precisely why we are seeking citizenship so that we can all be the same or equal." Rosaura echoed these beliefs: "It's like they say, the Latino vote counts a lot, and perhaps we can make a difference and help our people by voting," again, signaling a desire to redress community needs. When asked why he planned to vote, Don Ignacio, the only respondent who was retired, replied, "They say that one more vote *es la fuerza*."

This theme of Latino voting and collective political clout was perhaps most remarkable in my interview with Juan. While Don Juan acknowledged that he sought naturalization to legalize his son, he was also "aware of the needs of the Latino community. I think it is important for Latinos to seek citizenship so that we can exercise our rights, so that we can vote and so that we can be taken into consideration." Clearly, Don Juan's decision to naturalize is indicative of this dual stimulus: on the one hand, he wanted to legalize his son, and on the other, he had an added political motive that he felt he owed to his community. He later generalized the logic of reactive naturalization to other Latino migrants who were pursuing citizenship and those who are excluded from it.

> A lot of us are motivated to naturalize because of the discrimination that we face. Elected officials discriminate Latinos frequently. Latinos have such a strong presence here. Imagine if we were all citizens. We would have clout. If we were to unite, like we did May 1st, that would be powerful. I think it is good that Latinos are naturalizing. It is in our interest and in the interest of our children.

Don Juan concluded by stating, "The way I see it is that by becoming a citizen I will have more clout to defend the rights that many Latinos lack. I feel that it will give us more authority to speak out for our rights." Contrary to earlier research that found migrants who associate mostly with noncitizens to be less likely to naturalize, it appears that *because* all respondents were formerly un-documented, they are in solidarity with the millions of co-ethnics who currently have no legal pathway to legal residence or citizenship in the United States and seem to imagine future political action with community-wide interests in mind (see DeSipio 2006: 110; Zepeda-Millán 2017). Because the experience of "illegality" is so proximate, these Mexican migrant naturalizers are in some ways surrogate subaltern subjects for the undocumented.

Regarding the migrant rights protests of 2006, although none of my interviewees participated because of work or other obligations, most overwhelmingly sympathized with the cause and several cited the protests as an additional impetus for naturalizing. Felipe recalled feeling "terrible" when he encountered a promigrant march in San Bernardino County that he was unaware of.

> One day that I came here, there was a march that I did not know about and I felt terrible. I thought they were only going to have them in Los Angeles, but they also had one here. And when I saw the march proceeding here, I felt like, all of these people, and I wasn't even aware of it . . . But that time I did feel terrible. I didn't even want to go out because I thought they would say, "Why isn't this fool marching?" [laughter]

This echoes Don Juan's earlier statement of a shared racial responsibility that Mexican migrants owe their community. When asked whether the migrant rights protests motivated him to naturalize, Felipe said that on top of his urgent need to legalize his wife, the marches "pushed me further to do it." Don Juan, who was not present at the protests and who had already made up his mind to naturalize prior to them, candidly stated, "Honestly, no. I couldn't be there . . . I had already made up my mind [to naturalize] long before. But I thought it was great for the Latino population. It was a strong sign of unity."

Other respondents echoed such opinions. Dolores remarked,

> I did not participate, but my neighbors did. They were very excited to march. If I could have, I would have been there too. I thought it was a very good idea. It was a great cause, to ask for immigration reform. The more people we can unite, the better chances we have of being heard.

Likewise, Adela (age forty-three) and Doroteo were unable to attend because of work. "But if we had the time, we would have gladly been there. Especially because it was a great cause. It was very important for us Latinos," Adela

exclaimed. When asked whether the protests affected her decision to naturalize, Adela replied assertively:

> Yes. It motivated you. A lot of the people who marched do not have
> papers, and those of us who do have them, we should not let them go
> to waste, and we should not be complacent. We should strive to reach
> higher.

Clearly, there is evidence of a sense of collective action, solidarity, and
shared racial responsibility with migrants who are barred from participation in formal politics among their citizenship-eligible co-ethnics.
Doroteo, Adela's husband, reported feeling motivated by fellow legal permanent residents seeking citizenship: "I heard that a lot of people were
becoming citizens and that encouraged me even more. That motivated me
further." To borrow from Guidry and Sawyer, the 2006 protests and subsequent migrant solidarity and collective action have the potential to transform the meaning and possibility of U.S. democracy and citizenship, in
this case, via the legalization of millions of undocumented migrants and
their families. These statements also suggest that migrants' mythologies of
citizenship not only convey fear and anxiety about the naturalization process but also their desire to pursue it in the interest of their mixed-status
families and communities.

How Do Mexican Migrants Experience the Naturalization Process?

My interviewees shared how the naturalization process affected them in the
private sphere, in the intimacy of their family and personal lives. Additionally,
interview and observational data convey how the process was experienced
emotionally and collectively in classroom interactions. Returning students
added to this environment by sharing their experiences during the much
anticipated and sometimes dreaded citizenship interview, the decisive moment of the naturalization process.

The Private Sphere: The Value of Citizenship in Mexican Migrants' Working Lives

For the most part, legal permanent residents who make the decision to begin
the naturalization process do not take it lightly and make it a priority to

accomplish this goal. On top of class instruction, several respondents studied using audio aids and other materials at home or work. Doña María, for instance, stated, "I listen to a cassette at home. I go over the questions and listen to the tape when I am at home." Don Juan relied on a "CD to practice the citizenship interview" when he was in the privacy of his home. Others practiced their English with their U.S.-born children, like Dolores, who exhorted her nine-year-old son, "*Mi'jo*, teach me how to write in English. Speak to me in English at home. I have to learn." Dolores was so consumed by the naturalization process that she had "dreams about the questions. I stay up late at night studying, and I've had dreams about the immigration officer. He tells me I did not pass. He tells me I have to come back." Indeed, in their mythologies of this process, many students feared that their dreams of citizenship would turn out to be a naturalization nightmare.

While the anxiety, fear, and intimidation involved in Latino naturalization are well documented (see Alvarez 1987), these negative emotions are often assuaged by encouraging remarks from friends and family. Don Felipe recalled some of this motivation: "You can do it," his friends said to him. "Those who are already American citizens would tell me, 'You have to accomplish it. If we did it, why can't you do it? You can do it.' Thanks be to God, I passed my exam today," he remarked proudly. Likewise, Rosaura, who married a U.S. citizen, reported that everyone in her family supported her attempt to naturalize. She said, "Everybody is happy because there is now a possibility for me to help them," signaling the prospect of regularizing her parents and siblings' immigration status. "I have heard nothing but good remarks from friends and family," said Beatriz. "They tell me, 'That is great. *Échale ganas.* You can do it.'" Finally, Adela and Doroteo, the only married couple pursuing naturalization in the sample, were equally supportive of one another. When Doroteo was reticent to seek naturalization and suggested Adela go at it alone, she replied:

> "No, we are both going to do it. If I become a citizen, I don't want you to remain as a resident. I don't want one of us to be higher and the other lower. I want both of us to be equal." More than anything, we are motivating one another to accomplish this goal. I try to help him and motivate him to learn. I tell him, *sí se puede.*

This remark is consistent with early gender research in Latino politics, which shows Latinas as taking a collectivist approach to political participation (Hardy-Fanta 1993) and may hold implications for the Latino naturalization gender gap (Pantoja and Gershon 2006) if Latina women continuously encourage citizen-eligible men in their family networks to naturalize. When it came to naturalization among my respondents, not everyone was as supportive however. Adela and Doroteo decided not to inform other family members about their attempt to naturalize, "so that in case we don't pass, they won't make us feel bad." Perhaps fearing social pressure, Amparo (age fifty) said, "I don't comment this to anyone." Similarly, Don Juan avoided telling his co-workers, stating, "I am afraid to tell them because they will tease me if I don't pass the interview [laughter]." While in the past naturalizers may have feared being labeled disloyal to México for seeking U.S. citizenship, here it is fear of embarrassment at not passing the exam, indicative of a shift in the popular conception of naturalization as a desirable outcome for the community writ large.

Potential citizens invested considerable amounts of time, energy, and money in the naturalization process. Most respondents agreed that the naturalization process required a huge sacrifice in their family and personal lives. "I have not missed time from work but I have cut into my children's time and many other tasks I have to do around the house," Rosaura remarked. "I get out of work, I cook, and I come to class," Amparo explained. Similarly, Dolores stated:

> I wake up at five a.m., I clean my bathrooms and mop my floor, then I go to work [housekeeping], I pick up my children from school, I begin to cook for my husband once he returns from work. Then I bathe my children and I come to class. Sometimes my back hurts but I keep going. *Sigo adelante.* That is the only way.

These statements reveal the gender disparities and difficulties of Mexican migrant women seeking naturalization as they balance citizenship acquisition with their employment outside the home and their caring and labor inside the home.[18] Adela and Doroteo described a similar situation:

> We are making a huge sacrifice. I get up at four a.m. each morning, my husband at five a.m. I leave before he does, and I try to make it home before he does and wait for my children to get home from school. It is hard. But God willing, we will make it. *Tenemos que salir adelante.*

On top of their long workdays, students attended the citizenship course Monday through Thursday from 6 p.m. to 8 p.m. Remarkably, Adela and

Doroteo offered their home for additional sessions on Friday evenings, suggesting the value that citizenship had assumed in the lives of these migrants.

Monetarily, most respondents felt they had paid a handsome fee (then $400 for the application alone). "It is a little expensive because of the application fee, $400," Rosaura said. To make matters worse, "you only have two opportunities. If you do not pass in two attempts, you lose the $400," she lamented. Together, Adela and Doroteo paid double that cost. For some, the rising fees are a real impediment to naturalization. Doroteo encouraged his brother to apply, "but he says he can't come up with the $400 fee. He is living paycheck to paycheck. It is not easy." Dolores agreed that the naturalization process was expensive, but said, "It doesn't matter. Even if we had to pay $1,000, so long as we become citizens, it is worth it," a sentiment echoed by most interviewees and indicative of the importance of citizenship in their lives. Acknowledging she was fortunate to have applied before the fee increased from $400 to $675 (effective July 2007), Beatriz stated, "I do not think it is expensive because we are taking a very important step that I think is priceless." As these interviews show, the value of citizenship in the lives of migrants has expanded beyond the quality-of-life benefits already noted in the literature, to include an added motive of collective political action.

"We are like a family": The Citizenship Classroom

Without a doubt, the classroom was the most propitious site to get at the question of how Mexican migrants experience the naturalization process collectively. Academically, most students started off timid and performing low when it came to the history and government content of the naturalization exam. Not surprisingly, English proficiency was an obstacle. In the case of Doña María, she stated:

> I am concerned because I still don't know English very well. That is my main concern. I have a hard time understanding what they are asking me. Of course, in Spanish I understand perfectly. I know the material. But I have a hard time when they ask me in English.

The fact that persons with low English-language skills have decided to begin the naturalization process suggests a sense of urgency to become citizens.

Among my interviewees, Dolores was the student with the lowest level of English skills. Regarding her decision to naturalize, she commented:

> I hesitated until my sister-in-law told me that it was going to get more difficult. There were rumors that after this January [2007] they were going to require perfect English for citizenship and that is why I submitted my application promptly. I thought, if I don't do it now I never will and that is why I am here.

Again, we see migrant mythologies of citizenship (rumors, hearsay, banter, etc.) informing and mobilizing legal permanent residents to seek naturalization. Additionally, the federal government's effort to make the naturalization process more demanding has motivated eligible migrants to seek citizenship immediately. If this trend endures, we can expect the time lag between when Mexican migrants become eligible to naturalize and when they begin the process to narrow.

Political Emotions and the Naturalization Process

The naturalization process has been described as one rife with "intense emotional overtones" (de la Garza, Falcon, and Garcia 1996: 347). My study revealed that a great deal of emotions unfolded collectively in the classroom. One memorable example was when two returning students shared their naturalization interview experience with the rest of the class. The following is an excerpt from my field notes on this occasion.

Pozole & Tears

   Rosa and Sandra arrived carrying a large *olla* [pot] of *pozole*, tostadas, beverages, and other treats. At this site, it is customary that students who take their interview return immediately (most of them returning the day of) to share their experience. The fact that Rosa and Sandra walked in with big smiles and carrying treats made it obvious to the class that they had passed their interviews and were now American citizens. Sandra had passed the day prior but waited to come in with Rosa, who passed on this day. It was clear that Rosa's interview had been that day as she was dressed more formally than usual. As the women walked in, the students jubilantly remarked "*¡Pasaron!*" [you passed!] and they congratulated their former classmates. At this point, as is customary on these occasions, the instructor asked the women to come to the front of the classroom and share their experiences with their classmates, who were eager and full of questions.

The first question coming from the group was "*¿Quién te tocó?*" [Which officer did you get?] "*Una Americana*" [a white woman], Rosa replied. She proceeded to tell in detail the course of her interview. "*¿Tráes tu green card?*" [Do you have your green card?], the officer asked Rosa. "*Estaba nerviosa*" [I was nervous], Rosa admitted. "*¿Cuantas preguntas te hicieron?*" [How many questions did they ask you?], an impatient student asked. "*Once*" [eleven], Rosa replied. The officer also asked Rosa to read and write a total of five sentences. "*Cuando recién llegué a esta clase no sabía nada*" [when I first came to this class I didn't know anything], Rosa remarked. At this point, Rosa began to cry. "*Se me hacía tan difícil, pero el maestro nos levanta el ánimo*" [It seemed so difficult, but the instructor always gets our spirit up], she said as she wiped her tears. The students agreed, sympathized, and cheered for Rosa. "*Dale un abrazo*" [give him (the instructor) a hug], the students remarked. They all cheered as Rosa and the instructor embraced. Rosa smiled and wiped the remaining tears from her face. After sharing their thoughts and tears, I returned to my duties of serving and distributing refreshments to the students, who waited patiently in their neatly aligned desks. People chatted, joked, laughed, and enjoyed warm bowls of *pozole*. "*Parece cenaduría, como en México*" [It looks like a restaurant from México in here], somebody shouted from the back of the room. Once everybody was served, Rosa handed me a bowl; "*come*" [eat], she said. So I did. I sat and pondered about my project and the wonderful people around me who made it all possible over *pozole* and tears [Félix, "*Pozole* & Tears" Field Notes, 1/16/07].

This incident was as memorable for Dolores as it was for me, as she recalled in her subsequent interview weeks after the event:

When somebody has his or her interview, I pray for that person. I pray, "Dear Lord help them pass" because they are in the same position as me. I pray to God that he gives luck to all of them, because at that moment we are all going to be the same, just as nervous. All of the people who come and give their testimony encourage the rest of us. They say, "*Sí se puede, sí se puede*" and that is very encouraging. Do you remember Rosa? She cried, and she told us that she owed it to the instructor. I agree, we have a great instructor. And when we saw her cry, all of us also cried. Because like she said, when she first arrived to the class she did not know how to write, like myself. But she had the support of her husband, as do I, and thanks be to God she passed. And all of us are just as happy for her.

That Dolores mentions having the "support of her husband" alludes to the gender disparities discussed earlier and to the gender double standard of having her husband's "approval" for taking on this endeavor, which in hetero-patriarchal households may not be allowed. Nevertheless, such observational and interview data capture the collegial environment and general rapport that characterized the classroom for both male and female students. As evidenced above, the anxiety, joy and tears shed during the naturalization process are shared among the group, suggesting that the solidarity and synergy of the classroom can counteract and perhaps overcome the negative emotions that have long discouraged the process among Mexican migrants.

It is important to highlight the instructor's role in creating a welcoming and vibrant learning environment for migrants. When asked about relations in the classroom under Benjamín, Adela replied: "I think we are like a family. We all help each other. Nobody will make you feel bad. I hope it continues that way as new students arrive." During my follow-up visit to this class however, a younger instructor replaced Benjamín, much to the dismay of the students. Educated in the United States and hardly bilingual, the new Latina instructor demanded that students speak English only. Immediately, the vibrant classroom dynamic that made it such a productive learning and cultural space diminished.

Instead of being a conduit for "Americanization," the citizenship classroom can be a critical public space for forging a sustained "oppositional counterpublic," or what Schmidt Camacho calls an "alternate pedagogy" (2008: 106), where migrants negotiate and understand the naturalization and political socialization processes on their own cultural terms. Given that noncitizens are excluded from voting and other forms of electoral politics, the citizenship class constitutes an "alternative public sphere" for migrants to debate politics and new ideas about democracy more broadly and the naturalization process specifically (Guidry and Sawyer 2003: 276; see also Rocco 2014). As the following section illustrates, this citizenship class is a counterpublic insofar as it is a space for the production of a counternarrative that exposes the bureaucratic arbitrariness of the citizenship process and challenges the central contradiction of U.S. citizenship, namely that ethnic Mexicans are continuously racialized as "illegal aliens" whether they are naturalized or not (see De Genova 2005). The production and validation of these alternative sets of knowledge in the classroom create a transnational, rather than assimilative, relationship to citizenship and national identity, since both are denied to many migrants legally and in everyday social interactions.

Negating Naturalization: Racial Knowledge and the Citizenship Interview

Despite its standardized format, citizenship applicants perceive the naturalization interview as arbitrary and unpredictable. According to the accounts of those who have experienced the interview, the outcome is largely determined by the idiosyncrasies and prejudices of the immigration officers. While policy advocates have obtained some concessions in the citizenship process, including a redesigned naturalization exam, immigration officials still wield broad discretionary powers when handling the interview and its outcome, leading to wide-ranging experiences for migrants.[19] Some students are scrutinized; others are in and out in a matter of minutes. This adds to the anxiety of the students who await the interview and accounts for their desire to hear the experiences of others who have completed the process. When asked about the officers, Doña María replied: "Some people say that they are nice, others say that they are mean. So, I don't know what to expect for my interview." Rosaura felt that some officers were more discriminatory toward individuals who were ill-prepared or lacked English-language skills. Others who have completed the interview offered more mixed messages:

> I have heard different things. Some people say it is hard. Some say it is easy. Some people say they do not really speak English, and they passed it just fine. Others who do speak English have not passed it. So, I have heard both sides. Hard and easy.

Regarding the officers: "Well, some say that the person was not too nice. Others say otherwise. I have heard both sides." Adela echoed the unpredictability of the officers stating: "One young lady said that out of ten questions she only answered three and the officer let her pass. So, it depends on the officer." Indeed, Benjamín often responded to students' anxiety over the interview by stating, "Every officer is different, every interview is different."

This collective understanding of the interview as subjective is largely predicated on the view that the outcome is shaped by the race of the examiner. Tellingly, the first question asked of Rosa was *who* interviewed her. There is concern among the students about the race/ethnicity of the officers who administer the exam, as some are reputedly stricter than others. According to Don Juan, "there is one officer, an Asian American woman, who is particularly strict. Several people have said this." Beatriz recalled these statements in her interview: "They speak badly of an Asian American female officer. They say she does not pass anyone." When asked whether there were Latino officers, Juan replied, "Yes, there are Latino officers. They are racist [laughs]." On this point, Don Juan was not alone. Multiple times during site visits students remarked that Latino officers were customarily the hardest. When Luz, a student not interviewed, failed her exam, students attributed it to the unjust and antagonistic Latino officer who interviewed her. Reportedly, the first remark he made to Luz as she entered was, "How many lies are you going to tell me today?" Students were particularly dismayed about Luz's rejection as she was among the students with the greatest English-language competence and knowledge of the history and government content. In contrast to Sandra and Rosa, who returned to share their experience, Luz did not return to the classroom, perhaps out of shame or disillusionment.

Among her listed sources of anxiety over the interview, Dolores mentioned her English and writing skills. "Unless I get an officer who is a despot, egotistical. That has happened to a lot of people. Or a racist officer as well," she added, suggesting that this is a major concern that can ultimately determine the outcome of the naturalization interview. Conversely, Dolores recalled hearing about "two people who got a Filipino officer, and they said they are very nice." However, she concluded,

> The best we can do is to be ready. The officers can tell when a person is well prepared. Likewise, we can also tell how the officer is, how he looks at you, how he speaks to you, how he treats you.

The perceived racial gaze of the immigration authorities reminds us that the gender of the officer and test taker also play a role. These played out in Sandra's experience, as per my field notes. "I was interviewed by a Filipino officer. He was nice to me. I would say he even winked at me." Despite being a standardized process, race and gender dictate a big portion of the naturalization interview and in some cases the outcome. Given the significance of the naturalization interview in the lives of migrants, their experience may have lasting implications on their subsequent views and incorporation in the host country and in some cases may have the effect of "disenchanting citizenship" (Plascencia 2012). As Robert Alvarez suggested in a similar study three decades ago, "New and potential citizens deserve a stronger and more positive introduction to the governing institutions of the country" (1987: 347). In response to such "inconsistent bureaucratic treatment," the citizenship class enables students to collectively navigate the perceived arbitrariness and inequality of the naturalization process, an experience that can potentially inform future political action (DeSipio 2006: 110).

Citizenship Gatekeepers and Transnational Ciudadanas

Las pobres desterradas
   de Morelia y Toluca, de Durango y San Luis,
   aroman la Metrópoli como granos de anís . . .

—Ramón López Velarde, "Las Desterradas"

After the initial ethnographic research discussed above, I started facilitating a citizenship class in Santa Cruz, California, where I met Doña Chole a *michoacana* migrant whose encounters with naturalization I want to conclude this section with. But first, a story about the citizenship class out of which she emerged, a space we carved out with much love in the face of some unexpected surveillance. One typical Saturday morning, just as our citizenship class was about to begin, we received an unexpected visitor: the instructor from the only other citizenship class in town. Our citizenship classes and pedagogical commitments couldn't be more different. Her class was offered through the city's adult education program for a fee and was taught on a strict "English only" policy. Ours was volunteer run, free, and entirely bilingual. These radically different pedagogical approaches to citizenship education had a lot to do with our personal biographies. I, the U.S.-born son of Mexican migrants, one of whom is now a naturalized citizen; she, the archetype of a traditional citizenship class instructor: a middle-aged, white, retired teacher.

As I rushed to my citizenship classroom, running a few minutes late as usual on Saturday mornings, I was intercepted by the retired teacher-turned-citizenship-class-instructor, who literally blocked my entry at the door. "You must be the citizenship class instructor: Who are you?!" she blurted out demandingly. Caught off guard and feeling utterly disrespected by her overture, I replied politely but firmly, "If you want to talk to me, you are welcome to return at the end of my citizenship class." Realizing that she had rudely overstepped her boundaries at that point, the woman said she would return in two hours, in a nearly apologetic tone. My three fierce Latina undergraduate student volunteers witnessed the exchange from inside the classroom and looked at me with bewilderment. "We are in for an interesting conversation after our class today," I uttered as we began our civics routine.

The citizenship instructor arrived immediately after our class ended, giving my volunteers and I virtually no time to debrief. True to our open-door philosophy, we welcomed her in, and she instantly began questioning our citizenship class credentials and boasting about hers. "How long have you all been doing this? I've been teaching citizenship classes for years. I have a 95 percent success rate." Her tone and demeanor were off-putting, to say the least. She then inquired where each of us was from, with much curiosity. Growing irritated, my student volunteers replied tersely: "Los Angeles." "San Francisco." "San Diego-Tijuana." "I am from Orange County," the citizenship teacher replied, "the birthplace of the minutemen!" At this point my three Latina student volunteers were fuming, seeing this as a racial micro-aggression on her part. We knew all about the damned minutemen. We had just discussed their pernicious political rise in our citizenship class.

This is an example of the policing of citizenship classrooms and the monitoring of civics education as an exercise in coercive "Americanization," one that reminds Mexican migrants who are in pursuit of the elusive goal of political inclusion that they don't fully belong. This encounter with the citizenship class instructor was reminiscent of the "Americanizers" of yesteryear—white teachers and social workers determined to "go after the [Mexican migrant] women" in particular (Sánchez 1984). Our citizenship classroom, by contrast, was modeled after the one discussed in this chapter— a space for alternative political education for the community and an incubator of future young Latino leaders when it came to the student facilitators. As discussed in this chapter, our citizenship class was an open space where Mexican migrants could expose the central contradictions of U.S. citizenship and constitutionalism, one where we were equally critical of the Mexican government. On several occasions we received one-time "volunteers" who I can't help but feel were part of the surveillance of citizenship education. From this class emerged Doña Chole, a transnational *ciudadana* whose encounter with naturalization and citizenship gatekeepers I recount below.

After months in the citizenship class, Doña Chole and I arrived to the USCIS federal building in San José for her naturalization interview, feeling cautiously optimistic after her classmate Antonio's recent successful experience. Antonio had given Doña Chole some civics cheerleading in the days leading up to her exam. However, there were some key differences between the two citizenship interviews. Doña Chole is a senior from Michoacán with over fifteen years as a legal permanent resident, making her eligible to take the naturalization test in her native Spanish. For these interviews, the qualified applicant is expected to bring an interpreter to her citizenship test, in case the USCIS examining officer is not bilingual, which is most likely the case. There I was in the waiting room, subtly anxious at what would be only my second attempt serving as citizenship test interpreter, trying to conceal my innate nervousness before Doña Chole's usual gleeful self.[20]

Suddenly, a citizenship officer cracked the door open and called out: "Soooledad Pereeeez." Doña Chole and I jumped out of our seats and treaded across the waiting room in what seemed to me like a long, fateful march toward the officer. The middle-aged white officer looked up from the files he held in his hands and peered at me with bewilderment, as if demanding an explanation to my presence, nonverbally. "I am her interpreter," I uttered, somewhat anxiously under the uncomfortable gaze of the officer. Putting his hand up, the officer stopped me summarily stating, "She won't be needing you. I will be using a computer-based interpreter." With that, he turned his back and escorted Doña Chole into the entrails of the immigration building, shutting the door in my face.

Dejected, I walked back to my seat where Doña Chole's husband waited patiently and explained to him the situation, trying not to seem too disconcerted. On the inside, however, I was fuming. I pulled out my cell phone and typed out a text message to my brother, a much more seasoned citizenship class instructor in Los Angeles, who regularly served as interpreter for his eligible students. "Bro, I am at USCIS accompanying one of my students to serve as her interpreter and the f*$%ing officer told me he wouldn't need me! He said he would be using a computer-based interpreter! WTF?!?!?!?!" My brother's response only added to my anxiousness and anger: "Hmm, I have never seen or heard of officers using computer-based interpreters during a citizenship interview. . . . " This is bullshit, I thought to myself. This is precisely the kind of bureaucratic arbitrariness that I have been documenting in my research on the naturalization process, and it completely blind-sided me. How will Doña Chole respond to this unforeseen change in her interview? How does a computer-based interpreter even work? Will she be able to clearly hear and understand the translations? Will this derail her responses? Before I could fully process and assess the situation, Doña Chole emerged from her citizenship interview, with a big grin and a thumbs up, the universal sign of success, completely undeterred and ready to exercise her hard earned transnational citizenship.

What Does Naturalization Mean to Mexican Migrants' Transnational Identities?

What do naturalization experiences like those of Doña Chole mean in the context of migrants' transnational lives and identities? To conclude, this chapter addresses the question of how naturalization impacts migrant cross-border allegiances, affiliations, and attachments by returning to the ethnographic data from the first citizenship class discussed earlier. In contrast to studies that associate acquiring citizenship with "political assimilation," these interviews suggest that cross-border loyalties and attachments do not wane upon naturalization. Benjamín, who was the citizenship class instructor and a U.S. citizen for more than a decade, stated, "I think that we can take the [citizenship] oath [of allegiance] but never be completely loyal. I think that you can never deny your roots or origins." When asked how she will identify upon naturalization, Rosaura replied assertively, "Oh, well, Mexicana obviously. I will always be Mexicana. One hundred percent." Upon further probing, she elaborated,

> Well, I don't know, but I feel that, yes I am becoming a U.S. citizen, but I am Mexicana. Even if I was told that I can no longer be Mexicana, I will continue to be Mexicana. That is what I believe. If the government were to tell me, "You are no longer Mexicana," well okay, they can believe that if they wish, but I feel that my family is Mexicana. I am Mexicana.[21]

Rosaura concluded,

> To be Mexican is to be Mexican. Even if you become an American citizen, you have it in your blood, in you, in everything. You have to say it [the oath], you will say that you will renounce it, but you know that you cannot stop being what you are.

Similarly, Dolores argued, "I am Mexicana. I will always be Mexicana. Because of my roots. Just because I become a citizen doesn't mean that I will stop being Mexicana." This question was seemingly as important for Adela, who remarked:

> We will never stop being Mexican. You always have it in your heart. When I go to Tijuana, and I see the Mexican flag, I feel like crying,

because we are not in our country. When I see the American flag, I feel joy, but I don't feel the same way as when I see the Mexican flag. I think that even if you become a citizen, you will never stop being Mexican. No matter what you say in the oath.

While there is evidence of dual loyalties "under two flags" here, to use Michel Jones-Correa's language (2001), Adela's reaction to her native flag was more emotive than her response to the U.S. flag. Upon further probing, she offered an interesting metaphor:

Well, when I am in the States, I can say I am a citizen. But when you are in your country, all it is, is a piece of paper that makes you a U.S. citizen, but in reality you were born in México. And I think you are never going to leave México. It is like a marriage. Even if you are married, you cannot forget about your parents. It is very similar. Even if I become a citizen, I will never forget where I came from.

Mexican migrants may be "marrying the state," as Plascencia argues (2012: 161), however *without* abjuring ties to the country of origin. While critics have accused Mexican migrants of "civic bigamy," these interviews remind us that ethno-cultural attachments persist postnaturalization partly as a result of racial discrimination.[22] Adela's husband, Doroteo, agreed, "I will continue being Mexican. The papers have nothing to do with that. I will always be Mexican. Nothing can take that away from me."

The Prospect of Enduring Diasporic Roots

Furthermore, there is evidence that this apparent diasporic nationalism and cross-border loyalties can have enduring effects. This is best represented when respondents spoke about their children who were born and/or raised in the United States. Felipe stated:

I want my children to never forget their roots. I don't want them to forget where they came from. There are some people who don't want their children to speak Spanish, only English. But in my eyes, it is better for them never to forget their roots. Because this way, our children, if they are to one day make something of themselves, if they represent us in some government entity, they can do something for us because they are informed about the kind of life we have, how we come here, how much we suffer to come here. Otherwise, they will forget about their roots, and later on they could even be against us. So perhaps my grandchildren would say, "Throw out all those old people" [laughter]. Because he is not going to be aware of his roots, and he will not sympathize with how much we suffer to come to this country.

Don Juan, who said his children self-identify as Mexican, stated, "Well, I think they fight for their place in the U.S. and for establishing themselves in the U.S. but they also feel that they are Mexican." When asked why she identified her U.S.-born children as Mexican, Dolores replied, "Well because their parents are Mexican, and because of their roots. The same way we were brought up as children, we raise them in the same way." When asked whether she thought her children would have the same degree of ethnic attachment to México as she does, Dolores replied, "Yes, I think so. I am going to instill that in them. That they have to go to México, and visit their uncles and get to know all of México; it is beautiful." Likewise, Doroteo and Adela have four U.S.-born children. "They are Mexican," Doroteo said assertively. "If they are the children of Mexican parents, then they have to be Mexican. And they have to maintain our customs from México and our roots."

Racial Naturalization

Among respondents who said they would retain ties to México upon naturalizing, there is evidence of what the legal scholar Devon Carbado calls *racial naturalization*. Carbado defines racial naturalization as the social practice by which "all of us are Americanized and made socially intelligible via racial categorization" (2005: 633). Effectively, Don Juan stated, "We will never stop being Mexican. That cannot be taken away from you." Among the reasons for this enduring Mexican identity is the fact that "we will continue to face discrimination simply because we are Mexican. Even if we become citizens, we will encounter prejudice." Similarly, Dolores argued, "a person could very well be a citizen but he/she is treated based on [racial] appearance." While Don Juan and Dolores implied that their phenotypic cues overshadowed formal or legal citizenship, Mexican migrants are not "Americanized" in the way that Black migrants are (see Carbado 2005). In contrast to Mexican migrants, Carbado suggests that Black migrants' racialization (i.e., their Americanization) relegates them to the bottom rungs of the U.S. racial economy alongside African Americans.[23] By contrast, Mexican migrants are racialized as the United States' iconic "illegal aliens," making them vulnerable to detention and deportation (De Genova 2002; 2005). For Mexican migrants in the United States, de jure naturalization does not have the effect of *denaturalizing* Mexican migrant "illegality" in everyday social interactions and public institutions. To borrow from Lisa Cacho, "race is the methodology of social value" that renders ethnic Mexicans in the United States ineligible for legal personhood (Cacho 2012: 17).

Historical and present-day encounters with racialization largely explain why Mexican migrants retain strong ethnic attachments and cultural identifications once they become U.S. citizens. Of course not everyone agrees on the point of enduring ethnic identifications postnaturalization. While there was no one in my sample who resembled this adamantly assimilationist view, Rosaura described a fellow co-worker who recently naturalized as follows:

> There is one person at my work who became a U.S. citizen, and he says that although he was born in México, he is now one hundred percent American citizen. He says that since he became a U.S. citizen, he is an American. I always argue with him. I would fight him if he weren't a man [laughter]. I don't understand how he can be racist; I feel he is racist toward his own people. I ask him, how can it be that you feel this way if you came here like the rest of us did? You suffered like the rest of us. And now that you were able to obtain citizenship, you should thank God, but that should not make you feel that you are better than those of us who do not have papers. But he is the kind of person who is narrow-minded. The kind that lets it get to his head—the fact that he is a citizen gets to his head.

This discussion bears similarities to a comment made by Doroteo. With regard to whether he will change upon naturalization, Doroteo replied assertively, "In my opinion, I will be the same person, regardless if I pass or don't pass. A piece of paper is not going to change who I am." Doroteo was aware that other migrants, like Rosaura's co-worker above, did not agree. In a statement hauntingly reminiscent of the historical narratives captured by Arredondo (2008), Doroteo asserted:

> A lot of people think otherwise. They even change their name. They even use American names. But I think that is wrong. It is not like you can change your face. It is not like you can wear a mask. What are you going to do, wear a mask? If I have money or don't have money, I will continue being the same person.

Most respondents actively retained their Mexican identity and nationalism/regionalism upon naturalization and disapproved of co-ethnics who did not. In this context, migrants' enduring Mexican identity is a product of their perception of how race and gender structure both the naturalization process and their everyday life experiences in the United States more broadly.

The "asphyxiating politics of citizenship": Evidence from Focus Group Interviews

Playing the role of participant more so than observer, in the time following the initial ethnographic research described above, I volunteered at coordinating and teaching citizenship classes throughout Northern California. In Salinas, California, an agricultural region with a long history of Mexican migrant activism, I was able to volunteer and conduct multiple focus groups at a long-standing citizenship class founded by a local union in the mid-1990s (see Johnston 2004). Again, the imminent threat of a hostile political climate was cited as the main reason for seeking "defensive naturalization": "We should consider becoming citizens because the way the laws are changing, I wouldn't be surprised if they start throwing out legal permanent residents . . . legal permanent resident status does not guarantee security in this country," said a female migrant in the first focus group. In a remark reminiscent of Plascencia's understanding of naturalization as migrants entering the "circle of membership" (2012: 187), one male participant in the second Salinas focus group described migrants' political experience in the United States as an "ever-closing circle," akin to the "asphyxiating politics of citizenship" aptly described by De Genova (2010a: 102).

In this antimigrant political climate, naturalization did afford a measure of "political self-defense" (Pantoja and Segura 2003: 282) for these migrants, as they could "vote out of office . . . politicians who take it out against our race," as commented by another male migrant in the class (for more on the "electoral threat" posed by naturalized migrants vis-à-vis racist legislators see Zepeda-Millán 2017). Similarly, female migrants envisioned citizenship as providing a modicum of safety in a racially hostile political climate, especially for those in mixed-status families. As one woman remarked, "My family, my children are U.S. citizens and I am not," alluding to the ever-present possibility of family separation. Another female respondent offered a similarly gendered perspective: "I, as a mother, am becoming a citizen to vote and fight for the rights of my family, of my children who were born here." However, her struggles for U.S. citizenship did not mean relinquishing her Mexican citizenship or self-identification. Testament to her transnationality, she vowed to struggle "without denying my country [México] because I am from there, but here I am going to fight for the rights of my children" who are birthright U.S. citizens.

One of the methodological and pedagogical innovations of these focus group discussions was that I read aloud a Spanish translation of the citizenship oath of allegiance to the class, which states: "I hereby declare on oath, that I absolutely and entirely renounce and abjure all allegiance and fidelity to any foreign . . . state, or sovereignty, of whom or which I have heretofore been a subject or citizen." Almost without exception, Mexican migrants were extremely critical of the exhortation to renounce ties to their country of origin, precisely because they felt that their new country utterly rejected them. "They require us to swear by their country and by this constitution but at the end of the day they do not see us as fellow Americans," said a female migrant from Michoacán named Alina. Class participants critically reflected on the course material to expose this central contradiction at the heart of U.S. citizenship, what Plascencia describes as the Janus-faces of citizenship (2012). When a male migrant from Zacatecas asserted, "We also have rights, the constitution says so," Alina replied, "just because we become a U.S. citizen, it doesn't mean that we will be treated like an American." Perceived discrimination largely accounted for enduring ethnic attachment postnaturalization for these migrants. When the migrant from Zacatecas acknowledged that even after naturalization "we continue being Mexican," an elder *paisano* hauntingly foreshadowed the migrant political life cycle, stating that they would be Mexicanos "until we die, and even once we are dead." While an anti-migrant political context mobilizes migrants to seek citizenship, "suggesting a complex, almost contradictory relationship between their feelings of stigmatization and the process of naturalization" (Michelson and Pallares 2001: 66), discrimination also partly explains why migrants do not relinquish loyalties to their communities of origin. Under an antimigrant context, the so-called "political baptism" may, in effect, mark the political birth of transnational citizens.

Conclusion: Implications for Political Participation

Conservative policymakers and commentators in the United States vocally disapprove of Mexican migrant cross-border identifications and loyalties. The institutionalization of these transnational ties has evoked public outcries from political observers bemoaning the fact that dual nationality undermines national sovereignty and singular loyalty to the United States. An alternative explanation suggests that, for migrants, dual nationality can be a means to reconcile memberships in both their countries of residence and of origin, leading to higher naturalization rates in the United States, and making dual nationality consistent with membership in the U.S. polity (Jones-Correa 2001). Regarding allegiance, Don Juan, from the first citizenship class discussed above, stated, "By seeking citizenship I have to obey this country's standards. It would be contradictory for me to seek membership in a country whose principles I did not agree with." Dolores added, "Once you become a citizen you have to respect the laws of this country." Adela said naturalization is a commitment, "legally and before God, that you will accept that oath. No matter what, we want to be in this country, so we have to accept the laws the way they have them." As these statements suggest, ethnic attachment to the homeland postnaturalization does not necessarily equate with disloyalty to the host country. As Plascencia finds in his study of Mexican migrant naturalization, "Those participating in citizenship classes desire citizenship, want to be good citizens, and want their children to be good citizens" (2012: 114). U.S. commentators and policymakers who demand loyalty from migrants should focus on granting first-class citizenship to ethnic Mexicans rather than the noncitizenship or second-class citizenship historically conferred upon them regardless of nativity (see Gutiérrez 1995).

This chapter complicates the assertions that, regarding Latinos in the United States, "a traditional pattern of political assimilation appears to prevail" and that "the intention to become an American citizen increases identification with the United States," pointing to a sustained anti-immigrant context and discrimination throughout the naturalization process (Citrin et al. 2007: 41). From the perspective of Mexican migrants, there is more to naturalization—understood as the legal rituals of U.S. political belonging—than newfound patriotism and singular national allegiance (Kun 2005: 7-11). With regard to migration history, this chapter suggests that the decision to naturalize today cannot be understood as a sign of permanent resettlement in the United States or an indication that migrant mobilization in U.S. politics comes at the expense of participation in Mexican politics (or vice versa). Again, under hostile political conditions, the "political baptism" of Mexican migrants in the United States may be more accurately described as the political awakening of transnational citizens.

As these findings show, among migrants who were once reticent to seek U.S. citizenship, there is an emerging consensus in favor of naturalization.

Similarly, the newly eligible also share a sense of urgency to naturalize in an immigrant-hostile and increasingly precarious political environment. However, ethnic attachment to the homeland does not always wane over time or upon naturalization. Those naturalized retain cross-border identifications and attachments in a way that does not preclude political engagement in their new country. To put it in Jose Alfredo's words when asked how he will identify upon naturalization: "If I am in the United States, I am an American citizen. If I am in México, I am Mexican, upon entering. We can be both; they are not mutually exclusive. There is nothing unlawful there." Don Juan responded to the same question, stating, "I will be Mexican, but I will have the rights of an American citizen." Just like migrants who were civically minded in their home country are likely to be engaged in the host country, there is nothing to say that reactive naturalization cannot drive political participation across international boundaries. To conclude, in the words of Alicia Schmidt Camacho, "As migrants narrate a condition of alterity to, or exclusion from, the nation, they also enunciate a collective desire for a different order of space and belonging across the boundary" (2008: 5).

3

Enactments of Transnational Citizenship

MIGRANTS' ENTANGLEMENTS WITH
MEXICAN PARTY POLITICS

Prologue: Rigoberto Castañeda, Transnational Citizen

"I didn't want to do it! I didn't know if I was going to lose part of my mustache!" Rigoberto Castañeda explained his fear of becoming a naturalized U.S. citizen in these de-Mexicanizing, mustache-maiming terms. As Castañeda recalled, he became a naturalized U.S. citizen in mid-1990s California, when droves of his co-nationals were doing so as a protective measure against then Governor Pete Wilson's antimigrant political agenda (for more on the infamous Proposition 187, see Zepeda-Millán 2017). Castañeda shared his mythology of U.S. citizenship while sitting in the comfort of his legislative office in Zacatecas, México. Castañeda reminisced about his political experiences as a migrant in the United States during an interview I conducted with him in his capacity as "migrant deputy" in the state legislature of his native Zacatecas. His primary residence still in Los Angeles—he was the epitome of a transnational citizen. As this chapter will show, however, in many ways, migrants like Castañeda are the incarnation of transnational citizenship gone awry.

"Follow me," snapped Casteñada, as he pulled me out of his office and ran down a hallway and up a narrow staircase of the colonial rose-stone building that now serves as the state legislature in Zacatecas. He flung open two heavy wooden doors; I followed closely behind into a packed room for a press conference, all eyes on us. Unaware that I was walking into a press meeting underway, I sank into a seat near the back of the conference room, melting under the gaze of state legislators, reporters, and ex-braceros—elderly Mexican migrants, who were rightfully and righteously seeking their due from the Mexican government, *sombreros* in hand. Rigoberto took the seat at the head of the table, looking every bit the overly confident Mexican PRIista politician he had become. After a relatively brief meeting, where activists denounced Mexican officials, claiming they were deliberately mishandling ex-bracero's identity documents to delay their long overdue payments from the government, Rigoberto once again grabbed me saying, "Let's go," as if issuing an order to a political staffer. We rushed through another hallway and took a sudden, unexpected exit through a large window that lead to the rooftop of the colonial building, which formerly served as a convent. "Take a look at this," Castañeda mumbled, as he lit a cigarette expertly snuggled between his lips. Before me was a striking view of Zacatecas city, the capital of our eponymous ancestral state. As I took in the view, I could see the allure of transnational politics for men like Castañeda, who was subsequently appointed director of the state's Secretary of the Zacatecan Migrant, his reward for being a loyal PRIista. The city before us was his new political playpen, and it came with a whole lot of power, money, and influence. As a reminder of the ironies and contradictions of Mexican politics stood *El Cerro de la Bufa*, the capital's iconic mountain that was the site of an important revolutionary battle and that, in the prophetic words of the peasant, migrant poet Máximo Pérez Torres, towers over the mestizo migrant state whose topography resembles a huddled "sleeping indigenous woman."

Having previously laid out migrants' enunciations and mythologies of citizenship in the United States, I chronicle in this chapter U.S.-based Mexican migrants' enactments of transnational citizenship before the Mexican state and their ongoing struggle for representation in Mexican party politics. As the opening vignette suggests, the chapter documents the promise and potential of transnational citizenship in the orbit of the notoriously corporatist, clientelist, and increasingly cartelized Mexican political system, and also its political pitfalls and contradictions.

The Elusive Enactment of Migrant Representation in México: The Political Action Front of Mexicans Abroad

In the months leading to México's July 2009 congressional election, Salvador Pedroza and Fabián Morales, two Chicago-based Mexican migrants, aspired to be placed as migrant candidates on the proportional representation lists of their respective parties: the right-wing National Action Party (PAN) and the once hegemonic Institutional Revolutionary Party (PRI). Both migrants were proven and qualified party militants. As president of the Illinois chapter of PAN, for example, Pedroza had been a staunch supporter of Felipe Calderón in his bid for the Mexican presidency in 2006. Morales, a Chicago realtor and hometown association (HTA) leader, coordinated a personal meeting with the national president of the PRI at the time, Beatriz Paredes, seeking endorsement for his candidacy.[1] In spite of their efforts and proven partisan stripes, the PRI and PAN failed to provide either aspirant with a migrant candidacy, leaving them out of the congressional race.

In response to what they considered an egregious act of political neglect, Mexican migrant activists in the United States put aside their party affiliations to form the Political Action Front of Mexicans Abroad, with one goal in mind: to demand that political parties in México endorse migrant candidates and thereby guarantee migrant representation in federal and state legislatures. While the transnational movement to gain migrant political rights in México had gained important concessions, including the right to vote in presidential elections from abroad, the Political Action Front argued in a letter to Mexican political parties that migrant transnational enfranchisement was far from complete.[2] For one, the requirements for voting from abroad were unreasonably cumbersome; second, migrants lacked adequate representation in México's federal and state congresses, due in part to the parties' failure to place migrants in electable positions on their lists or to endorse migrant candidacies, period.

In their letter, the Front demanded Mexican political parties provide migrant representation, arguing, "social justice comes to fruition through the equal representation of society in our country's elected institutions." The Political Action Front made clear the high stakes involved in their call upon Mexican political parties. "Not only are our political rights at stake, but also our sense of belonging and loyalty, our duties and obligations as Mexican citizens." In the eyes of these migrants, not only was their transnational political membership in jeopardy, but also Mexican democracy itself was on the line: "The implementation of democracy in México via electoral processes will be fulfilled when anyone who is and identifies as Mexican can vote and be voted into office, wherever they may be!" The Front's claim was directed at México's political institutions and at civil society writ large.

Political parties and society: we have the opportunity to go down in history as the generation that ingrained human rights into our political institutions. Lest we be judged like the earlier generation that deemed women and youth unfit for involvement in México's public affairs.

This treatise of transnational citizenship from the Political Action Front raises an important set of questions regarding migrants' ongoing entanglement with Mexican party politics. First, to what degree are México's political parties "incorporating" Mexican migrants in their party discourse and in their power structures? Second, among those migrants who have contended for office, what have been their experiences with Mexican party politics and the challenges to their transnational political trajectories? In short, how do Mexican migrants enact their transnational citizenship before the Mexican state? This chapter addresses these questions by drawing on in-depth structured interviews with migrant deputies in the state legislature of Zacatecas and with migrant candidates in the 2009 congressional election (and subsequent election cycles), each representing one of the three major parties (PRI, PRD, PAN). In the lead up to the 2009 election cycle, I conducted interviews with the only migrant candidates in the race: Lupe Gómez (PAN) and Carlos Arango (PRD), in Southern California. Immediately after, I conducted in-depth interviews with the two migrant deputies in the Zacatecas state legislature at the time, Rigoberto Castañeda (PRI) and Sebastián Martínez (PRD). Additionally, I discuss structured interviews with local party representatives and leaders from two of the smaller parties in Zacatecas, Partido del Trabajo (Labor Party) and Convergencia (now Movimiento Ciudadano [Citizens' Movement Party]), and draw on ethnographic field notes from Lupe Gómez's campaign events throughout the state.[3] To call into question the idea of migrants being "incorporated" into a clientelistic and corrupt party system— and thereby highlight the contradictions of diasporic dialectics and migrant enactments of transnational citizenship in a corporatist political context—I briefly discuss the troubling pattern of cartelization in Mexican party politics and the collusion of its electoral institutions, which in principle are supposed to stay above the party fray.

The Cartelization of Mexican Party Politics: Migrants Confront México's Multiparty Electoral Autocracy

In response to the utter usurpation of migrant political subjectivity on the part of Mexican parties discussed at the outset of the book, Proyecto Migrante *Zacatecano* (a broad U.S.-based Zacatecan migrant association that seeks to promote the interests of migrants on both sides of the border) began lobbying for electoral reforms to allow for independent candidacies in local elections.[4] This would allow migrants a political avenue to run for office free of party hierarchies and patronage. At the local level, the municipality of Enrique Estrada in Zacatecas elected the state's first independent mayor, a small step forward in México's painful process of "democratization." With independent candidacies now on the books, it was time to see how the law would be implemented with regard to migrant candidates, a group of diasporic political subjects eager to enact their transnational citizenship free from party fetters and control.

In July 2015, one of the members of Proyecto Migrante from North Texas and I paid a visit to the Zacatecas State Electoral Institute, the local agency in charge of implementing electoral law in the state. Donning *tejanas* and cowboy boots—seemingly the irrefutable symbol of migrant subjectivity in the Mexican political arena, in this part of the country at least—we descended into the basement of the building, where the bureaucracy attends citizen grievances on "politico-electoral" matters in the state. Immediately, I felt the bureaucratic gaze of the staff of lawyers and data analysts, their business suits a sharp reminder of the cultural and class differences between Mexican migrants and Mexican bureaucrats and political elites. The lead lawyer in charge of attending to citizen grievances greeted us rather cordially and professionally in her office. We introduced ourselves as members of the political committee of Proyecto Migrante (the proud embodiment of the diasporic dialectic, I thought to myself, somewhat self-righteously). "We are here to inquire about the implementation of the new electoral reforms concerning independent candidates," we stated. She proceeded to give us a general overview of the requirements, campaign finance restrictions, and electoral timetable that independent candidates were subject to. When asked specifically how independent candidacies would apply to migrants seeking office in the state, she struggled to find a direct answer and implied that these two political subjectivities might be mutually exclusive—as if migrants could only run through party nomination. "Are you suggesting that these two categories, migrant candidates and independent candidates, are incompatible"? Scrolling haphazardly through her computer she replied, "Yes, that may be the case," tentative in her answer. Looking over at my comrade, I uttered with sarcasm, "That would be anti-democratic."

Unable to provide a direct response, the lawyer recommended we submit a formal information request to the president of the State Electoral Institute regarding migrant and independent candidacies. Upon my return to California,

I took to the task of conferring with the rest of the members of Proyecto Migrante to write up the inquiry. "We are seeking to uphold two hard-won migrant political principles," our letter concluded empathically: "self-determination and autonomy." The institute never formally replied to our query, meeting instead with a California-based migrant association widely believed to be loyal to the reigning PRI; our diasporic dialectics and migrant enactments of transnational citizenship seemingly stifled and suffocated by an increasingly cartelized Mexican political party system.[5]

To understand the challenges and possibilities of migrant involvement in Mexican politics, it is important to discuss the nature of the transitioning party system therein. In democratic and nondemocratic systems alike, political parties represent the "main institutional channel connecting people with their government" (Anderson 2009). As Htun and Ossa remind us, "Groups do not advance their demands in a vacuum but in the context of already-existing political institutions" (2013: 7), namely, political parties. In México, parties have and will continue to act either as facilitators or gatekeepers to the elusive possibility of migrant political representation. Indeed, "parties have inherent interests that shape their positions vis-à-vis policies to promote the inclusion of historically marginalized groups [e.g., migrants] . . . they are the primary agents of representation and hold a monopoly on access to elected office" (Htun and Ossa 2013: 7). Following Leslie Anderson's contention that "we can learn a great deal about new and developing democracies through studying the histories of more established and consolidated democracies" (2009), in this section I discuss party organizational development in consolidated democracies to project what Mexican party politics may look like in the twenty-first century and explain the likely impact of this system for the prospect of migrant political representation and their enactments of transnational citizenship. Specifically, with the rise of U.S.-style elections in México, campaigns have become increasingly candidate-centered and party presence has begun to wane at the grassroots level. Moreover, recently the party system in México has shown signs of what in other democracies has been described as the "cartelization" of competitive party politics. Either outcome will impact the prospects of migrant participation in Mexican politics and their enactments of transnational citizenship therein.

At the turn of the twenty-first century, policymaking and legislation in the context of post-PRI hegemonic politics would require alliances and coalitions across party lines like never before. Under conditions of single-party rule, the Mexican congress acted as a rubber stamp for PRI *presidencialismo* throughout most of the twentieth century. As Manuel Pastor and Carol

Wise have argued, with the removal of the PRI from the executive and its gradual decline in congress in the first decade of the twenty-first century, policymaking in economic and other key policy areas required greater statecraft and alliance-building capacity on the part of Mexican leaders and parties (Pastor and Wise 2005).[6] Initially, party alliances generally followed ideological lines, with the formerly hegemonic PRI siding mostly with the right-wing PAN and the leftist parties coalescing into a broad front made up of the PRD, PT, and Movimiento Ciudadano.

However, with the return of the PRI to power, México witnessed an ideologically incongruent realignment among its parties dubbed "*el Pacto por México*" (the pact for México). Upon its dubious return to power, the PRI picked up right where it left off at the turn of the twenty-first century—with a relentless agenda of neoliberal reforms and a spiral of political violence. With the support and complicity of the PAN and PRD in congress, the Peña Nieto administration fast-tracked a series of structural reforms, notable among them the partial privatization of the state-owned oil company Petróleos Mexicanos (PEMEX). Indeed, this alliance between the PRI, PAN, and PRD in congress rubberstamped neoliberal reforms in México's economic, educational, and energy sectors (the PRD would later partially back away from some of these structural reforms).

These inter-party alliances may be symptomatic of an early stage in the development process experienced by parties in more advanced democracies. In particular, two trends in party development in consolidated democracies may be applicable to the current party system in México. First, many advanced democracies have experienced a shift in party organizational structures and mobilization strategies. In many consolidated democracies, political parties have gone from extensive rural and urban machines to a tendency to withdraw their activities and presence at the grassroots level. In the case of the United States, Janelle Wong (2006) writes, "The party structure is weak at the local level, and outreach strategies have shifted dramatically . . . The potential for mass-mobilization efforts . . . has been overlooked in favor of party activity confined primarily to the airwaves" (52). Technological innovations in U.S. and Mexican political campaigns have "increased the importance of mass media marketing" (57). While there was a limited revitalization of political parties at the end of the twentieth century in the United States, this consisted of "technical and professional sophistication rather than grassroots organization." By the turn of the century, Wong states, "personal contact by neighborhood party activists had become largely a thing of the past" (57). Overall, there is a weakened local party structure and a shift in favor of mass-mediated, candidate-centered campaign tactics. Speaking to the experience of Western European democracies, Katz and Mair state it summarily: "The Mass party is dead" (2009: 760). With the rise of U.S.-style elections in México, we may expect a mobilization vacuum to develop at the local level, especially in rural communities. Indeed, the conventional political wisdom in rural México is that parties only rear their heads during election time.

More troubling for an unconsolidated democracy like México is the related trend that as parties gradually move away from civil society, they may move closer to the state. In their research on parties in developed, mostly Western European, democracies, Katz and Mair (2009) identify a second pattern related to the diminishing role of parties at the local level: the "cartelization of ostensibly competitive political parties" where "parties increasingly function like cartels, employing the resources of the state to limit political competition and ensure their own electoral success" (753). The cartel party is likely to emerge in political systems "characterized by the interpenetration of party and state and by a tendency towards inter-party collusion" (755). Conditions of cartelization allow for greater "inter-party collusion or cooperation" (755), leading to a sort of depoliticization of party politics, insofar as parties become less distinct in terms of ideology and policy positions (e.g., *Pacto por México*). As Katz and Mair note, "Competition between cartel parties focus less on differences in policy and more—in a manner consistent with Bernard Manin's notion of 'audience democracy'—on the provision of spectacle, image, and theater" (755). Ultimately, under conditions of cartelization, the cartel parties form a "ruling coalition" that enjoys the resources of the state (758).

In addition to the risk of cartelization, Leslie Anderson points to two characteristics particularly important for parties in an unconsolidated democracy: (1) whether the dominant party has an authoritarian past, and (2) the degree to which the party is internally democratic. With the ominous return of the PRI, both indicators cast a troubling shadow for the prospects of democratization in twenty-first-century México. That said, it is unlikely México will experience a return to single-party hegemony in the twenty-first century. A more likely outcome is that México will transition into a predominant/cartel party system. As Anderson reminds us, either scenario is injurious to the democratization prospects of an unconsolidated democracy (2009). Yet, if the latter case materializes, it can open political opportunities for the creation of new opposition political movements and institutions, where U.S.-based migrants can play a strategic role.

Katz and Mair note that cartelization creates fertile ground for the emergence of "anti-party system parties that appeal directly to public perceptions that the mainstream parties are indifferent to the desires of ordinary citizens" (2009: 759). At the time of the initial research for this chapter, it was politically in vogue for migrants to flirt with the remote possibility of a "migrant party," an unlikely proposition today. As such, the specter of a migrant party looms in some of the interviews that follow. Of course, the party that actually emerged to fill the political void left by the cartelization process is Morena—Movimiento Regeneración Nacional (National Regeneration Movement). The opposition party Morena has begun to make inroads into the Mexican diaspora in the United States, as reflected by the episodes discussed briefly below.

On November 19, 2013, a day before the anniversary of the Mexican Revolution, a cross-border contingent of Mexican migrants and activists from California, Nevada, Chihuahua, and other places planned a public protest and press conference outside the Mexican consulate in San José, California, to denounce the privatization of México's state-controlled oil company Petróleos Mexicanos (PEMEX)—one of the last standing vestiges of the country's postrevolutionary economic nationalism. I arrived before the convoy of activists and Univisión cameras rolled in, and I approached Mexican migrant families as they shuttled in and out of the consulate to inform them of the impending rally and press conference regarding an amendment to the Mexican constitution that would allow foreign corporations to meddle in Mexican oil. One migrant shrugged his shoulders asking incredulously "¿Y qué podemos hacer de aquí?" (What can we possibly do from here?). I explained that many U.S. oil companies are eager to profit from Mexican oil, and that the group of activists would personally deliver a letter from Mexican leftist leader Andrés Manuel López Obrador to Chevron headquarters (where we were later run-off by police) immediately following the protest. "Is this being put on by a [Mexican] political party?" another migrant from Jalisco, who waited with a group of his *paisanos* in the parking lot outside of the consulate, asked somewhat suspiciously. Indeed, this protest was organized by members of the incipient antiparty system party Morena (and its U.S. affiliates). When the Morena activists arrived—megaphones and banners in hand—I signaled to the group of migrants from Jalisco, who remained standing in the same place, to join us in the rally. Staying put, instead they nodded in approval of the activists' resounding message against privatization from afar.

This diasporic distancing and ambivalence toward Mexican party politics notwithstanding, Morena continues to make appeals to Mexican migrants in the United States. In March 2014, Morena's cofounder and now México's president-elect, Andrés Manuel López Obrador, held a political rally on the lawn of City Hall in downtown Los Angeles where he denounced Obama's failure to put an end to the record-breaking deportations of Mexican migrants and their families (on this point see Gonzales 2013). Less promising was a 2015 visit to Southern California by the Morena candidate for the gubernatorial seat of Zacatecas, David Monreal, who cajoled migrants to patiently wait their turn at the migrant deputy position in the state legislature, stating metaphorically: "If you don't dance this time, you'll dance the next time"; as if these migrants are power-hungry opportunists eagerly waiting their chance at the spoils of office. Monreal ultimately handpicked the migrant nominee, overlooking the U.S.-based candidate that Proyecto Migrante *Zacatecano* internally vetted and democratically selected. Such are the potential political pitfalls and possibilities of diasporic dialectics and the contradictions of transnational citizenship in a clientelist party system traced in this chapter.

Having briefly discussed the possibility of a "socio-electoral coalition" between migrants and Morena, where the latter can evince "important institutional voices for publicizing allies' demands and denouncing violations of the human rights" (Trejo 2014: 337) of migrants on both sides of the border, the following sections of this chapter return to the question of migrant representation in México's dominant parties and explore questions of migrant party identities and policy priorities, calling into question what it means for migrants to be "incorporated" into an increasingly cartelized party system.

Return of the Hegemon: The "New" PRI and Migrant Deputies

Given that the transition to a multi-party democracy in México is still unfolding and the fact that migrant involvement with Mexican party politics is part of that ongoing, iterative process, the degree of loyalty or attachment to a given party varies considerably among migrants, with some ambiguous about their party identification and others zealous partisans.[7] In order to tap into party identities, each of the migrant deputies and candidates interviewed was asked about their thoughts regarding the implications of forming a migrant party. This counterfactual served as a proxy for party attachment—those migrants who were strong partisans would likely not support the formation of an opposition migrant party. Conversely, their counterparts who were not as committed to an existing party might be more sympathetic to the idea of a migrant party.

Take, for example, the experience of the local migrant deputy in Zacatecas Rigoberto Castañeda, a committed PRIista. Castañeda—a long-time member of the PRI—felt it was difficult to form a migrant party and suggested that, instead, migrants should work within the existing party system. Castañeda explained his party affiliation as follows. "Given the fact that you have the existing parties, and based on my PRIista predispositions, is how I arrived at my conviction and at my party affiliation. My party chose me to be its representative under proportional representation." In Zacatecas, political parties must make concessions to migrant candidates by law since La Ley Migrante (Migrant Law) established a quota in 2004.[8] Castañeda's comments imply that existing parties are a satisfactory and sufficient mechanism through which migrants engage in Mexican electoral politics. "That is how we [migrants] become involved in the politics of Zacatecas and in the politics of México, through the parties, through our party affiliation." Castañeda was well aware that a migrant candidate needs party backing to get into office since parties control the migrant-candidate nomination process. "That is the way we made it here," he said about his position in the Zacatecas state legislature. Of course Castañeda failed to mention the inherent political risk involved in migrants entering party politics, which in a notoriously corporatist system like México can compromise their "demands, identities, and independence and can jeopardize" (Trejo 2014: 333) their very legal personhood, as we saw in the introduction to this book. As Htun and Ossa remind us, while political systems have implemented quotas and "other mechanisms to improve the diversity of elected legislatures," the degree to which "quotas and other institutional interventions actually improve the political presence of excluded groups" is an open question. Indeed, "participation in political office" does not necessarily lead to "legislative advocacy of group interests," as we will later see (2013: 4).

"Voluntary and Altruistic"? Migrant Deputy Policy Priorities

With regard to his policy work in office, Castañeda identified a series of migrant "causes" and needs as his political raison d'être. When asked what motivated him to run for the position of migrant deputy, he replied, "What motivates me is to continue working for the migrant causes that have long been part of our struggle." In fact, Castañeda began his trajectory in migrant civil society as part of migrant HTAs in California in the early 1990s (see Smith and Bakker 2008). Castañeda described the work of these organizations as "voluntary and altruistic," aimed at benefiting migrants' communities of origin. As Castañeda pointed out, migrants have long been coordinating projects in their hometowns with the goal of spurring economic development and improving the standard of living therein (Fox and Bada 2008). Castañeda's role as a migrant deputy has been to "follow-up, support, and strengthen" such projects from "this new front" (i.e., political office). For example, as a migrant deputy Castañeda submitted a policy proposal with the goal of "fomenting migrant investments." The broader objective of this proposed legislation is to create a safe environment for those migrants who are interested in making investments in Zacatecas.[9] The goal, Castañeda explained, "is to ensure that the migrant investment is a success, so that he/she does not return defeated." Lastly, Castañeda has worked to stimulate migrant investments in social infrastructure and economic development projects by providing oversight, transparency, and quality control for these endeavors.

> When they request it, I am here to work with them [migrants]. Take for example the stalled construction of a dam in El Ranchito in the municipality of Juchipila. Thanks to the assistance of this office and that of my party, we have helped the migrants complete that project.[10]

The Diaspora-as-District Approach

In the political discourse and policymaking of Castañeda and other migrant politicians, the Zacatecas and Mexican diasporas emerge as an extraterritorial constituency. Castañeda envisions his work on behalf of this cross-border constituency as follows:

> As a matter of political participation, it is my job to provide information for all of the [migrants] that I represent. I have to be in frequent contact with them and let them know that I am here to help them by legislating. That is my main objective. Additionally, my goal is to have an improved relationship with them so that they are well aware that

they have a representative in the state legislature for any issue they may want to address.

Indicative of the cross-border span of diasporic dialectics, the work of Castañeda is not exclusively aimed at assisting migrants with their activities *within* México but also with their civic, social, and political inclusion in the United States (for a discussion of how the Mexican government can aid migrant integration in the United States see Délano 2010).

> We have a field office in the U.S. for addressing migrant grievances, with a full-time staffer in charge of this office. Through this office, we provide any kind of support that may be needed. We gather migrant petitions there and send them over here [Zacatecas]. In turn, we are providing a service for our people. Take for instance issues of immigration status; we provide legal assistance from Zacatecas. Later this afternoon someone is coming to see me because he is trying to sponsor his family for legalization in the U.S. but is being charged the excessive amount of five thousand dollars [USD] for the paperwork. I made an appointment with him in my office here, and I am going to put him in touch with my advisor in Los Angeles, California. He will provide my advisor with the case number, and my advisor will follow-up, and we will proceed to help them from there.

Furthermore, Castañeda has also reached out to California politicians for the benefit of Mexican migrants therein. "As soon as I took office, I sent an official communiqué to state senators in California and local politicians in Los Angeles, to inform them about my new position and establish a working relationship with them." Reportedly, Castañeda submitted an initiative proposing that U.S. authorities accept the consular-issued *matrícula consular* as an official identity document, one to which then California State Senator Alex Padilla was initially sympathetic. On top of this, Castañeda also worked with Los Angeles City Council member José Huizar in order to deliver four ambulances to the municipalities of Jerez, Villanueva, El Salvador, and Tlaltenango in Zacatecas. "José Huizar is from Jerez," Castañeda explained, "and he wants to do something for his land." On top of this, Castañeda also coordinated a visit to Zacatecas by Los Angeles Council member Gil Cedillo. Castañeda concluded by emphasizing the bilateral implications of these diplomatic interactions:

This is proof that we can work together. This is proof that we can provide ideas to senators and assembly members in the U.S. We can provide the tools to understand the issues that affect our community so
that we work to resolve them.

Clearly, the interview with Castañeda suggests that migrant elected/ap-
pointed officials envision their constituency as residing on both sides of
the U.S.-México border: both in migrant communities throughout the
United States and in Zacatecas proper.[11] The conversation with Castañeda
also reminds us that these returned migrant politicians can be agents of
transnational citizenship, if they resist the allure of Mexican party patronage and its "token economic subsidies and financial support" (Trejo
2014: 342).

Beyond Token Representation

To what degree has the notoriously clientelistic PRI "incorporated" migrants
into its party structure? As a committed PRIista, it is not surprising that
Castañeda believes that his party has proactively recruited migrants. However,
as discussed in the introduction to this chapter, the experience of Fabián
Morales suggests that party discourse is not always implemented in practice.
Of the three major parties, the PRI was the least willing to offer concessions
to migrants, such as the right to vote in presidential elections from abroad,
when these issues were being debated in congress in the late 1990s (Martínez-
Saldaña and Ross Pineda 2002). In an effort to improve the party's image,
the national leader of the PRI, Beatriz Paredes, made a campaign stop in
Zacatecas during the July 2009 midterm congressional elections. Castañeda
was sitting awkwardly at the edge of the stage, quite visibly the PRI's token
migrant. Addressing a large crowd in the migrant-sending *municipio* of Jerez,
Paredes emphasized the party's commitment to stemming out-migration and
made emotional appeals to the women who often stay behind. Outside of
this political rally, an indigenous *huichol* family—perhaps the most egregious
symbol of PRI neglect in this region—sat under "mute" Alamo trees, those si-
lent witnesses of the injustices of Mexican political history, entirely unnoticed
(author field notes, June 2009).[12] While the "new" PRI can strategically use
migration in its rhetoric to reinvent the party's image, it remains to be seen if
that will actually produce spaces for migrants within the party, beyond token
representation.

Transnational Training Grounds: HTAs as a Pathway to Migrant Political Participation in México and the United States

As the interview with Castañeda suggests, HTAs can be organizational vehicles for migrant involvement in Mexican and U.S. politics. Indeed, survey research reveals that HTA membership can have spillover effects into other arenas of civic life in the United States, with migrants who are members of these ethnic associations more likely to be part of other U.S. civil society organizations compared with migrants who are not HTA participants (see Ramírez and Félix 2011; see Pantoja 2005 for evidence of how HTA membership spurs U.S. civic engagement among Dominican migrants). Moreover, in-depth ethnographic case studies of these organizations reveal the internal dynamics whereby HTAs "scale-up" and expand their agenda to include migrant rights activism in the United States (see Bada 2014; see also Zepeda-Millán 2017 for the role that Dominican migrants played in the immigrant rights mobilizations in New York City, for example). Here, it is instructive to briefly examine the state-diaspora interface from the perspective of one such organization: the Federation of Zacatecan Clubs in Northern California (FCZNC).

An interview with then president of the FCZNC, Fermín Luna, in 2011 revealed the organization's work in México and the United States and provided insight into how HTAs can serve as conduits for transnational participation, especially for migrants who may be *disinclined* to participate politically, as was the case with this migrant turned HTA leader. I began by inquiring about the transborder work of the FCZNC. On top of the usual public infrastructure projects destined for communities of origin in Zacatecas (public roads, electricity), Luna explained that the organization was prioritizing "productive projects" that have the added benefit of job creation. "Upon completion, productive projects continue offering employment. What we are trying to do is create employment over there [Zacatecas]," Luna explained from the office of his successful shipping business in San José, California. When asked to offer an example of one such project, Luna pointed to *invernaderos* (greenhouses), "which are a bit more costly but they yield increased production and they generate jobs. We want our projects to create employment . . . considering that many migrants are returning," alluding to the climate of increased deportations in the United States.

Luna lamented that the work of HTAs had been halted by the lack of political will on the part of municipal authorities in Zacatecas. As he put it:

The biggest challenge that we face comes from the mayors . . . many of them don't want to contribute, they only want to promote their own projects and when we propose a project they try to use it to their own benefit . . . many of the HTAs are facing this problem. The mayors don't want in. I don't know what they are doing with the money, but they are not willing to support our program.

When asked if there was a particular political party that was unwilling to collaborate with migrant HTAs, Luna replied that mayors were uncooperative irrespective of party. This created serious setbacks that the HTAs attempted to resolve:

When mayors are not willing to work with us the HTAs, the Federation [FCZNC] has offered to contribute the municipality's share. But if the municipality does not approve the project, the state and federal governments cannot see it through. The mayor has to approve it, and they aren't willing to do that. We currently have two projects that we are proposing to mayors and the federation or the clubs are offering to lend them their share of the money because they allegedly don't have the funds, they don't have the budget. We are offering to lend them their share so that we can see the projects through and still we can't get the projects cleared . . . this is irrespective of party, I am talking about all four parties [PRI, PAN, PRD, PT] not just one party.

If these state-diaspora tensions persist, Zacatecan home-state federations may go from being "consolidated civil society counterparts" of their state government (Fox 2006: 45) to being cross-border critics and agents of accountability and democratization at the (sub)municipal level (Bada 2014).

Despite these challenges, Luna felt that, internally, the HTAs within his federation were working well and that, in turn, his federation was collaborating successfully with other Zacatecan federations throughout the United States (California, Texas, and Illinois). "The Zacatecan Federation of Northern California is on the right track. All of the clubs support me and they are all working very well." Luna was equally optimistic about inter-organizational cooperation across Zacatecan federations:

I don't believe we had ever seen this degree of collaboration between the federations. Currently, there are about seven federations—I would say they are the largest federations—that are working very closely [including federations from Chicago, Fort Worth, Los Angeles, Oxnard, San José, Orange County]. We communicate on a weekly basis; we exchange e-mails. We are achieving something that we had not previously accomplished. There were previous attempts to create a confederation but they were unsuccessful. Why? Because every- body wanted to be a leader and it never materialized. Now we are all working without leaders. We are working together. Nobody is going to be higher than anybody else. We all work and collaborate as equals, on the same level. This has given us *fuerza* [strength].

These collaborative efforts were not only targeted at the community of or- igin in Zacatecas but they also sought to address migrant rights in the United States. According to Luna, the FCZNC, for the first time, is turning to is- sues that concern migrants in the United States. "Now that I am president, I have become deeply involved in this." Again alluding to intra-organizational cooperation and broader partnerships, Luna stated,

we are uniting with migrants from Michoacán, from Jalisco, with the Mexican consulate . . . When it comes to Zacatecas migrants, we are working with the state government, with UC Berkeley and with the FCZNC around the issue of migrant public health . . . we participated around the issue of public health for three days during the Binational Health Week here in San José [for more on this see Zavella 2011] . . . There are health-care programs that people are not aware of, in case they become ill, where they can be treated. We have all of the information here, what clinics can attend to their health needs. What they can do if they don't have money for healthcare.

Luna's path to a leadership position within this transnational association is striking considering that, like many fellow migrants, he was initially *dis- interested* in joining the HTAs. Luna left Zacatecas for the United States at a young age in 1979. "We came out of necessity not because we wanted to," Luna stated, echoing his compatriots' view that international migration is a necessity not an option. Like many other labor migrants, Luna began working low-end jobs. "I started like every other migrant, as a dishwasher, that is how we start off." Luna recalled being invited to join the Zacatecan federation as early as the 1980s, by migrants in Los Angeles. He remembered attending two meetings in Los Angeles and being encouraged to establish a federation in San José, where he now resides and operates his successful business. "I was young at the time," Luna said. "I didn't give it much consideration. I didn't think it was important. When you are young, you want to invest your time in other matters," he said with laughter. A decade later, once the FCZNC was already established, Luna was invited to participate in an event organized by an HTA from a village near his community of birth. Luna attended and once again was encouraged to participate by other HTA members. Still he declined. Only after attending these events for two consecutive years did Luna finally decide to participate.

> I decided to start my own HTA. From that point forward I became involved and I liked it. If I am going to become involved, I will give it my all, otherwise I don't get involved. That is how I started, and now I am going on my second year as the FCZNC president. I guess people liked the way I worked. When I was the president of my HTA, I had a good working relationship with members of the Zacatecas government. I guess they saw something in me that they liked.

Luna fondly recalled being nominated for FCZNC president.

> I didn't see it coming until that day at the meeting; someone proposed me as the next president. They caught me by surprise. "Do you want to do it?" They asked me. And I replied, "If you believe in me, I will do it." But I really didn't know much about the federation. I told them, "If you are willing to elect me, I will do it, and I will give it my all." Up to this point, I think we have accomplished a lot. Every day I learn, I never stop learning.

If political participation is habit-forming and if engagement in one national context (México) is transferable to another (United States), this thickening of transnational citizenship hasn't fully solidified for Fermín Luna. When asked about his political participation in the United States, Luna regretfully acknowledged that while he is a naturalized U.S. citizen, he has not participated in U.S. elections, yet.

> That is one of the main problems that we have, I speak out of personal experience. I have been a [naturalized] U.S. citizen for many years now, and up to this point I have yet to participate in a single U.S. election. I am ashamed to admit it because that is the whole point of becoming a citizen. I think there are a lot of people like myself who don't

participate. I would like to encourage people to participate, that we all participate. This is truly embarrassing. We have the tools to participate, and we don't do it. I wish I could give you a different answer, but I am not going to sit here and lie to you and tell you that I do participate when I do not. But I do want to encourage people to begin to vote. Getting involved is very important.

His federation also lagged behind when it came to organizing for migrant political rights in the United States. When asked if the FCZNC participated in the recent migrant rights mobilizations calling for comprehensive immigration reform in the United States, like its counterparts in other cities did (Los Angeles, Chicago) (on this point see Gonzales 2009; Gonzales 2013; Zepeda-Millán 2017), Luna replied negatively. "We have not participated. In recent years there has not been much mobilization. I have a good relationship with one of the organizers, but we have not participated." However, if Luna's personal trajectory, from reluctant to active participant, is an indication of the FCZNC's organizational development, we might expect this trend to change. As we will see with the migrant deputies interviewed in this chapter, HTAs can serve as the transnational training grounds for migrant involvement in Mexican and U.S. politics. However, HTAs need to remain vigilant about not being brought back into the partisan fold of Mexican clientelistic politics, a process already well underway. The following section recounts a similar migrant journey, albeit one entrenched in the fractured terrain that is Mexican leftist party politics.

"To Live Migration in My Own Flesh": The Embattled PRD and Migrant Deputies

Since its inception in the late 1980s, the Party of the Democratic Revolution (PRD) has been an important source of political opposition for the PRI, often reaching out to migrants in the United States as part of its electoral strategy. As the major left-of-center party in México until recently, some political observers believed there was greater ideological affinity between migrants and the PRD. In recent years however, the party has faced serious internal strife that may impact its ability to appeal to the Mexican diaspora. In the following section I discuss the political trajectories of Sebastián Martínez, former migrant deputy for the PRD in the Zacatecas state legislature, and Carlos Arango, proportional representation migrant candidate for the PRD in the 2009 congressional elections.

Like many of his fellow Zacatecans, Sebastián Martínez is intimately familiar with the experience of Mexican migration to the United States. "I am the son of a former bracero," he explained in an interview, "my older brothers were all migrants. Their absence was a big part of my family life." At the age of twenty-five, Martínez left Zacatecas for the United States to, as he put it, "live migration in my own flesh."

Like fellow migrant deputy Rigoberto Castañeda and the experience of Fermín Luna discussed above, Martínez joined the federation of Zacatecan HTAs in north Texas, where he settled and currently lives. Martínez said the following of *Zacatecano*/a migrants' propensity to organize.

> There is a very unique characteristic among *Zacatecanos*—in fact I hardly see other state-of-origin groups as organized as *Zacatecanos*. This degree of social organization may even be unique on a global scale. Historically, you had Irish migrants, but *Zacatecanos* have demonstrated their extraordinary unity via migrant associations.

Martínez explained that it was the "needs that exist within the community" that motivated him to join the Zacatecas federation of HTAs in Texas. Like many of his colleagues, his work within this migrant association served as a pathway into Mexican politics: "My work within the HTA allowed me to venture into the political sphere," he explained. "In turn, that experience allowed me to take on the responsibility of becoming a migrant deputy, based on my familiarity with the needs of the community."

The "Second Face of Transnational Citizenship"

Consistent with the idea of diasporic dialectics, Martínez envisioned "community needs" in terms of migrant's role in Mexican civil society *and* U.S. civil society. Again, the related diaspora-as-district concept implies that migrants are a constituency with simultaneous needs on both sides of the U.S.-México border. Smith and Bakker (2008) describe migrants' involvement in U.S. ethnic politics as the "second face of transnational citizenship." With regards to the needs of the community in the United States, Martínez stated:

> The principle need has to do with education. I left for the U.S. with a high value for education. My work within the migrant associations in Texas allowed me to see that the majority of our youth only obtained a high school education. This did not make sense. In a first world country,

schools, even public schools, are in better condition than the ones we had in Zacatecas. Therefore, there was a need to motivate students and their parents to make the most of their educational possibilities. The future of our children depends on it. That was the main need—to motivate folks to take advantage of the opportunities they have in the U.S. Education begets a lot of positive outcomes: income, development, and the ability to live with dignity.

Far from being solely concerned with securing migrant loyalties to México, these interviews suggest that transnational policy entrepreneurs within the Mexican government can also contribute to migrant inclusion in U.S. society and politics (see also Délano 2010). These migrant deputies have the potential to bridge migrants' political needs on both sides of the border, if they can resist the "domestication" of U.S. and Mexican citizenship regimes.

"The Entire State Is Binational": Migrant Deputy Policy Priorities in Zacatecas

In addition to his concern with migrant issues in the United States, as a migrant deputy, Martínez's policy priorities have also been focused on México. Martínez explained that his work within the state legislature has always favored "migrants and the communities within the state with a high migration rate. Typically, these are rural communities with high levels of migration." With regards to public policies, Martínez stated:

The purpose of our public policies has been to stimulate development, at all levels, for example, through scholarships and other social programs designed to benefit migrants. Programs focused on education, culture, and sports for example. We have established music schools in high-migration regions within the state. We have built sports facilities, as requested by many of our *paisanos* [migrant countrymen]. These policies are aimed at the regions with a high migration rate, for example Jerez, Sain Alto, Sombrerete. In fact, there are hardly any regions within the state that do not have high emigration. It is virtually the entire state that is the target of these public policies. The entire state is binational.

Like other migrant officials, Martínez also prioritized policies of migrant investment in Zacatecas. Martínez concluded by explaining that these policies have compelled all government agencies and institutions, at the state level, to develop a plan of action for providing attention and services to migrants.[13] "In almost every government agency, you will find a space for migrants," Martínez stated.

"We Work a Whole Lot and We Devote Little Time to Political Life": Understanding Migrant Partisanship

Martínez also provided insights with regard to the challenges of forming a migrant party. "The possibility of a migrant party has always been on the table," he said. "However, I believe that you need solid bases in order for it to come to fruition and for it to last and not simply be a flash in the pan." In Martínez's eyes, part of the challenge of forming a migrant party has to do with issues internal to the migrant community itself. "Politically, migrants are not very participatory, in the U.S. or México, due to our labor market participation. To put it simply, we work a whole lot, and we devote little time to political life." Internal and external obstacles notwithstanding, Martínez did not rule out the possibility of a migrant party, "Nevertheless, the possibility of a migrant party depends on having the right circumstances at the right time; if the circumstances are there, then so be it." Martínez concluded his discussion on constituting a migrant party by stating: "It is important to remember that one of the criticisms that migrants have of Mexican politics is the existence of too many political parties that are run like *businesses*" rather than legitimate political institutions that represent the interests of civil society. "To add another party to the system as migrants might be counterproductive or at least contradictory to what we have been critiquing about Mexican politics." However, if conditions of cartelization between the PRI, PAN, and PRD continue, Morena may prove to be the alternative for migrants as the "anti-party system" party (Katz and Mair 2009: 759).

As a PRD migrant deputy at the time, Martínez provided insight into the relationship between his party and fellow migrants.

The PRD provides one alternative for migrants, just like the other parties do. However, historically, the bases of leftist parties tend to come from the most marginalized classes. We [migrants] fit this category: we became migrants because there were no opportunities in our country, there were no jobs, there was extreme poverty, and there was an overall lack of development. The PRD offers solutions to these problems that migrants face. The exodus of migrants was a consequence of under-development in our communities. As a result, there is an inclination towards leftist currents . . .You have to consider that for many years we were governed by one party: the PRI. It follows that many people who rejected the PRI were absorbed by a party on the left. This allows migrants to align themselves with parties on the left rather than parties on the right.

Martínez's discussion suggests an ideological affinity between migrants, as a displaced, rural/working-class extraterritorial constituency, and the left-of-center PRD. However, recent conflict within the party and the attendant desertions of its members have led many observers to question its commitment to a leftist ideology and policy agenda (for a discussion of the political development of the party see Özler 2009). Given the divisive internal dynamics, it will be important to observe whether PRD-inclined migrants will become disillusioned with the party and withdraw from politics altogether or realign themselves with another party, possibly Morena.

"Jail, Death or Exit": The View from Leftist Migrant Candidates

Aside from interviews with the two migrant deputies in the Zacatecas state legislature, this chapter also draws on in-depth interviews with the only two migrant candidates in the 2009 elections for México's federal congress. This section will discuss the political trajectory of the PRD proportional representation migrant candidate Carlos Arango, a Chicago-based community activist.

A lifelong political organizer, Carlos Arango has advocated for migrant political rights in both México and the United States since the mid-1970s. Arango's political activism began with the México City student movement in the late 1960s.[14] As a militant of the most radical wing in this movement, Arango protested for student rights, labor rights, and the liberation of political prisoners in México at a young age. In the face of political violence and repression from the Mexican state, Arango explained, "Your options were jail, death or exit."[15] Arango left for Los Angeles in 1974 where he continued his community activism alongside Bert Corona, the renowned Chicano activist (see Zepeda-Millán 2017). Once in the United States, his political work focused on an emerging migrant rights movement. Subsequently, Arango moved to Chicago where he worked with Casa Aztlán, a pro-migrant community based organization.

On top of his migrant activism in the United States, Arango never left his connection to Mexican politics. During the late 1980s, Arango was part of the political movement that led to the formation of the PRD (see Özler 2009). In fact, he had previously been placed as a migrant candidate on the party list, only to be replaced by a California migrant, who served in the federal congress from 2006 to 2009.

In 2009, as the PRD migrant candidate for a proportional representation seat in congress, Arango had a very clear political agenda, with several migrant priority issues.[16] Most of the agenda focused on regaining or securing extraterritorial political rights for Mexican migrants in the United States. The first item was to grant migrants the ability to register and vote directly in the United States for elections in México. Arango described his activism around this issue as follows:

> We have been working for migrants' right to vote for some time now. Our objective was to pass legislation that would really allow migrants to participate in elections. What the Mexican congress ultimately approved was what we have called a "partial vote," whereby you have the right to vote, but you really don't have a way to enact it. It is a right that you cannot exercise. Take for instance the issue of voter registration in the U.S., which we did not obtain.[17] Prospective voters have to travel to México to register and then return. That is the most costly vote imaginable. Secondly, you have to vote by mail. A lot of migrants were not able to cast their votes via mail. So you see, there are a lot of barriers. In other words, the law is designed so that the extraterritorial vote fails. It is a law that tells you that you have a right to vote, but in practice you really don't have that right.

Aside from extraterritorial voting rights, Arango also prioritized improving remittance-sending services for migrants, reforming the North American Free Trade Agreement (NAFTA) to include migration as a provision within the treaty, and lobbying the U.S. government to regularize the millions of undocumented migrants living and working therein. On this last point, he said:

> The Mexican government has never negotiated the issue of migration with the U.S. on equal terms. The reason for this is that the Mexican government does not fully understand the migration issue. That is the problem. The political parties don't fully understand it.

In fact, originally, the Mexican government deliberately left the migration issue off of the NAFTA agenda to not spoil negotiations with the United States (Délano 2011). As such, Arango felt it was important to initiate bilateral negotiations with the United States regarding immigration reform: "We can't meddle with U.S. sovereignty, but we can certainly negotiate with them." Of course, the prospects of such negotiations have become even less tenable under Trump (for a longer history of the "asymmetrical codependency" between the United States and México around migration issues see Menchaca 2016).

As a migrant candidate, Arango also followed the diaspora-as-district approach and the pattern of diasporic dialectics in his policy proposals.

> One of my goals, if elected, is to arrange spaces, especially in U.S. cities with high migrant concentrations, where people can receive assistance with their needs. There are a host of issues that people need assistance with and the Mexican consulate pays no attention to them. In the absence of other government institutions that they can turn to, the Mexican congress can provide this service. At the very least we could gather their grievances and process them . . . We can have a deputy visit, hold constituent meetings and collect recommendations . . . This would be like a *diputado móvil* like the *consulado móvil* . . . Binational politics is complex. You have to follow the domestic agenda within México but you also have a whole lot happening to our people over here [in the U.S.].

In general, Arango felt that there had been a rollback of migrant rights within Mexican electoral and party politics. He described his second attempt as a migrant candidate as unfolding under even more unfavorable conditions than before: "Now the circumstances are even more adverse given the fact that parties do not want to acknowledge migrants." As the introduction to this chapter illustrates, there were migrant partisans from the PRI and PAN, as well as migrants with no party affiliation, who were left on the sidelines, with no candidacies or party endorsements in the 2009 midterm election cycle. Even within his own party, the PRD, the role of migrants has been adversely impacted.

> This is an unfavorable situation for migrants, even within the PRD itself. We had won so much, and we lost all of it in the last congress. We had won affirmative action, we had won spaces for migrants. Now all of that is gone. Part of the problem is that if you are not in México, you can't keep vigilance.

This suggests that it is difficult to keep the parties accountable and the political process transparent from abroad. With migrants and Mexican civil society at large growing increasingly disillusioned with their current parties, the circumstances may be ripe for Morena to mobilize disaffected migrants.

Arango provided a sobering account of his own party vis-à-vis migrant deputies. Arango described the PRD as "a party of the left, sort of." He continued, "At the very least it is predicated upon issues that the left fought for. It is the closest party to this ideal anyway." On a more personal level, Arango stated, "I come from the student movement, and all of the movement activists are in the PRD or are now critics of the PRD" (see Özler 2009 for a related discussion). Arango concluded candidly,

> The PRD is not the best political institution, it has a lot of problems. It has a lot of internal currents and interests. But at the end of the day it is the party that ran López Obrador for the presidency.

With regards to the PRD's view on migrants, Arango explained:

> The PRD has an open space. By virtue of its own statutes, the party has open spaces and it recognizes migrants. In fact, by Mexican electoral law, the PRD exists in the U.S. It is a recognized entity there. The problem is that it lost its political legs . . . Because we had five state committees which got collapsed into a single national one throughout the U.S., which did not function.

Arango explained that domestically, the PRD is too consumed with its internal power struggles to be concerned with migrants. "There are a series of struggles within the party over different positions, over who controls the national executive committee, the political commission, over who selects deputies and senators." When the party confronts the issue of migrants, it is seen as simply adding more complexity to the already strained internal party dynamics. "Migrants sure contribute a whole lot to society, but politically the party is too preoccupied with all of this infighting to make concessions to them." While the parties often acknowledge migrants in their rhetoric, they are not always vested in opening permanent spaces for migrants within their power structures. Because migrant candidacies are subject to the political will of parties and politicians, Arango insisted it is important to secure a permanent space for migrants. "We need to legislate a space exclusively for migrants. Rather than fighting over the same pie, that pie should be distributed according to the proportion of Mexicans residing abroad." To borrow from Htun and Ossa, as long as parties control the candidate nomination process and as long as migrants continue to have unfavorable placement on party lists, they will have a hard time challenging the partisan balance of power in México (2013).

Lastly, Arango also offered insights regarding the question of constituting a migrant party, paying close attention to both external and internal barriers. Arango described the challenges of forming a migrant party as follows:

> First of all, is this migrant party going to be for México or will it be concerned with the U.S.? That is the question. If it is for México, we can form a party that is not officially registered. It would be a political party predicated on migrant issues, but it would not be a registered entity. I think we could get that far. But even a movement of that nature would have its share of problems because of competing ideologies. We may all be part of this party, but at the end of the day we each have a different vision or outlook. It would be more like a front. Historically, the Partido Liberal Mexicano had a clear mission, it was anarchist, it had a clearly defined ideology, it had a newspaper. Migrants today do not have an internally consistent ideology. That is on the Mexican side. On the U.S. side, this migrant party or bloc issue might be a good idea because we are excluded from politics here. It would be a good idea to run migrant candidates for congress and local politics in the U.S. This would be part of a two-pronged strategy. That is binational politics.

While migrant political mobilization raises a series of complex issues in México and the United States, there is no indication that the two cannot occur concurrently, as Arango emphatically concluded. As the following section illustrates, these migrants have the *militancia* and critical consciousness needed to democratically engage on both sides of the border and enact their diasporic dialectics in the exclusionary citizenship regimes of the United States and México.

Mexican Migrant Marxists: The Comité PRD of East Los Angeles

Another possible institutional mechanism whereby migrants can bridge their civic involvement in Mexican and U.S. politics is through Mexican party organizations that operate in migrant communities in the United States. Migration scholars have noted that "political parties often maintain foreign branches in which emigrants can participate" (Waldinger 2009: 9), but not much is known about the impact that these organizations have on migrant involvement in the home country or in the U.S. context.[18] In order to gain insight into Mexican party activity among Mexican migrants in the United States—which can be expected to vary ideologically by party—I turn to an interview with a migrant couple active in the leftist Comité PRD (PRD Committee) of East Los Angeles.

According to my informants, the Comité PRD of East Los Angeles was formed following the highly contested 2006 Mexican presidential elections in which the PRD candidate, Andrés Manuel López Obrador, lost by a narrow margin. The Comité PRD was organized by a group of Mexican migrants who, as my female informant Ines put it, "needed to unite and to be heard." At the time of the interview, the Comité PRD met weekly, had a membership of sixty to seventy people, and was undergoing efforts to secure its own meeting space.

Ines described the Comité PRD as an open and inclusive organization, one that welcomed alliances with other groups including other racial/ethnic minorities. For example, the Comité was approached by Filipino migrants who "identified with us and with many of the same economic problems and human rights violations."[19] According to Ines, this is what sets the Comité PRD apart from other groups: "We open our doors to any other Mexican national or any other group because that is how we learn together . . . There are other groups that are extremely exclusive." Interestingly, when asked about alliances with other Mexican migrant associations, such as HTAs, both interviewees responded negatively. "We are not interested because they are pro-government," explained Ines's husband, Pablo. "They work with the [Mexican] government, and we don't. We are in the struggle against those governments that oppress us." Ines added that the Mexican government attempts to "control your right to speak up. Your freedom of expression." In class-conscious terms, Pablo elaborated, arguing: "Political parties in México are influenced by the bourgeoisie. The bourgeoisie will side with whoever is in power. They are currently embedded in the PAN . . . Previously they were with the right, the PRI, now they are with the ultra-right, the PAN." According to Pablo, these parties "have the same methods of electoral fraud . . . and armed repression." This class critique also seemed to suggest evidence of party collusion, corruption, and cartelization. According to Ines, "These are parties that work for their own self-interest not for the people. They work for the upper classes." Her partner extended this critique to the competing currents within the PRD:

The current leader of the PRD in México is in that position for the business in it. He treats it as any other paid job not as a position as a representative of the people . . .Those party members sell-out, they don't defend [the party] . . .They want the pay that comes with being in power . . . they could care less about the public's interest.

Asked about analogous organizations in the United States linked to other Mexican parties (PRI, PAN), my respondents said those committees enjoyed the spoils of official support and were "encouraged by the Mexican consulate." In the eyes of Pablo, this influenced the group members' mission: "They are there out of self-interest not for the greater public good." With official ties come greater patronage resources and opportunities for clientelism: "All they do is move money. In our organization there is no money, just hard work . . . It is easier for them to appeal to people because they can give out computers . . . With us, it is all work. Unfortunately, people are less interested when you have to put in work. They show up when they are going to receive [handouts]." Despite access to official resources, Ines felt that their group had greater membership and migrant *militancia* (for a discussion of "migrating militants" see Zepeda-Millán 2017: 35). "Even then we have more people than they do. The people know our purpose and our honesty. That is what attracts them to our group, and they spread the word and invite more members."

When asked about their group's mission, my respondents envisioned the Comité PRD as serving a purpose in both Mexican and U.S. politics. Among its long-term goals, the Comité PRD had its eyes set on the 2012 Mexican presidential elections. According to Pablo, the Comité's short-term goals consisted of holding regular political "study groups," which sought to raise consciousness among its members. "We need study groups not only to defend our own candidates" he stated, "but to defend the party as well." More importantly, the study circles were part of a strategy to "develop consciousness" among its members. "Without consciousness, people tend to give up," he said. By joining the study groups, however, "people become aware of what is happening, what is wrong and what action needs to be taken . . . they become *concientizados*." In this manner, participants "will not abandon the struggle; they keep moving forward. They not only keep moving forward but they cannot sell-out, they commit to their [political] line."

Ines responded to the same question by emphasizing the role that the Comité plays in demanding migrants' political rights in México. In her eyes, the goal of the Comité was to "allow emigrants to be heard . . . to have our needs met and to have our rights respected as Mexican citizens." Consistent with the idea of diasporic dialectics, those rights were not limited to México proper but also included migrant rights in the United States. According to Pablo, the Comité was partly created to elect migrant representatives in México who would redress migrant grievances in the United States, including criminalization on the part of U.S. immigration authorities, pointing to "raids and human rights violations perpetrated by *migras* [U.S. immigration officers] against migrants who are detained and are mistreated and abused" as examples. Pablo identified these as the policy priorities that a migrant deputy should address; however, he felt that the PRD migrant deputy in congress at the time didn't "do a thing." To further underscore the plight of Mexican migrants in the United States, Ines added the issue of driver licenses for undocumented migrants: "They don't want to issue driver licenses to those of us who are undocumented . . . that is why we want representatives who will support us, who will defend us, who will fight for our rights."[20] Clearly, for the migrant activists of the Comité PRD of East Los Angeles, migrant rights encompass political entitlements on both sides of the border. In a statement representative of diasporic dialectics, Pablo concluded on the following note:

> As immigrants we suffer. First of all, we did not have access to jobs in México, we did not have access to education and we had to migrate here. Once we are here, we continue to suffer all sorts of abuses. For example, poor jobs—if we sell oranges, the police arrive and take everything away from us. We are discriminated, to put it simply, by the authorities and by the system in which we live in here. This is why we need to do something about it. Nobody is going to come and address our needs, only by organizing ourselves can we address them. I hope that by 2012 we are better organized and that we have greater voice . . . our voice will depend on the representatives that we have.

In the view of the militants of the Comité PRD, migrant representatives in México need not limit their policy work to domestic affairs but must also address migrants' political condition and experience in the United States. In this light, this cross-border Comité is a transnational public sphere (Rocco 2014), one that simultaneously foments migrant involvement in Mexican and U.S. politics. Having discussed the experience of migrants in Mexican leftist party politics, let's turn now to migrants in the right-wing PAN.

Crashing the Party? The Conservative
PAN and Migrant Deputies

Among progressive academic circles in Zacatecas, there was enthusiasm that the migrant Lupe Gómez was running for a single-member-district congressional seat in the state, but there was also an unspoken view that he had run with the wrong party—PAN. As México's right-wing party, these observers felt there was a rift between the policy priorities of the PAN and the work being done by migrants in the state. As the only party running a plurality migrant candidate, however, the PAN was savvy enough to capitalize on its "commitment" to pressing issues like migration and gender equality throughout the course of the campaign.[21] Noting the tensions inherent to diasporic dialectics and the contradictions of transnational citizenship, the following sections draw on structured interviews with Gómez before, during, and immediately following his campaign, as well as ethnographic observations from his campaign rallies in Zacatecas.

Lupe Gómez left the small ranching village of Santa Juana in Jalpa, Zacatecas, for California at a very young age. As mentioned in the introduction of this book, Gómez achieved important personal and professional goals while in the United States: he obtained a college education, became a naturalized U.S. citizen, and established a successful business in Orange County, California. Building on his ties to his hometown and state, Gómez also became an active member of Zacatecas HTAs in Southern California. In 2001, he became the president of the prominent Federación de Clubes *Zacatecanos* del Sur de California (FCZSC) (for studies of this organization and its members see Goldring 2002; Smith and Bakker 2008). During his term as president of this migrant association, among Gómez's most celebrated accomplishments was the expansion of the 3x1 matching funds program from a Zacatecas-based initiative to one that would be implemented across the nation (see Smith and Bakker 2008; Duquette-Rury 2014). Like other FCZSC leaders, Gómez's work within this migrant association served as a pathway for subsequent involvement in Mexican local, state, and federal politics. Aside from Carlos Arango, who was a proportional representation candidate, Gómez was the only migrant candidate in the country running for a single-member-district seat in the 2009 congressional elections.[22]

Going into his campaign, Gómez had very clearly defined policy proposals, both for the second federal electoral district in Zacatecas, which he would represent if elected, and for the Zacatecas diaspora in the United States. With regard to policies for Zacatecas proper, Gómez prioritized education and economic development for the municipalities within the second federal district in the state, a goal that he had been working toward since he was a member of the FCZSC. Gómez explained his transnationalized neoliberal vision as follows:

> My focus will be on education and development. Education is important because an educated society can prosper. We have to educate our youth so that they can compete at a global level. We need our youth to learn different languages, especially English. We need to train our youth in business administration so that global companies can realize that our youth are well trained and so they will bring their business to our state . . . We need to create the right conditions for this; we need to create special funds to develop the district that I am going to represent because that is the district that has the highest out-migration rates due to unemployment. We need to focus development efforts on this region . . . We need to create programs and coalitions to attract resources from different places. We want to attract people in the U.S. who are potential investors, but before we can do this, as a government, we need to create the conditions for this investment. The government needs to do its part. For example, it can participate in a two-for-one matching funds program, which is already in existence by the way. We need to promote and improve it such that investors can have the confidence that their money will be safe.

As a businessman himself, Gómez's pro-investment vision was very much in line with the pro-business, pro-trade preferences of the PAN. When Felipe Calderón was campaigning for president of México, who would go on to unleash México's seemingly endless cycle of violence, he addressed the issue of migration in his native Michoacán as follows.

> [R]ather than have *Michoacanos* leave to work in a cannery in the Imperial Valley or a factory in Chicago, I much rather that they stay here. I rather have the cannery here, in the Michoacán countryside. I rather have the factories here, where our people are. (Calderón 2006: 59)

In addition to education and development for the district in Zacatecas, Gómez also had policy recommendations destined for *Zacatecanos* in the United States, underscoring the contradictions of diasporic dialectics and the pitfalls of transnational citizenship. Gómez suggested that the Mexican government has failed to deliver on its promises to migrants in the United States. "Government officials come to migrants to see what they can get from them. I happen to believe that if we empower migrants, this is better in the long run." For one, Gómez suggested that the Mexican congress help the children of migrants who are students in the United States. Secondly, he suggested that the Mexican congress assist HTAs in the United States to create multi-purpose community centers to be used for the clubs' events.

> I think we can construct community centers in different cities in the U.S. This would foment unity among Mexicans in the U.S. and this, in turn, will help México in the long run. Mexican governors come here all the time and offer crumbs in comparison to the millions that we are contributing.

"I Am the Only Migrant Candidate in the Nation": Makings Sense of Mexican Partisanship

As a prominent member of the FCZSC, Gómez had multiple offers to participate in Mexican politics in the past. In his time as leader of this organization, Gómez worked with different governing parties in México. "As a leader of the organization, I had to work with whoever was in power," he explained.

> The purpose was to deliver the public goods, no matter what party was in power. In my view, the party was Zacatecas. That experience allowed me to observe how each of the parties works . . . Based on that experience, I chose the PAN. Why the PAN? Well, because the PAN was the party that opened its doors to us. Suffice it to say that I am the only migrant candidate in the nation today. The PRI did not consider migrants, nor did the PRD. They are too busy fighting over public office. In México, public office is seen as a profitable business. That is why México has not prospered, because that is all politicians care about. That is what is different between them and migrants. Migrants are not after the money. Rather, we are getting involved because we believe that we can do politics differently.

Like the PRD proportional representation candidate Arango, Gómez agreed that Mexican political parties have not done enough to include migrants. "We have 20 million Mexicans living in the U.S. They should give us a minimum of five congressional seats per party. But do you think they want to let go of their grip on power?" Gómez suggested that migrants are agents of political development, institutional change, and democratization within México. "They fear us. If we return to do politics differently, we are going to make them look bad." Exemplifying the Mexican side of diasporic dialectics, Gómez continued, "From the moment that we [migrants] began contributing to our communities, we learned that the government was not going to do a thing unless we took the initiative." Alluding to entrenched antimigrant interests in Mexican political institutions, Gómez concluded as follows:

> If we [migrants] do not return to México to try to change the status quo, it will never change . . . I hope that this gives way to a new political class of migrants, who are socialized in the U.S. and who have learned how to run a democracy differently . . . Many people have told me that the hope for the *Zacatecano* people is to have a migrant return to govern Zacatecas. I don't mean to get ahead of myself, but I hope that in our lifetime a migrant will return to govern Zacatecas.

El Migrante *as the Antipolitician: Lupe Gómez hits the Campaign Trail*

In his coverage of one of the first migrant politicians, journalist Sam Quinones described the late Andrés Bermúdez as the "antipolitician" (Quinones 2008). A successor of Bermúdez himself, halfway through his campaign, Gómez upheld the view of migrants as constituting a new political subjectivity in México. When asked what the advantages and disadvantages of being a migrant candidate were, Gómez explained to me, "The disadvantage is that my opponents have been campaigning for years. I've been campaigning for five weeks. But the advantage is that I am not a politician. I've never been a politician. I don't make a living from politics," speaking loudly over the boisterous crowd at a *charrería* arena during one of his campaign rallies. With regards to campaign strategy, Gómez said:

> I am learning day by day. I try to offer the best of me. I maintain my essence: a humble *ranchero* who left Zacatecas a long time ago and now has returned to do things better than today's politicians. I want the people to believe once again in a politician. A politician who is committed to Zacatecas and has proven it with actions, not with promises.

In the course of his campaign, Gómez was exposed to negative campaigning, or what he described as the "cruel and ugly side of politics," in Zacatecas. When asked what the toughest campaign moment or experience had been up to that point, Gómez replied, "The most unpleasant moment was during the first debate, when everyone attacked me. They directed unfair questions at me . . . Obscure legal codes that not even lawyers could address." Gómez perceived this as a strategy by his opponents to discredit him in the public view as the migrant who is out of touch with Mexican politics. "That was a very bitter experience. They tried to cast doubt in the people's mind that I am not *Zacatecano* like they are." In fact, a common criticism among those who oppose granting migrants political rights in México is that migrants have become disconnected from the domestic affairs of the country (for a rendition of these views see interviews in Fitzgerald 2000). Despite the gains on behalf of migrants over the last decade, this antagonistic view is alive and well. During a heated conversation I sustained with a local journalist and the running mate of the PRD candidate in Gómez's district, both expressed their belief that the migrant era had come to an end and the migrants were out of touch with the day-to-day political reality of México (author's field notes July 2009).

Despite the opposition from México's dominant political class, Gómez remained optimistic. "I am going to be the voice of migrants in the Mexican congress," he said. Gómez explained that his objective was to "strengthen migrants over there, by making policy on their behalf here. I think that we can be a great team," he said. "We are going to work with the migrant associations . . . I am part of them." Gómez, the seemingly organic migrant candidate, concluded the interview on a positive note:

> There may be some folks who don't fully understand my campaign. But there are also a whole lot of people who have believed in us. I began from zero and within a month, we are ahead in the polls. We will win.

"A Setback for Democracy": Mexican Electoral Fraud—PRD-Style?

To the dismay of Gómez and his supporters, the election outcomes did not favor him or his party in any of the federal electoral districts in the state. Amid rampant accusations of vote buying and improper electoral conduct on behalf of the state government, the PRD—the governor's party in Zacatecas at the time—won all four federal districts. Defying most electoral forecasts,

Gómez came in third behind the PRD and PRI candidates. When asked what this election outcome meant for the PAN and for migrants, Gómez replied, "This is a setback not only for the PAN but especially for migrants because I was the only migrant candidate in the nation." Gómez continued, "This is a setback for democracy and a setback for Zacatecas and for México." In Gómez's eyes, these elections were proof that democracy in México had not advanced much and remained in its infancy. So long as corrupt political practices, such as vote buying, did not cease to exist, Gómez commented, "we will continue without having the outcomes we want: security, peace, development." While some polls had him ahead leading up to the election, Gómez stated, "You can't beat a political machine and a government as corrupt as the one we have. One in which hundreds of thousands of public pesos are diverted" for electoral ends.

Electoral fraud notwithstanding, Gómez remained committed to his vision of migrant political empowerment. Asked if there had been electoral mobilization on his behalf among migrants in the United States, Gómez pointed to the limits of diasporic dialectics:

We formed a support group, but we have to work harder to make people aware of how important it is to participate actively in order to change things . . . If we really want to make a difference in México, we [migrants] need to get involved.

Gómez described the support group as

a collective of HTA leaders, not just from Zacatecas but from other states as well, who are committed to changing things down here. Who want migrants to be taken into account and to be considered part of the solution to México's problems.

When asked if these group members were PANistas, Gómez replied, "No I think the support group over there is not wedded to any party. The only party is migrants themselves . . . What we want is the public good for the entire nation."

Regarding his future political objectives and orientations, Gómez stated that he planned to continue working without a formal party affiliation. "I plan to continue working without an affiliation. I will continue to work towards the same causes within Mexican politics: development projects, the expansion of the 3x1 program, scholarships and the implementation of a job-creation strategy." In anticipation of his trip back to the United States, Gómez reflected on the election:

> We witnessed an election manipulated by the state government. This government is not willing to allow people to vote freely, without meddling and buying their votes. There is no respect for people's dignity here. But it is up to the people to change all of this. I hope one day we have the political consciousness to make those fundamental changes that are necessary for us to take a new path.

Indeed, anticorruption was a recurring theme in Gómez's campaign speeches. With the slogan "Take what you CAN, but vote for the PAN," Gómez often exhorted constituents not to give into bribes from other parties. Despite Gómez's efforts and media campaigns informing voters about "*el voto secreto*" (ballot secrecy), vote buying was seemingly rampant, as the election results appear to indicate (for a thorough discussion of Mexican clientelism see Fox 1994).[23]

Livening the Party? México's "Third" Parties and Migrant Deputies
PT and Convergencia

In addition to understanding the role of migrants in México's three major parties, it is important to consider their influence on the country's smaller parties. This section examines how the Labor Party (PT) and Convergencia Party (now Movimiento Ciudadano)—active since 1990 and 2000 respectively—envision migrants both as potential militants and as party officials. It draws on structured interviews with the Zacatecas state leader of the PT at the time, Saul Monreal, and then local congressman for Convergencia, Félix Vázquez Acuña.

Saul Monreal, national political commissioner of the PT in Zacatecas at the time of my interview, described his party as a leftist institution closely linked to social struggle, the working classes, and the Mexican peasantry. The party emerged from popular social associations such as unions and peasant organizations. Monreal claimed the party's ranks were growing thanks to its "dual mobilization strategy," which he described as follows. The first is the "mass-based strategy" which is a bottom-up, grassroots mobilizing strategy whereby party organizations operate in barrios and communities, formulating social infrastructure and social policy. The second strategy is the "electoral strategy" where the focus is strictly political: securing offices for the party at the municipal, state, and federal levels of governance. The two approaches are complimentary, Monreal argued, because during nonelection years, the focus is on the mass-based mobilization strategy. "The party is constantly working," Monreal stated, "like its name suggests. Not only in campaign years but also during nonelection years, the party is advocating on behalf of peasants, workers, and students."[24]

In addition to these social actors in Mexican society, the PT has also turned to Mexican migrants residing in the United States as a potential pool of party militants. Monreal described the PT's rapprochement with migrants as follows:

> We have established dialogue with migrants. Previously, the PT did not count on migrants in Zacatecas. The case of Zacatecas is unique for the party because, as you know, there are a lot of *paisanos* who live in the U.S. As a result, we have been opening up spaces within the party and giving them plenty of attention. In fact, since I joined the party, the PT has extended to Southern California. It has extended to Chicago. We now have PT committees in the U.S., in places like Texas. We are working on consolidating the party in more U.S. cities among our migrants. There is a lot of enthusiasm around the party; it has been well received. We are currently working on building a strong migrant base for the PT.

With regard to offering elected or appointed party positions to migrants, Monreal replied somewhat vaguely, "Of course we support them in this end. We are in solidarity with migrants and at the appropriate time we will deliver on our commitment to them." When asked how the PT has attempted to recruit migrants into its ranks, Monreal said the focus has been around a mutual concern over development in Zacatecas. "Many migrants still have their families here and there is a lot of poverty in Zacatecas." Since the interview was conducted in the middle of campaign season, Monreal made sure to deride the PRDista government (the PT and PRD split in Zacatecas during this election cycle). "There has been complete neglect on behalf of the government since 2004 around that migrant concern, which is also our concern: the development of neighborhoods and communities." Monreal made the electoral aspirations of his party very clear:

Migrants have been more than willing to contribute to local development. But the state authorities have failed them. [Migrants] have implemented infrastructure and other projects that have been stalled. In this sense, we have been in solidarity with them, and we have been more than willing to generate such projects and advance toward the governorship. Let's say it, the governorship is the only mechanism to work effectively to this end, which is reflected in our *paisanos* and in their people who live here in Zacatecas.

While Monreal did not specify when and how the PT would allot positions to migrants, what was abundantly clear was that the party needs them to make it to the governorship. Alternatively, given the conditions of party cartelization mentioned earlier, migrants may begin to gravitate toward the newest of these opposition movement parties: Morena.

Like the PT, Convergencia (as noted, now Movimiento Ciudadano) can also be characterized as a leftist party. The local congressman Félix Vázquez Acuña described his party as a leftist institution concerned with social democracy. As such, Convergencia believes that the primary role of government should be focused on social programs and public goods aimed at the most marginalized classes. Vázquez juxtaposed his party's position with that of the right, which, in his eyes, is primarily concerned with stimulating the private sector. By contrast, Convergencia believes that the primary concern of public policy should be directed at the urban and rural poor.

As a leftist party open to political empowerment, Vázquez explained that Convergencia "by its very principles, is sympathetic to the possibility of migrant participation." However, Vázquez identified an additional structural factor that compels parties to endorse migrant candidates, namely the quotas established by the Migrant Law of 2004. "In compliance with the electoral law of Zacatecas, in the previous local elections, we included migrant candidates within our proportional representation list." As mentioned, the Ley Migrante, or Migrant Law, in Zacatecas requires parties to include migrant candidates in their party lists and reserves two seats, out of thirty, for such candidates in the local congress. Vázquez explained:

According to the rules of assignment, two out of thirty seats are reserved for migrant deputies in local congress. Those are assigned to the first and second place parties in terms of overall state votes. The two parties that obtained the largest percentage of the vote were the PRI and the PRD, that is why the two current migrant deputies are from those institutions [both interviewed earlier in this chapter].

While Convergencia is sympathetic to the migrant cause, and while the local election laws oblige it to include migrants in its party lists, the party is far from reaching the vote threshold to successfully place its migrant candidates into office.

When asked what actions Convergencia has taken to attract migrants into its ranks, Vázquez replied:

> At the level of our national executive committee, my understanding is that the party has coordinated meetings with migrant communities in the U.S. In Zacatecas, I could point to more personal examples of constituency services. There are many people who have migrant relatives in the U.S. who, unfortunately, have died there. What we have done in response to this situation is coordinate with the State Migration Institute in order to facilitate the process by which the bodies are returned to the place of origin [on this point see chapter 4].

Vázquez acknowledged "a more concerted action consists of coordinating meetings in the U.S. However, our biggest challenge is limited economic resources—that is what prevents us from having direct contact with migrants in the U.S." While Convergencia views migrant political participation favorably, it offers a smaller payoff to migrants in terms of electoral success. Furthermore, as a younger and emerging party, any efforts at mobilizing migrants in the United States directly are handicapped by limited party funding. The experiences of these smaller parties offer strategic lessons for newer parties on the political horizon interested in reaching out to migrants, such as the newly triumphant Morena, which will ascend to federal power in 2018.

Mujer Migrante: Giselle Arellano Grapples with Mexican Gender Politics

As made painfully obvious by this chapter, men have occupied most of these appointed and elected seats for migrants. In the case of Zacatecas, only three migrant women have run for or held political office: congressional candidate Giselle Arellano, former migrant deputy Estela Beltrán, and the current migrant deputy María Guadalupe Adabache Reyes. Below I reflect on the most polemicized of these campaigns, Giselle Arellano's run as migrant candidate for México's federal congress.

In the 2013 Mexican federal elections, Giselle Arellano—a young Nevada-based Zacatecas HTA president who resembles more its pageant contestants than the old-guard migrant leadership—took a decisive step to enter the male-dominated world of Mexican transnational politics. Already she was at the helm of her Las Vegas home-state federation, a position usually occupied by men. Now, she would make a run for México's federal congress as a migrant candidate with the conservative PAN, a party that pays a great deal of lip service to gender equity. The duplicity of Mexican gendered transnational politics would soon become evident with a controversial video that launched Giselle's campaign into infamy. Modeling angel-themed lingerie, a video Giselle had previously filmed in Las Vegas would go viral on social media, winning her accusations of being an "escort" and calling into question her "moral integrity" in the eyes of the socially conservative PAN. After intense gendered political wrangling, Giselle's campaign would continue, relegated to a tough district in her native Zacatecas, where she would confront organized crime, all kinds of sexual stereotypes, and ultimately come up short in the election.

In February 2015, what I anticipated would be a short, formal interview in Las Vegas turned out to be a dizzying day in the life of Giselle Arellano. Giselle scheduled me for an interview about her transnational political experiences at a coffeehouse in one of Las Vegas' posh hotels when only a few minutes into the conversation she said, "Come, I'll give you a tour of the town." I followed her as she worked her way to valet parking, receiving VIP treatment by seemingly every casino employee she encountered. We jumped into her new pick-up truck and after a quick tour of the strip, we ventured toward one of the real estate agencies she works with. Unfamiliar with the racial geography of the region, she explained to me the demographic shifts that have transformed greater Las Vegas, describing where Latino communities reside and how she confronts and challenges everyday anti-Latino discrimination wherever she encounters it. At the real estate office, we chatted informally with a Mexican and Central American married couple that moved to Nevada from Texas who were interested in buying a home. After sharing some lending advice and bidding them farewell, Giselle explained to me that she always looks out for Latino families' best interest as they navigate the real estate market with steep information asymmetries.

Switching effortlessly back to the plight of migrants in Mexican politics, Giselle explained her campaign as migrant candidate as part of a rough, rigged, contact sport. Recalling her conversations with the male leadership of México's major political parties she said: "It's a fixed game where they tell you what role and what position you are going to play and how you are going to play it." Asked if she would ever run for political office in México again, she replied pensively, "Maybe once I am married and have a family," as if heteronormativity would somehow shield her in a second potential run through Mexican gender politics. Realizing that our interview had turned into an afternoon-long outing, Giselle drove me back to the casino as we chatted some more about the plight of Mexican migrants in the United States. "You and I should write a book," Giselle said playfully, about the political struggles of Mexican migrants on both sides of the border.

Giselle's apt metaphor of Mexican politics as a fixed gendered game controlled by men at the helm of the dominant parties was reminiscent of my interview with Estela Beltrán when she served as the first female migrant deputy in the state legislature of Zacatecas. Beltrán's two male political advisors responded to seemingly every question I asked of her, at times literally interrupting the congresswoman, who was otherwise candid about the gender inequities in Mexican party politics. Months later, when I casually encountered her at the FCZSC annual fundraiser in Los Angeles, what I hoped would be an informal exchange was once again intercepted by her male advisors, who flanked her on either side at the dinner table. Since her term as the first female migrant deputy in the Zacatecas state legislature is completed, I intended to catch up with Beltrán in Northern California, but she was nowhere to be found, seemingly alienated from the male-dominated world of Mexican transnational politics.

Conclusion

As this chapter illustrated, political parties in México support migrant representation in discourse but have generally failed to systematically "incorporate" them into their power structures. In summary, the chapter finds that the PRI, as part of a long-term strategy to reinvent itself, has symbolically incorporated migrants into its rhetoric but has done little to offer candidacies or spaces in its party list for migrants. While PAN was the only party to field a migrant candidate for a single-member-district seat in the 2009 elections for federal congress, it seems to be ideologically antithetical to those who envision migrants as a political force of the left. By contrast, given its origins, the PRD may seem like an ideological ally for migrants but currently faces profound internal cleavages that have adversely impacted its electoral prospects. Moreover, México's smaller parties, like the PT and Convergencia (now Movimiento Ciudadano), have attempted to recruit migrants as party militants but offer less of a payoff to them in terms of electoral success.

The chapter also discussed the institutional barriers and potential implications of constituting an extraterritorial "migrant party." Like other marginalized sectors of Mexican society (women, indigenous communities), migrants are not fully represented in México's political institutions. As a result, migrants have tentatively aligned themselves with existing parties and momentarily entertained the idea of constituting a migrant party. With recent signs of party cartelization in México, however, the more likely scenario is that migrants may gravitate toward the emerging antisystem party, Morena, which is currently making inroads into the Mexican diaspora in the United States.

The interviews presented in this chapter also have important implications for the broader research question driving this book: How does migrant engagement in Mexican politics impact their engagement in U.S. politics? In spite of the fact that these migrants have affiliated with different political parties in México, and in some instances consider each other to be political adversaries in that context, in the United States they share striking political commonalities. In the United States, the migrants interviewed here are naturalized U.S. citizens, registered Democrats, and proponents of comprehensive immigration reform. While they may disagree with their party affiliations and policy preferences in México, there is one point on which they all agree: there is no contradiction between their simultaneous participation in Mexican politics *and* U.S. politics, the limitations of transnational citizenship notwithstanding.

In their everyday lives, their involvement in Mexican politics is consistent with their civic-political engagement in the United States. In the days leading to the historic election of Barack Obama in 2008, Rigoberto Castañeda—the migrant deputy discussed earlier in the chapter—flew from Zacatecas to California to vote for the first African American president of the United States. "I had five eligible voters in my household who would not vote unless I returned to vote. As soon as I arrived, I located the polling place and on Election Day, I took the entire family to vote." When asked how holding political office in México has impacted his civic and political life in the United States, PRD migrant deputy Sebastián Martínez replied:

> This experience has had a very positive impact. It has allowed me to develop a deeper understanding of the social and political dimensions of public life. It has provided me with a framework to further grow in the U.S. It has allowed me to develop businesses and educational exchanges . . . It has allowed me to strengthen the bilateral relationship between México and the U.S. This personal experience has been very enriching, and it has taught me to value civic engagement, for instance, the right to vote. In the U.S. many of us cannot vote, so this allows those of us who can to actively participate in choosing our candidates and when possible, to vote in both countries. Not every citizen has the privilege to vote in two countries, like we do, thanks to our binationality, which ultimately allows us to be more committed to both México and the United States.

Martínez alluded to the staying power of migrant cross-border political participation, stating:

> I think we are privileged citizens to have the opportunity to cast our vote in México and in the U.S. I think this is historic, and we should pass this on to our future generations so that they may reap the benefits of that privilege . . . I dream that one day a Latino will be president of the U.S. I also dream that a U.S. Latino will be president of México. My goal, as an ordinary citizen, is to help shape that consciousness so that one day one of our children, of Latino origin, will govern México and will govern the U.S. This is a constitutional right that we have, by law. All we need to do is build that dream. All you need to do is to construct that dream and say, *sí se puede.*

In contrast to conventional wisdom regarding dual nationals, these migrants are contributing to and enriching democratic life in both their country of origin and of residence. Far from fitting the prevailing stereotype of Mexicans as the United States' "iconic illegal aliens" (see De Genova 2005; 2004), these Mexican migrants are in practice exemplar transnational, and by extension, global citizens. To borrow from Luis Cabrera (2010), these migrants are "exemplar practitioners of global citizenship" (7) who can "enact significant aspects of global citizenship by seeking to protect the core rights of others who do not share their state citizenship" (258). Short of the supranational reforms or normative change in the global citizenship ethic that Cabrera calls for, however, Mexican migrants will remain caught between imperial citizenship in the United States and clientelistic citizenship in México as they continue to deploy their diasporic dialectics to democratize political belonging in both exclusive membership regimes.

4

Embodiments of Transnational Citizenship

POSTMORTEM REPATRIATION FROM
THE UNITED STATES TO MÉXICO

"nuestras vidas son un continuo peregrinar entre el aquí y el allá"
—OCTAVIO PAZ

The Diasporic Demands of Migrant Mortals

At a public library in a Latino neighborhood in San José, bearing the early signs of the impending gentrification sweeping through Silicon Valley, members of Proyecto Migrante *Zacatecano* (PMZ) and migrant activists from Michoacán awaited a special visiting guest: a PAN migrant federal deputy from the Mexican state of Guanajuato. I arrived a few minutes shy of the scheduled community forum and already members of PMZ were grilling the migrant deputy outside the venue. "Did you vote in favor of the energy reform?" asked one *paisano* demandingly. "Yes, I did, and let me explain to you why," the migrant deputy replied. Before the migrant deputy could justify his support of the reform that would open Mexican oil to private investment from national and transnational corporations, the *paisano* yelled to his face: "Then you are a fucking traitor to the *patria*!" The migrant deputy snapped back, "If you are going to insult me, I will leave," visibly surprised that this wasn't just another group of migrant leaders who would indulge the migrant-turned-politician and greet him with congratulatory pats on

An earlier version of this chapter was published as "Posthumous Transnationalism: Postmortem Repatriation from the United States to Mexico." Latin American Research Review 46 (3): 157–179.

the back. "It's not an insult," I interjected. "You came here to debate and dialogue with the diaspora, and this is what diasporic political dialogue is all about," I said ushering the group into the library to impede the migrant congressman from leaving before the rest of us could have a piece of him.

Once inside, the migrant federal deputy comfortably slipped back into his "leadership" role, taking the seat at the front table ready to preach to the room full of *paisanos*. Before he could do this however, Juan Castro of PMZ took the stand and delivered a scathing and incisive presentation exposing just how corrupt and politically bastardized diasporic policies such as the 3x1 matching-funds program had become. The purpose of Juan's prelude was to introduce the special guest and the audience to two of the organization's guiding political principles: transparency and accountability. Like the migrant organic intellectual that he is, in an impromptu pedagogical exercise Juan Castro began randomly calling on audience members to provide examples of transparency and accountability (or lack thereof) in their encounters with Mexican bureaucracies and political institutions. "Adrián, can you give us an example of transparency and accountability?" Not expecting that Juan would call on me, I instinctively invoked what is in my mind the clearest manifestation and embodiment of the tragedy of transnational citizenship: the repatriation of deceased Mexican migrants from the United States to their communities of origin in rural México. While Mexican consulates in the United States have funds for these postmortem repatriations, I stated, they were not always forthcoming about this aid or transparent about the budget for this and other services. To this, the migrant deputy instantly replied, "You should do as the migrants from Guanajuato, we don't leave one cadaver behind," sounding more like the PANista politician he had become than the migrant representative he professed to be. Ironically, toward the end of the meeting, migrant leaders from Casa Guanajuato, an ethnic association in Greenfield, California, arrived to remind their migrant representative that he had not yet delivered on his promise of expediting birth certificates to migrants from his home state toiling in the fields of the Salinas Valley. With that, we were reminded of how Mexican migrant mortals demand and embody transnational citizenship, from the cradle to the grave.

Introduction

> *No soy más que una nave . . .*
> *nave en que se celebran eternos funerales,*
> *porque una lluvia terca no permite*
> *sacar el ataúd a las calles rurales . . .*
>
> —*Ramón López Velarde*

This chapter discusses the increasingly institutionalized practice of repatriating the bodies of deceased Mexican migrants from the United States to their communities of origin in rural México, the final phase of the migrant political life cycle. Strikingly, this practice has not been confined to migrants who die in attempted border crossings into the United States (De León 2015). In addition to the hundreds of migrants who die at the border each year, there are also thousands of temporary, long-term, and settled migrants who form part of this posthumous return migration from the interior of the United States. Since 1997, the number of migrants who die in attempted surreptitious crossings of the México-U.S. divide has averaged over 300 per year (Inda 2007: 148). By comparison, posthumous repatriations averaged around 10,000 annually in the early 2000s (Lestage 2008). The vast majority of Mexican migrant deaths occur not at the border but inside the territorial United States as a result of work-related or vehicular accidents, homicide, natural or other causes (Lestage 2008; Hayes-Bautista et al. 2002). There are a wide variety of circumstances under which posthumous repatriations occur, and the deceased repatriates span the full gamut of legal statuses—undocumented migrant, legal permanent resident, naturalized U.S. citizen. In some instances, it is a decision made by the remaining family in the village of origin who, lacking legal entry into the United States, wants to see their loved one for the final time. Other times it is the decision of the immediate family in the United States, planning on eventually returning permanently to México. Yet in other circumstances, it is the expressed desire of migrants in life to be returned to their community of origin in death, thus exercising more decision in the matter.

Posthumous repatriations should not be seen as a strictly private form of transnationalism. As Osman Balkan states in relation to this practice among Muslim migrants in Europe: "While death is undoubtedly a universally shared human experience, for minority communities in migratory settings death is a rupture that foregrounds questions that are central to every migratory experience: Who am I and where do I belong?" (2015a: 132). For the scholars of México-U.S. migration who document the cross-border flows of financial and social remittances and transnational politics, it should not be difficult to accept postmortem repatriations as yet another form of migrant transnationalism (see for example, Rouse 1991; 1992; 1995; Goldring 2002; Fox 2005; Smith 2006; Fox and Bada 2008; Smith and Bakker 2008; Schmidt Camacho 2008; Moctezuma 2011; Bada 2014). However, for the skeptics of transnationalism, this practice raises a set of theoretical and normative questions. There is an insistent critique of the transnationalism literature, which suggests that over time, migrants in the United States experience "foreign detachment." The political sociologist Roger Waldinger makes a compelling case that international migration is not simply a social phenomenon but a political one as well. "States seek to bound the societies they enclose," he writes, "they strive to regulate membership in the national collectivity as well as movement across territorial borders" (Waldinger 2007b: 343). Correspondingly, "Nationals, believing in the idea of the national community, endeavor to implement it, making sure that membership is only available to some, and signaling to the newcomers that acceptance is contingent on conformity" (344). Thus, the "bounded community" or "container society" exerts a series of assimilatory pressures on migrants, leading to foreign detachment over time. "[A]s the ex-foreigners nationalize, they accept and internalize the social models prevailing among the nationals, replacing old country with new country solidarities" (347).

In a more recent iteration, Waldinger further nuances his argument suggesting that the degree and nature of "trans-state activity" depends on where migrants stand on the trajectory of political or social incorporation. "Given the rise of massive state apparatuses *controlling* population movements between states, not everyone can move from 'host' to 'home' country and back with equal ease" (2008: 9). Further advancing his political caging hypothesis, Waldinger insists, "states 'cage' the populations residing on their territory, constraining social ties beyond the territorial divide, while reorienting the activities toward the interior" (2008: 9). In this view, settlement is the end result. Over time, "ties to the home environment wither: the locus of significant social relationships shifts to the host environment as settlement occurs" (2008: 9). In his most recent book, Waldinger refers to these migrants as "bordered," stating that when they enter the space of the receiving state "they enter a cage, where their home country ties inexorably wither" (2015: 81). If this account is to be accepted, then the transnational practice of repatriating the bodies of migrants who have died in the United States, particularly long-term migrants, becomes even more intriguing and worth examining, especially if this practice tells us something about migrants' sense of political belonging. Death in the diaspora raises political questions. As Balkan reminds us, "By conferring a sense of fixity or permanence to identities that are more fluid or ambivalent in life, determining where a dead body belongs helps demarcate social and communal boundaries" (2015a: 120).

How common is the practice of repatriating the bodies of Mexican migrants who die in the United States? While posthumous repatriations appear to be a minoritarian affair—like other forms of transnationalism—the numbers are not insignificant. Lestage estimates that one out of every six Mexican migrants who dies in the United States is repatriated to México (2008: 211). At one point, figures from México's Secretaría de Relaciones Exteriores (Foreign Ministry, or SRE for its Spanish acronym) reported an average of thirty deceased Mexican migrants repatriated from the United States per day. From 2004 to 2006, the recorded transfer of deceased Mexican migrants increased from 9,877 to 9,913 to 10,398, respectively. Mexican consulates throughout the United States are responding to co-nationals' need to repatriate their dead daily, not to mention the self-help of HTAs and informal social networks in migrant communities. As Alicia Schmidt Camacho states, "The space of death is not confined to the border . . . Mexican consuls have had to apportion ever-greater percentages of their budgets to the forensic identification and repatriation of bodies, both of migrants who perished in transit and of those who died in the United States" (2008: 290). These patterns raise a couple of interrelated questions. Why do Mexican migrants desire and realize a burial in their communities of origin, and what does this practice imply for transnational political membership and belonging? Second, who are the government and institutional actors involved—on either side of the border—and what is their role and view of this practice? Drawing on transnational ethnography between Southern California and Zacatecas, México, this chapter presents interviews with elected and appointed officials, repatriation data from the Mexican consulate in Los Angeles, and qualitative interviews with the families of twenty-two deceased repatriates to provide preliminary answers to these questions.[1]

Focusing on Zacatecas offers a number of analytic advantages. Located in north-central México, Zacatecas is one of the historic migrant sending-states and has had among the highest out-migration rates relative to its population size. As discussed in the previous chapter, the state government of Zacatecas has taken a pioneering role on issues related to the diaspora, ranging from job-creation schemes utilizing migrant remittances to allowing migrants to run for office in state and municipal elections. In that sense, Zacatecas has been at the forefront of issues concerning migrant rights, even though the question of migrant "representation" is highly contested. In order to determine whether the same pattern applies to posthumous repatriations—the transnational practice that marks the end of the migrant political life cycle—it makes sense to select Zacatecas as the initial case of research. Additionally, Zacatecas represents, in some respects, a microcosm of the broader landscape of migration in México as a whole, exhibiting variations in migration historicity across municipalities. While the central and southern municipalities have seen recurrent circular migration to the United States for over a century (e.g., Jerez), some of the northern municipalities, such as Río Grande, have only experienced U.S.-bound migration on a large scale since the 1980s, allowing for rich comparisons at the municipal and submunicipal levels.

In providing an account of how the Mexican government has institutionalized this practice, I avoid reproducing the dichotomized debate regarding whether this is state-led transnationalism or strictly migrant-led transnationalism, and instead show how the two are dialectical and in constant tension with one another. In other words, while this demand has existed among migrants well before the Mexican government responded to it in a systematic fashion, the recent effort by the Mexican state to institutionalize these repatriations certainly provides a political opportunity structure that will facilitate them in the future. Rather than being a unidirectional argument of institutionalized repatriations driven by the Mexican state, I make the case that it is a dialectical process or "synergistic loop" negotiated by migrants and Mexican state institutions and bureaucratic actors (Iskander 2010: 255). Indeed, policy change around posthumous repatriations involved power struggles between migrant deputies, who prioritized this and other diaspora demands, and political actors not as concerned with migrant affairs, while the Mexican state overall seems to follow its tendency to capitalize on such programs, if not co-opt them altogether. As Robert C. Smith puts it, "The increasing creation of extra-territorial or diasporic bureaucracies, and laws regulating diasporic behaviour, enables greater and more effective channeling of migrant demands, but also their regulation and limitation" (2008: 709).

This final chapter is divided into three sections. First, I develop a cultural analysis to illustrate that posthumous repatriation is a recurring theme in the diasporic imaginaries and cultural production of rural Mexican migrants in the United States—that is, in their mythologies of transnational citizenship. Second, I present ethnographic material from interviews with bureaucratic actors to document how the Mexican state has institutionalized posthumous repatriations at the transnational, national, state, and municipal levels of governance, as part of its broader effort of rapprochement with the Mexican diaspora. Third, I discuss the role of migrant family and social networks in the cross-border process of repatriating cadavers and in the making of a posthumous transnational tradition.

Understanding Posthumous Repatriation
"Culture of Departure," Culture of Return

A sustained exodus over decades in villages throughout rural México has set in place not only the social networks necessary for emigration but also an entrenched "culture of departure" that has proven difficult to break (Quinones 2008; Cohen 2004). A constant influx of dollars has made local economies dependent on remittances to the extent that residents have few economic alternatives other than leaving for the United States (Menchaca 2016; Moctezuma 2003; Rouse 1991). Migrant purchasing power on display in their home villages in the form of homes and other goods entices other villagers north (see Lopez 2015). Journalist Sam Quinones chronicles how the homes that migrants build in their communities of origin are a reminder to the locals of the "difference between emigrating and staying put." Every year, migrants return and add to their homes, "intending to retire to them one day." The homes, Quinones observes, "are immigrants' promise to return for good one day." "Yet, amazingly," he writes, "few immigrants ever retire to them." With urban jobs and school-age children in the United States, for example, the trip home becomes increasingly difficult for these migrants (Nichols 2006). Though few migrants keep the promise of return, "the dream nevertheless lives on," as Quinones describes it, "surreally filling México with empty houses."

    Quinones's observations resonate with the academic literature on the "myth of return."[2] While Mexican migrants often express and plan for a return, scholars suggest, few return for good, *in life*. However, as this chapter unearths, many Mexican migrants are indeed returning permanently, albeit deceased, thus fulfilling that dream posthumously. As Osman Balkan states, "The myth of return, a powerful and almost universal trope in narratives of migration, influences not only life but also death in the diaspora" (2015a: 124). Because a return in life is uncertain, the desire for a posthumous return to the community of origin is a recurring theme in the collective memories, everyday exchanges, and cultural production of rural Mexican migrants. The following section describes how migrants express their desire for posthumous repatriation in their music. To borrow from Pat Zavella's work on "transnational cultural memory," Mexican migrant songs are important "cultural texts" that represent "archives of feelings" and "repertoires of memory," where expressions of "migrant mourning" and "melancholia" are collectively inscribed (Zavella 2011; see also Schmidt Camacho 2008).

Migrant Music, Memory, Mourning, and Melancholia

The Mexican migrant "embodies a melancholic condition" writes Alicia Schmidt Camacho (2008: 12), and music often offers "narrative coherence" and "narrative closure" to the "psychic wounding" that is migration (2008: 106). An enduring desire for a return to their *tierra*—even after death—is a recurring trope in the transnational imaginaries of rural Mexican migrants. While posthumous repatriation involves private and kinship-based decision-making, the sentiment behind this practice is a common theme in the cultural production of the Mexican diaspora.[3] Mexican regional music and its diasporic reproductions are a particularly rich social text where one can find repeated references of a desire for a burial in México. Posthumous repatriation and diasporic nostalgia are recurring expressions in the lyrics of *ranchera* icons Vicente Fernández and the late Antonio Aguilar, whose songs are ubiquitous in the Mexican diaspora.

In the heart wrenching lyrics of *Mi Ranchito*—a song not necessarily about international migration but certainly about departure and conceptions of homeland—Vicente Fernández describes the two as follows:

> *Allá atrás de la montaña, donde temprano se oculta el sol, quedó mi ranchito triste y abandonada ya mi labor . . . Ay corazón que te vas para nunca volver, no me digas adiós.*

> Over there, behind the mountain, where the sun sets,
> is my sad little ranch and abandoned my labor . . .
> Ay dear heart that departs to never return, do not bid me farewell.

Far from being mere romantic or pastoral language, Fernández's lyrics speak to the nostalgia shared by many Mexican migrants displaced from their agrarian lives in México's destitute ranching states. In contrast to conventional accounts of a voluntary labor migration, these lyrics illustrate the difficulty of abandoning the community of origin and the loved ones therein. Like many of Fernández's songs, *Mi Ranchito* is a long-time favorite in Mexican regional music. True to the timeless quality of the song, Cumbre Norteña, a Los Angeles *norteño* band made up of U.S.-born Mexican musicians, covered the song and perform it regularly in nightclubs throughout the city to audiences of recently arrived and U.S.-native Mexican youth.

Similarly, in their song *Zacatecano*, Conjunto Río Grande, a *norteño* band similar to Cumbre Norteña but whose members are Zacatecas natives, describe the reasons for migrating and subsequent diasporic identity:

Adiós amigos, adiós mi linda tierra. Me voy muy lejos, la pobreza me lleva.... Cuanta tristeza al dejar a mi familia, con la esperanza de darles mejor vida . . . Hoy que me encuentro muy lejos de mi tierra, por un destino en un lugar lejano, te juro hermano por Dios que no es mentira, que orgullo siento de ser Zacatecano.

Farewell friends, farewell my beautiful land. I leave to a distant place, poverty takes me away . . . How sad I feel to leave my family, with the hope of providing them a better life . . . Now that I am far from my land, in a distant place, I swear to you brother, how proud I am to be Zacatecan.

Again, these lyrics challenge the notion of Mexican migration as an autonomous process by pointing to rural poverty as the condition of exit. Additionally, the song conveys the enduring nostalgia for the local homeland (in this case Zacatecas), as well as the invigorated ethnic pride and diasporic identity migrants experience when they are displaced from their land. While the members of Conjunto Río Grande reside in Zacatecas, their music is popular in the Zacatecan diaspora and they often perform in migrant communities in cities like Los Angeles, Dallas, Denver, and Chicago. Not surprisingly, Conjunto Río Grande and the L.A.-based *norteño* bands like Cumbre Norteña take after one another and share their musical repertoire. In this manner, musical forms between cultural actors in México and the diaspora synergistically interact around notions of homeland and identity.

In addition to the recurring themes of diasporic nostalgia and attachment, explicit references to posthumous repatriation are not uncommon in Mexican regional music. To cite one of Vicente Fernández's most popularly known songs, *México Lindo y Querido*:

México lindo y querido, si muero lejos de ti, que digan que estoy dormido y que me traigan aquí . . . Que me entierren en la sierra, al pie de los magueyales.

México beautiful and adored, if I die far from you, let them say I am asleep and have them bring me to you . . . Bury me in the sierra, by the maguey plants.

Here, Fernández makes a specific reference to posthumous repatriation that also invokes pastoral imagery. To connect this to *Mi Ranchito*, these lyrics suggest a posthumous return to the rural landscape that was initially abandoned. While Chicano historians such as Gilbert González and others have borrowed directly from these lyrics to argue that "México lindo" migrants were historically at the whim of government-orchestrated nationalism and thus politically demobilized at the interest of the Mexican and U.S. governments (1999), I argue that migrants' attachment to their homelands represents an autonomist connection that develops free from—if not against—the influence of the Mexican state, such that migrants' loyalty is to their local political communities not necessarily their government.[4]

References to posthumous repatriation occur across the different genres of Mexican regional music. From the *corrido* sphere, the late Chalino Sánchez sings[5]:

Adiós rancho de Las Milpas, del estado de Durango. Nunca te voy a olvidar, yo siempre te he recordado. Cuando muera me sepultan, allá en mi rancho adorado.

Farewell rancho Las Milpas, from the state of Durango. I will never forget you, I have always remembered you. When I die, bury me in my beloved ranch.

Here, we see a similar diasporic memory and longing for the home locality. In this *corrido* the homeland is specified beyond the state level to the particular *rancho*, indicative of migrants' tendency to identify primarily with their *patria chica*.

Lastly, Los Tigres del Norte make reference to posthumous repatriation as follows:

Como el águila en vuelo, como la fiera en celo desafiando fronteras defendiendo el honor, he pasado la vida explorando otras tierras para darle a mis hijos un mañana mejor. Si la muerte me alcanza en su loca carrera, envuelto en mi bandera que me lleven allá. Que me canten el himno de mi patria diez meses o me muero dos veces si me entierran acá . . .

Like the eagle in flight . . . defying borders, defending honor, I've spent my life exploring other lands to provide my children a better future. If death meets me in its frantic race, draped in my flag, I ask that I be taken over there. Sing my country's national anthem ten months or I will die twice if I am buried here . . .

A desire for a posthumous return to the community of origin is a recurring theme across several of the musical genres of rural Mexican migrants, spanning multiple generations of migration from the 1960s to the turn of the twenty-first century, as seen in the selections discussed above. While posthumous repatriations cannot be directly attributed to the return ideologies expressed in these lyrics, they are not solely a function of the political opportunity structure recently created by the Mexican government either. A look at the historicity of posthumous repatriations in one classic migrant-sending municipality reveals that this practice predates the Mexican government's efforts at institutionalizing them, revealing a sustained postmortem transnational tradition dating back to at least the 1980s (see figure 4.1). Before discussing the Mexican government's institutionalization of these repatriations in greater detail, however, a discussion of gender and migration is in order.

Gendered Accounts of the Homeland

It is important to consider that these accounts of the rural community of origin are mediated by transnational "gendered memory" (Goldring 1996). In other words, recollections of the rural landscape of origin are informed by the social relations and gender dynamics therein, producing contrasting return ideologies between male and female migrants. To this we add the transformative effect that international migration can have on gender norms and ideologies within Mexican migrant families (see Hondagneu-Sotelo 1994; Rosas 2014). From the perspective of female Mexican migrants, for example, memories of the village of origin are associated with the surveillance of women and the social sanctions reserved for behavior deemed deviant from *rancho/* rural normativity (Goldring 1996: 311). With the feminization of Mexican migration to the United States, women's entry into the labor force and their increased recourse to social-institutional outlets for redressing issues, such as domestic abuse, are among the factors challenging men's patriarchal authority in Mexican migrant households.[6] Important life-cycle events experienced in the United States also seem to consolidate settlement for migrant women therein. As Goldring states:

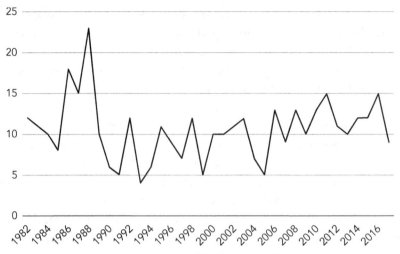

FIGURE 4.1 Posthumous Repatriations from the United States to Jerez, Zacatecas, 1982-2017

Source: Death certificate data collected by author from the Notaría Parroquial archive in Jerez, Zacatecas, and the Los Angeles Family History Center archive in California. Out of 381 deceased repatriates accounted for between 1982 and 2017, 67.5 percent were male and 32.5 percent were female.

> Being a mother in the United States tends to strengthen ties to the country—women who migrate are likely to bring their children to the United States or have children there. As children grow up and go to school in the United States, they too will most likely remain, marrying and raising their own families there. Women said it is very important to them to be near their children and grandchildren. (313)

This and other factors partly explain why migrant women envision their futures in the United States.

Concomitantly, "gendered memory" also partly explains male migrants' divergent return ideologies. In Goldring's and other ethnographic studies (Rouse 1992), Mexican migrant men envisioned the United States as a site for work and increasingly settlement, while they viewed the community of origin in México as a site to visit for leisure, relaxation, and eventually retirement. Unlike women, most men in these studies expressed a desire to permanently return to México upon retiring. The factors described above, whereby male's influence over the micropolitics and gender norms of the family diminishes, may partly account for the desire to return. Related to this point, male migrants remember the rural community of origin as a place where they are free from the social and spatial discipline of life in the United States. Additionally, the village of origin also offers the opportunity for male migrants to recreate and partake in traditional rural cultural activities—*coleaderos* (Mexican rodeo), *peleas de gallos* (cock fighting), and so forth. Whether the desire to return constitutes nostalgia for reclaiming male migrants' diminished *ranchero* masculinity or, conversely, their ethno-territorial identities—which are bound up in gender, class, and so on—is open to debate. Nevertheless, the transnational feminist critique is well taken: "The romanticization of rural place is belied by women's experiences there and should be guarded against to the extent that it privileges some voices and plans for the future while ignoring others" (Goldring 1996: 323).

Having discussed the recurring trope of posthumous repatriations in the transnational cultural memories of Mexican migrants earlier in the chapter, the following section shifts focus to the view of bureaucratic actors involved in the process of repatriating cadavers from the United States to México in order to trace how the Mexican government has institutionalized this practice at the transnational, national, state, and municipal levels of governance.

Transnational Ethnography: The View from Institutional and State Actors
The Transnational Level: Mexican Consulate—Los Angeles, CA

Interviews with bureaucratic and state actors at the transnational, national, state, and municipal levels of governance proved useful in understanding the logistics, requirements, politics, economics, and culture behind posthumous repatriation.[7] At the transnational level, a joint interview with the consul in charge of administering these repatriations and the public relations director at the Mexican consulate in Los Angeles, California, revealed that this was the first of fifty consulates to offer a subsidized program whereby Mexican families who are financially disadvantaged can receive material assistance to repatriate their dead. To facilitate this process, the consulate partnered with six mortuaries in the county. The consul described the development of this program as follows:

> Each consulate has diverse needs. I don't have the same demands as the [consul] in Calexico, Chicago, Atlanta, or Salt Lake City. Here [Los Angeles], given the demand and thanks to the general consul's efforts, a partnership was established with several mortuaries in the county. This

is the only consulate with such an agreement. Thanks to this agreement, six funeral homes in the county have offered a basic service at a very low cost. This basic package includes a coffin made of compressed wood, processing of all documentation necessary for the repatriation, embalming and transportation of the body to an international airport.

While the Mexican government has invested considerable funds for these repatriations, upward of half of consular budgets in some instances, as we will see later in the chapter, this is not a unidirectional story of state-incentivized "necropatriotism" (see Balkan 2015b). Unlike Lestage's interpretation, which suggests that these repatriations occur as a result of the Mexican government's efforts to institutionalize them (2008), the consul describes posthumous repatriations as a diaspora demand that emerges from migrants and their families; one to which the consulate subsequently responds. Lestage's analysis suggests that the Mexican government's efforts at institutionalization began during the Fox administration. However, figure 4.1 illustrates that migrants' demand around this issue precedes the Mexican government's institutionalization, suggesting that state-led transnationalism and migrant-led transnationalism are mutually constitutive (but also dialectic).

In order to qualify for this subsidized program, "the applicant must prove that he/she is financially disadvantaged and cannot cover this cost," the consul stipulated. "Aid is authorized for Mexican nationals," he added.

> Part of the requirements is to accredit the identity and Mexican nationality of the deceased. Those are the two fundamental requirements: identity and Mexican nationality. Identity can be established by an official document belonging to the deceased, and nationality can be established with a birth certificate, Mexican passport, a declaration of Mexican nationality, or even a certificate of Mexican naturalization.

When asked about dual nationals, the consul responded, "So long as you come to me and prove that the deceased is a Mexican national, not an American citizen, I can provide the aid."

"Why Invest in the Dead"?

Regarding the politics behind this program, the consul provided a detailed account. In 2004, the Mexican congress provided consulates with funds specifically designated for subsidizing posthumous repatriations. Under this arrangement, the "central authorities" established a spending cap for the aid destined for repatriating a cadaver.

> No consulate can provide more than one thousand five hundred dollars [USD] in financial support for this end, except for exceptional cases. What are those cases? Well, for example, if there are two or more deaths in the same family, in which case the financial cost for the survivors is too great. Under such circumstances, the appropriate consulate solicits authorization, and the central authorities decide whether financial assistance will exceed the established amount.

It was apparent from the consul's tone that the legislation allocating aid specifically for posthumous repatriation was not well received by all policymakers involved:

> There may be officials who prefer to invest these funds elsewhere. Some have inquired, "Why invest in the dead instead of on migrants who are still alive?" A lot of money is invested in these repatriations. In 2004, out of the 120 million pesos authorized by congress, 55 million was designated for the dead. It does not make sense. Half of the budget to transfer the dead? That money could be utilized to facilitate legal processes.

México's Ministry of Foreign Affairs has been committed to assisting posthumous repatriation since the 1980s, according to the consul. "However, the budget was limited then. If an applicant received two hundred dollars, that was generous." Again making reference to the increasing demand, the Consul added:

> But the issue became more and more salient. And of course, it also matters how some legislators or state governing bodies view this issue. If legislators have made it an issue to allocate fifty percent of the consulate budgets exclusively for posthumous repatriation, then so be it.

The consul concluded on a sarcastic tone: "These are matters that we mortals shouldn't question." To this the public relations staffer remarked tongue in cheek, "You wouldn't want their ghosts to come back and haunt you." The earlier comment by the consul also suggests an important role played by certain legislators, likely those from high-emigration regions in México, a point we will return to in the interview with the late federal congressman Andrés Bermúdez.

Regarding the large sum devoted to posthumous repatriation, the consulate provided the following data. In 2005, the consulate in Los Angeles assisted a total of 216 families repatriate a deceased loved one, spending USD$277,636. Additionally, the overall number of bodies repatriated with and without financial assistance from the Mexican Consulate in Los Angeles during 2003-2005 increased from 1,344, to 1,361 to 1,418 respectively.

Regarding where posthumous repatriation happens more often, the consulate provided the number of deceased repatriates by state of origin for the years 2004-2007. Not surprisingly, high-emigration states, such as Jalisco and Michoacán, were near the top of the list. However, other traditional sending regions such as Zacatecas were relatively lower. This could be a function of mortality rates or, more interestingly, it can also be an indication of socioeconomic status and/or migrant "incorporation" in the United States. As the director of public relations suggested:

It also depends largely on the amount of time spent in the U.S. by Zacatecans. For instance, there may be a lot of Zacatecans who no longer have links to Zacatecas and thus are buried here. Not everyone wants to be buried over there because the whole family is now here.

Considering an alternative explanation, she stated, "Or perhaps Zacatecans have enough money to repatriate their dead without support from the consulate." While this research is an initial attempt at addressing this question, the idea that burial site may be an indicator of migrant loyalty/attachment merits further consideration. As Osman Balkan states, in the context of death in diaspora, "Soil is endowed with extraordinary significance when it receives a dead body" (2015a: 123; see also Balkan 2015b; 2016).

When asked about the motives behind posthumous repatriations, the consul responded:

Some say, "It was his/her last wish to be buried in the community of birth" . . . but I believe that one of the reasons why they do not bury them in the U.S. is simply the cost. It is much more expensive to bury them here.

The view that the decision to repatriate a cadaver is the result of a simple cost-benefit analysis is at odds with the cultural framework presented in this chapter, as expressed in the interviews with the relatives of deceased repatriates. Before discussing the view of migrant families however, the following section scales down to the state-level of analysis and focuses on two institutional sites central to the process of repatriating cadavers: the Zacatecas international airport, and the State Migration Institute.

The State Level: General Leobardo Ruiz International Airport—Calera, Zacatecas

Indicative of the Mexican government's effort to institutionalize this process at the state level, in January 2008 public health authorities in Zacatecas appointed a full-time medical doctor to the state's international airport to oversee and administer the arrival of cadavers on international flights, reportedly making this the first international airport in the country with such an arrangement.[8] The doctor described the nature of his work as follows:

> Over the course of the last six months we have coordinated with the airport authorities, through committee meetings, and we requested that we receive all official medical documents concerning every cadaver that arrives at this airport. Previously there was no such coordination or no established process . . . Now there is a commitment on behalf of the actors involved in carrying out these repatriations and those receiving the cadavers. Thanks to our committee meeting and our request per the Zacatecas public health services, they are now following these guidelines and honoring the commitment on behalf of the agency that processes these repatriations.

The doctor also described the work of the different actors involved in the international process of repatriating a cadaver:

> The transfer of the body is coordinated by a foreign funeral agency, via the consular network which approves of the participating funeral agencies and the persons in charge of preparing the preservation of the body. Thereafter, the body is transferred from the place of death, which is often their place of residence abroad, back to the place of origin, which in most cases is here in Zacatecas or in a neighboring state like

Durango or any other state that may not have access to an international airport. Finally, from this airport we hand the body over to a local funeral home.

Upon arrival at the airport, the doctor and his staff expect that each cadaver will have the appropriate medical documentation, ranging from the death certificate to the funeral that prepared the preservation of the body. "We also corroborate that the body is transported in an appropriately sealed container so that it can leave the airport to the cemetery."

Documenting the Deceased

Although the international airport in Calera, Zacatecas has taken a leading role on this matter, the doctor said, "We still have challenges to overcome and actions to consolidate." Ideally, the doctor detailed, every cadaver should arrive along with a series of documents accrediting not only the death certificate but also "a signature from the preparer and the procedure they followed for the preservation of the body. In this manner, they are in some ways guaranteeing that the body will not arrive in a state of decomposition." Regarding this documentation, "some are very thorough," he said, but most are not.

> All cadavers should arrive with the necessary documentation, they should not simply arrive and hand them over to me. They should first furnish all of these documents, including the note from the Mexican consulate, the certificate from the embalmer, and an official document from the doctor who certified the death. Only upon reviewing these three key documents should I authorize the exit of the cadaver from the airport and its transfer to the cemetery. This should be the process for the reception and exit of each cadaver. But it rarely happens this way. In some cases many of these documents are missing. I need these three documents as per the official procedure of repatriating cadavers. This should be consolidated not only in this country but in every country and in every state of this country. This is fundamental for public health and for the repatriation of cadavers.

My informant suggested that the increasing institutionalization of this transnational practice was in large part due to the efforts of the Zacatecas state government.

When a *paisano* dies abroad and there are no resources for the autopsy, the embalming of the corpse, its repatriation to this airport and to its place of origin, part or all of the costs are absolved and the process on the U.S. side is expedited. It has been the prerogative of the governor of Zacatecas, Amalia García, that when somebody dies in the U.S. the state government assists the family members here who otherwise might not have the resources to repatriate their loved one for burial in their place of birth.

As my interviewee described, and as we will see in greater detail in the following section, the Zacatecas state government has invested considerably in this process.

I think this is due to the sensibility of two key actors: the *gobernadora* Amalia García Medina and the director of health services in our state to take proactive action to guarantee the health of our citizens in Zacatecas and beyond.

The Cultural Politics of Posthumous Repatriation

In contrast to my interview at the Mexican consulate in Los Angeles, my respondent at the international airport in Zacatecas had a very different opinion regarding the reasons why migrants and their families repatriate their loved ones who have perished in the United States. Whereas my informants at the Mexican consulate suggested a simple cost-benefit calculation, the doctor in Zacatecas felt the reasons were profoundly cultural.

There is a popular proverb that says that where you bury your *ombligo*, that is where you ought to grow, reproduce, die, and be buried.[9] As a result of international migration, however, which is a multicausal phenomenon due to economic or ecological factors, people are displaced. However, to leave a loved one in a distant place once he or she is dead would be like never accepting their death. People here say, "I want to see him/her to know for certain that he/she is dead." It is a common experience of mourning to not accept death. Having the corpse before you helps relatives accept death. On the other hand, this also allows them to share the last moment with the body, the *velorio* [wake] attended by the deceased's family, friends, and neighbors before burying him/her in the land of his/her birth; often times next to the tombs of his ancestors, father, mother, or brothers. In some cases, when a body was buried in a place other than the place of birth, there have been family disputes over this.

My respondent substantiated his observations with the nature of his work:

> We have worked not only behind our desks, we have worked for many years in the field. We know the collective sentiment of the people, the cultural beliefs that they cherish during this process of immense loss and pain. I have seen people crying for their deceased loved one to be repatriated, and they continue mourning until they bury the body, and they continue crying for days thereafter. They do not accept the person is dead until they have the body with them.

As Rosa-Linda Fregoso and Cynthia Bejarano cite in their separate but nevertheless related discussion of disappeared and murdered women in Latin America: the "right to mourn the dead, for bereavement is 'one of the most deep-seated fundamental needs in all human cultures' and it 'require[s] that the location of the loved one's remains be known and that the mourners have a body to mourn'" (quoted in Fregoso and Bejarano 2010: 24).

Instituto Estatal de Migración—Zacatecas

My interview with the director of the Instituto Estatal de Migración (State Migration Institute, IEM) in Zacatecas revealed the degree of policy convergence and increasing coordination between the Mexican federal and state governments regarding posthumous repatriations.[10] According to the director at the time, Fernando Robledo, "The state government and the federal government have the same policy regarding the repatriation of cadavers." As stated earlier, the federal government provides support via the Ministry of Foreign Affairs and its consular network in the United States. Correspondingly, Robledo explained, state governments have followed suit and attended to this "social exigency concerning the repatriation of cadavers." In the view of Robledo, this demand "is gradually increasing year after year."

"De la no intervención a la institucionalización"

In response to this demand, the IEM in Zacatecas, like the Mexican government at the transnational and national levels, has taken steps to institutionalize and streamline the process of repatriating deceased migrants by establishing a bureaucratic protocol.[11] IEM did its part by making an effort to systematically document these repatriations on a case-by-case basis. "In this office," Robledo shared, "we have statistics for years 2005 and 2006, including cause of death, which show an annual increase." In 2005, IEM attended to fifty-four repatriations in the state, whereas in 2006 the figure increased to seventy-six. Prior to 2005, the numbers were less reliable, again indicative of the recent efforts to institutionalize the process of repatriating deceased migrants. On record, IEM showed fourteen repatriations for year 2004, although Robledo suggested the figure was closer to thirty-six and probably around thirty for 2003. "I was appointed to this office in November 2004 and that was all we could document because we did not have prior records or data," suggesting that the earlier groups of civil administrators had not thoroughly streamlined, institutionalized, or documented these repatriations since the IEM was founded in 1999.

As per the protocol, "and as a matter of principle," Robledo explained, "as soon as family members walk into this office seeking aid, the staff immediately contacts the family in the United States, in the presence of the party who is seeking assistance." Second, the staff contacts the corresponding consulate in the United States. "We don't leave it for another day, we attend to this issue at that very instant," Robledo continued. "This is an issue of principle and humanitarianism because death is a severe matter," he concluded.

Robledo emphasized that the state government of Zacatecas has established clearly defined criteria for administering posthumous repatriations.

> The *gobernadora* [Amalia García Medina] determined that we provide all the assistance possible. The earlier protocol required participation from four parties: the participation of the family of the deceased repatriate, the participation of the consulate, participation from the municipal government and from the state government.

When García Medina took office, she streamlined this protocol by eliminating the role of the municipal government, "due to the delay in providing funds on its part and the conflicts this would generate." Thus the governor streamlined the protocol into three contributing parties: "contribution from the family, from the consulate, and from the state government" via IEM. Robledo mentioned that there are exceptional circumstances under which family members can go directly to the governor who can then determine how to redress the relatives of the deceased repatriate(s). In large part, these cases would be determined according to the "magnitude and social impact" of the repatriation(s). "For example, in case of collective deaths," Robledo explained. Under these circumstances, the governor may determine to cover most or all of the costs based on her discretion. When it is a border death, the Foreign Ministry covers the cost of the repatriation in its totality. Exceptional cases notwithstanding, the point is that there is an institutional "mechanism to provide assistance for families who seek it," he emphasized.

These "exceptional" cases of collective deaths, as Robledo suggested, often provide state actors the opportunity to respond in ways that can be widely construed as "humanitarian." "When there are collective migrant deaths, say for instance a car accident in the United States, this becomes news and this news takes on a different connotation," Robledo stated.

> For us [IEM], there is no difference administratively speaking. Relatives seek assistance from us in the same way that anybody else would. But when we are talking about collective deaths, the matter becomes politicized by municipal presidents and other officials, and it becomes newsworthy. It becomes of political interest and you see the intervention of deputies, municipal presidents, and even the press requesting assistance, in some cases, before the family has sought us out.

"What is very clear in the state government, thanks to the *gobernadora*," Robledo underscored, "are clearly defined institutional procedures for repatriations."

Robledo concluded the interview by returning to the point of humanitarianism. "There is an administrative predisposition during this difficult process for families that is deeply humanitarian on the part of the public servant. There is profound humanitarian conviction here, and it shows in how we deal with this process administratively," he emphasized. The irony of course, is that historically the Mexican government has failed to sufficiently address the structural causes of migration in the first place (e.g., poverty and unemployment).

The Federal Level: Migrant Deputy Andrés Bermúdez

Policy Tracing

To understand posthumous repatriation at the federal and municipal levels, I interviewed Andrés Bermúdez and Serafín Bermúdez respectively.[12]

As migrant elected/appointed officials, posthumous repatriation was a priority on the Bermúdez brothers' policy agendas. At the time of my interviews, the late Andrés Bermúdez was a *diputado migrante* in México's federal congress representing the second district of the state of Zacatecas, while Serafín filled his former position as mayor of Jerez, Zacatecas. As federal congressman, Andrés Bermúdez lobbied for an additional 12 million pesos on top of the already existing funds destined for posthumous repatriation in January 2007. When asked what his fellow congressmen made of his proposal to funnel more funds for repatriating the bodies of deceased migrants to México, Andrés replied: "Many of them did not agree with the destination of these funds because, to put it simply, they do not know what it means to be a migrant." The congressman continued: "They need to know what it is like to be a migrant. What it is like to have your son, your brother, or your father's body arrive so that it can be buried in his *colonia* or *pueblo* along with his other family members," signaling the gap between Mexican rural migrants and the elite political class that governs their country.

As a migrant himself, Andrés knew firsthand what the process of posthumous repatriation was like. In 1992, Andrés and his eldest brother José suffered a car accident in Oregon. José was fatally injured, and shortly before dying he requested to be buried in Jerez, alongside his parents. The lyrics of a posthumous *corrido* capture this as follows:

> *Adiós hermanos queridos: Pancho, Serafín y Andrés. Mi esposa Petra y mis hijos ya no los veré otra vez. Les encargo que me lleven a sepultar a Jerez.*

> Farewell my dear brothers: Pancho, Serafín and Andrés. My wife Petra and my children, I will not see you again. I ask you to take me to be buried in Jerez.

Andrés described the process of repatriating his brother's body to Jerez as emotionally draining and bureaucratically cumbersome. For this reason, "We made it an issue to facilitate and speed up the process of repatriating a body," he said.

> We spoke with Mexican airlines so that they can prioritize the space for transporting cadavers. Having a cadaver in an icebox is an ugly

feeling . . . For a mother to know that her son is dead but not know where he is or if he is frozen somewhere . . . this is why it is best to speed up the process.

At the municipal level, Serafín Bermúdez agreed stating:

There ought to be three contributing parties for this process—the federal, state, and municipal governments. Even if it is a minimal contribution, there ought to be some aid because the families, on that side or here, do not have the resources to transfer their dead.[13]

When asked why migrants wish to return to their land even after their deaths, Andrés responded:

Every migrant, from the moment we depart, from that very instant, we think, "I am going to return. I will return rich, I will return different, I am going to help my *colonia*, I am going to help my mother." We miss our land so much that when we are in the United States, we ask each other, "Hey, if something were to happen to you, where do you want to end up?" "Well, I want to return to my land. I want to be where my parents are; I want to be where my children are. I want to know that I returned to my *pueblo*. Alive or dead, but I want to return to my *pueblo*." Some unfortunately return in a casket. But their last wish was to be in their land. And that is exactly what we are trying to help them do.

Like the lyric analysis presented earlier, this excerpt captures migrants' nostalgia for their land and describes their dreams of return migration. To connect this to the gender analysis discussed earlier, Bermúdez seems to imagine the deceased repatriates as males and frames his policy work around this issue with emotional appeals to the grieving mothers. Additionally, Bermúdez suggests that in the context of emigration, when a return in life is uncertain, migrants' desire for a posthumous repatriation is commonly expressed in the quotidian conversations and exchanges of the Mexican diaspora.

Bermúdez felt it was important to spread the word about the funds at the Mexican consulates to repatriate bodies home.

I want it to be known that there are funds available at every consulate. The easiest step for people in this situation is to go directly to the consul and to tell them that there is money there to take my loved one back to our land. We have to get the word out otherwise the consulate keeps whatever funds are not used at the end of the year.

Bermúdez concluded on the following note:

> I am here to represent my people. I always tell [elite politicians] that in order to do away with migration, they need to have been migrants themselves. I am tired of hearing *políticos* talk about migration this, migration that. Know it, live it, in order to do away with it. Nobody can do away with that which they have not felt.

Indeed, as the embodiment of a transnational citizen himself, Bermúdez understood the issue of posthumous repatriation firsthand, both from the perspective of a migrant and as a migrant representative. Having discussed the views of institutional actors in this section, it is important to conclude by discussing the views of migrants and their families. The following section discusses interviews with family members of deceased repatriates in villages across two migrant-sending municipalities in Zacatecas, one classic-sending (Jerez) and one recent-sending (Río Grande).

The View from Migrants and their Families
Jerez

As a region with a long history of emigration to the United States, the migrant-sending villages in the *municipio* of Jerez have developed strong transnational social networks over time. These migrant networks prove to be an important mechanism in facilitating cross-border activities ranging from sending remittances to repatriating a deceased migrant. In the absence of such robust networks, an institutionally complex process like repatriating a body can become even more cumbersome for the relatives involved. This point emerged in my fieldwork in the migrant-sending *rancho* of Los Haro, a community that has witnessed multiple posthumous repatriations over time (for a history of this community and its migrant network in the United States see Nichols 2006). The following group interview with the family members of a deceased repatriate illustrates the central role of migrant social networks.

RESPONDENT 1: Several migrants from Los Haro who have died over there [U.S.] have been buried there. I think this is due to the fact that previously the migrants who were over there did not know how to proceed in these circumstances. There was nobody to guide us on how to complete the paperwork. We were helpless. It was as if the world came crashing down on us. Today there is a lot of *raza* [migrants].

RESPONDENT 2: [interjecting] Who offer a helping hand.

RESPONDENT 1: They are young migrants who were born here [in Los Haro] but they speak English well and they guide us.

1: Were there others who helped you guys with the repatriation process?

RESPONDENT 2: Yes, they are migrants who have lived through similar situations, and they already know what action to take, they have some experience, and they all come together to help and guide us on how to proceed.

Migrant social networks can provide information and also resources necessary for repatriation. A woman in Los Haro who lost her youngest son in an automobile accident while on his way to work in Napa, California, gratefully acknowledged this point.

The people over there helped us . . . they helped us with money. A lot of folks donated money, including my son's boss, my nephews, and all of our people who reside over there. They all raised money and helped out so that we could bring my son back. May God bless them. Without their help, it would have been very difficult to bring my son back.

The solidarity characteristic of migrant networks manifests itself in multiple ways when a migrant dies in the United States and is subsequently repatriated to the community of origin.[14] Because they have established communities on both sides of the border, it was not uncommon for Jerez migrants to hold two vigils when a migrant died: one prior to repatriation, and one following when the body arrived to the community of origin. Another interviewee in Los Haro, whose son died in the United States from health problems, described the U.S. vigil as follows:

A lot of people showed up over there. The service was held in a big chapel. It was full of people—his friends, acquaintances, and others all closely united. The woman who was saying the prayers said, "This young man was a good person, a good friend. It shows from all the people who are present."

The solidarity around a migrant's death in the United States was also expressed transnationally, as it was also common for loved ones in the United States to accompany the body back to México. Such was the case described by another man in Los Haro whose son was murdered at his workplace in Colorado, who said that one of his son's co-workers traveled to attend the burial. "As well as another one of my sons who was over there," he explained.

This issue was further discussed in my interviews in the neighboring ranching village of El Durazno. When discussing the comparative costs of repatriation versus burial in the United States, one interviewee whose twenty-one-year-old brother died in Los Angeles, California, due to health complications, suggested that while the cost of a funeral and burial in the United States is greater, you have to account for the collective expenditures of the people who make the trip to México for the burial of the body. "It's not just the cost of repatriating the body, you have to account for the costs of the family members who come." When asked who accompanied the body from the United States to México, he recounted, "Within the family it was my mother, my father, plus four of my brothers, that is six, plus a brother-in-law, seven total." In my interviews in the village of El Cargadero, this pattern was particularly striking. With entire nuclear and extended families relocated in the United States, there were often considerable amounts of people who made the trip for the repatriation and burial of deceased migrants.[15] One interviewee recalled that when his son's father-in-law perished in the United States, all of his children came. "It must have been fifteen or twenty people," he recalled. He added, "But two months ago, one of my sons died over there and fifty-two people came. Ten of my children who reside in the United States came and all of their children and grandchildren . . . the entire airplane was full."

This section illustrates the important role of migrant social and family networks in providing support for posthumous repatriations—material and moral. However, no matter how robust these networks, certain migrants are barred from returning due to financial and legal constraints. In my group interview in Los Haro, respondents said that while it was typical that people return along with the deceased repatriate, it is usually those "who have the means to go back," alluding to legal reentry into the United States. When asked whether there was anybody who wanted to travel to México but was unable to, my respondent in El Durazno stated:

> Yes, of course, there were. One of them was my brother's wife who could not leave the U.S. for legal reasons, and others who were in the process

of regularizing their immigration status but had not yet attained legal permanent residence. And also there were some nephews who could not come because of the costs.

Another man in El Durazno whose son died in a vehicular accident in Van Nuys, California, in the early 1980s responded to the same question with a clear recollection: "Nobody came. My in-laws could not come because some of them didn't have papers and others because their jobs did not permit it. Back then there was a lot of work . . . that is why nobody came."

Río Grande

The municipality of Río Grande is comparable to Jerez in population size and migration intensity, but the families there had a qualitatively different experience with posthumous repatriations. While Jerez is a historic migrant-sending region, Río Grande is a much more recent source of international migration to the United States. Among the more recent Río Grande migrants—particularly those who were undocumented—the process of repatriating a body proved considerably more difficult institutionally and financially. When a migrant circuit is in formation or nonexistent, migrants have little or no established social network to rely on for support. The bureaucratic and financial hardship of repatriating a body in such low-information contexts was expressed in my interviews in the Río Grande villages. On top of the personal grief, one respondent in Las Esperanzas described the process of repatriating an extended family member as fraught with "countless sacrifices." The surviving children of the deceased repatriate went into debt to finance the repatriation and were still paying off the costs at the time of the interview. Likewise, in Las Piedras, one respondent stated, "Two of three of my family members who have perished in the United States were brought back. Sadly, my father stayed over there because we did not have the resources to bring him back," alluding to the financial and institutional resources needed for repatriation. A second respondent in Las Piedras, whose son was murdered in Houston, relied on his sister, who had a visa and happened to be visiting her daughters in Texas at the time of the homicide, for assistance with the repatriation from the U.S. side. One interviewee in El Fuerte put it thusly: "*Los mojados* [the undocumented] have no assistance whatsoever except for that offered by all the other *mojados* who reside over there."

Even with less-established migrant networks, the Río Grande respondents relied on strategies of self-help for processing and financing the repatriations of their loved ones. Aid for repatriation often came from relationships that had been established in the United States with other individuals from their hometowns and beyond. One woman in El Fuerte who lost two of her sons from smoke inhalation when a fire consumed their living quarters said it was their friends in the United States who helped repatriate them to their village. "Their friends took care of everything," she said, "[My sons] had many friends, they were very friendly." In addition to coordinating the repatriation from the U.S. side, two friends accompanied the bodies for their funeral in El Fuerte. In the nearby village of La Almoloya, a woman whose son was murdered in Texas was grateful to the persons who assisted with his repatriation. When I asked her if the aid came from individuals from La Almoloya who resided in the United States, she replied, "People from all over the place helped us, may God bless them."

While Río Grande as a whole is an emerging site of mass international migration to the United States, I did encounter a smaller subset of long-term and established migrants in my interviews in the village of La Almoloya. Among the more established migrants who had attained legal permanent resident status in the United States, there was a qualitative difference in the process of repatriating a deceased migrant whereby the bureaucratic and financial burdens were considerably reduced. One woman in La Almoloya recounted the repatriations of several migrants in her immediate and extended family. About her brother-in-law's migration experiences, she said, "He left for the other side from a very young age. Initially he would migrate undocumented, but he later managed to legalize his status as part of the amnesty." Widowed at an early age with no children, he lived with some of his nephews in Texas, where he worked until retiring at the age of sixty-five. He visited La Almoloya one to two times a year for a few weeks at a time. According to my interviewee, "When he was on his deathbed he asked that they not leave him over there [in the U.S.]. He wanted to return even though he had lived in the U.S. and had a mobile home there." After all, she concluded, "His wife, his parents, they are all buried here," suggesting that family and kinship ties also factor into migrants' desires to return. Upon his death, several of his nephews coordinated the repatriation. Once it was arranged, "seven of his nephews along with their families" accompanied the body for burial in La Almoloya.

Additionally, her son had two repatriations in his immediate family: both his wife and his son died in the United States and were repatriated to La Almoloya. A long-term migrant to the United States, her son married a woman from his native La Almoloya and they had three children. Initially, his family lived in La Almolya while he migrated to the United States seasonally. Once he regularized his status, he was able to sponsor his wife and young children to migrate to the United States Thereafter, the family moved to the state of Washington where the father worked on a ranch. Tragically, the twenty-year-old son died in a car accident in 2003 and was repatriated to La Almoloya, as was agreed upon by both parents. When his mother developed cancer thereafter, she expressed her wish to die in La Almoloya so she could be buried close to her son. As her condition worsened, she became confined to a hospital and was not allowed to travel to México for medical reasons. "She said that if all she had left was a few days to live, she wanted to return to México, but she was not allowed to return." There was no other choice but to await her death in the United States and repatriate her posthumously. If this had been an undocumented family or one with less robust migrant networks to turn to for aid, the repatriations may have been considerably more straining financially and emotionally. Lastly, it is also important to note that the main impetus for this repatriate was a desire to be close to her son, suggesting that ties to kinship and place may play out differently depending on the gender of the migrant, a looming factor in this practice, as we will see in the section that follows.

The View from Migrant Families in the United States
Repatriation to El Tesorero, Jerez

To conclude, it is important to discuss how migrant families in the United States experience and navigate posthumous repatriations. This section will discuss how mixed-status migrant families in the United States emotionally and collectively arrive at the decision to repatriate a deceased loved one, beginning with the case of eighty-year-old Angel Escobedo, who passed away in Los Angeles in January 2007 and was repatriated and inhumed in Los Haro, Jerez, Zacatecas.[16] His son Ramiro offered insight into his father's life, death, the process of repatriation, and the reasons behind the decision.

Don Angel was born in rancho Jomulquillo, Jerez, during the tumultuous postrevolutionary period in rural México, when former hacienda lands were being redistributed to impoverished peasant farmers and their families. Don Angel's family was bestowed a plot of land in El Tesorero, not far from his birthplace, where he was raised, married, and started his own family. Don Angel, like most of his peers, did not have access to a formal education. He and the other men in El Tesorero would learn to read and write from the only literate person in the *rancho* at the age of thirty.

Don Angel and his brothers made their first trip to the United States as contracted laborers under the Bracero program. They toiled in the fields of the Southwest in Arizona, Indio, and San Joaquín, California. They worked for a year at a time and then returned to their families in El Tesorero, Jerez. It was not until the 1980s, when Don Angel's children were grown, that they began migrating to the United States more permanently.

Never obtaining a pension for his work in the United States, Don Angel remained in El Tesorero until he developed Alzheimer's disease. With nobody to care for him in México, Ramiro and his siblings decided to bring Don Angel to Los Angeles in 2003. Don Angel would spend the last four years of his life with his children in Los Angeles, unable to communicate with them because of his condition. That is, until shortly before his death.

According to Ramiro, Don Angel had a "moment of clarity" during which he understood he was going to die. "Even though he could not speak," Ramiro shared, "we would ask him questions and he would respond, nodding yes or no. We told him we were going to take him to México, and he understood and he agreed with our decision to take him back." This is why Ramiro and his brothers agreed to repatriate their father's body to Jerez after his death.

However, Ramiro's sisters did not agree with this decision. In anticipation of Don Angel's death, Ramiro's sisters had invested in arranging a burial in Los Angeles. "We knew the day was going to come," said Ramiro, "we had everything ready to bury him here. After his death however, my brothers and I, acting on sentimental considerations, decided to repatriate him." Despite being more difficult to send his father to México than bury him in Los Angeles, "we thought it was best to take him over there. That is what he would have liked. That is the reason why we took him back." As Ramiro and his siblings have settled more permanently in Los Angeles, his sisters wanted to have their father close to them. "They wanted to be able to visit him and take him flowers," Ramiro explained. "But we thought it would be best to bury him over there. We wanted to give him that wish. We think that is what he would have liked, even after his death."

In the context of emigration, Ramiro discussed an element of posthumous family reunification or a kinship dimension intimately connected with notions of homeland that factor into the decision to repatriate a body. "We wanted the family to be united once again. My grandparents, my uncles, they are all buried in México. They are all in the same cemetery; their tombs are next to one another. The family has reunited after their deaths. They have been returned to their land," Ramiro explained. As Balkan reminds us, "The act of burial represents a performative practice of place-making par excellence" (2015a: 123).

On this point of connection to the land, Ramiro offered some insight when discussing his desire to be buried in México. Despite being a more permanent migrant in the United States and having two U.S.-born daughters, Ramiro expressed, "if I die here [the U.S.], I would like to be buried in México, in the place from which I departed. I want to return to the place I once left, my land. Even if I die here, I would like to be buried over there." Just like sustained migration has created a "culture of departure" in many of these regions, Mexican migrants seem to maintain a culture of return in their transnational imaginaries, which often materializes posthumously.

Repatriation to Lo de Salas, Jerez

My second oral life history was strikingly similar to Don Angel's. Don Lino Espitia was born in Lo de Salas, Jerez in 1925. He was raised, married, and fathered "nearly two dozen" children there, as his widow Josefina and daughter Martha shared with me. Don Lino came to the United States as a bracero "around 1958," his widow lucidly recalled, worked in Las Cruces, New México for a short period of time and returned to his family in México. It was not until his children grew and migrated to the United States in the 1970s and 1980s that Don Lino and his wife, Josefina, began visiting them periodically in California and Nevada. In 2004, Don Lino suffered a stroke that left him in a wheelchair, unable to care for himself and unable to speak. Shortly after, his U.S.-based children decided to care for him and their mother collectively, taking them into their homes on a rotational basis. Don Lino passed away in June 2007.

When asked why the family decided to repatriate Don Lino's body to Jerez, his daughter Martha replied, "When he died, we had already made the decision that he was going back to his land. He loved his land. He did not want to be here, he did not want to die here." When asked why she felt it was her father's desire to return, Martha stated, "He wanted to return because he was a *campesino* [peasant] who loved his land. He loved his fields, his animals. He enjoyed his land; he lived from his land." Like many rural Mexican migrants who want to escape the asphyxiating entrapment of the carceral metropolis, "Whenever he was in the U.S., he longed for his home, he longed for his land." After all, as Alicia Schmidt Camacho argues, historically, the receiving "state itself functioned as a carceral space for racialized migrants who were denied full membership to the sphere of rights" (2008: 91).

Among Martha's siblings in the United States, those who have secured legal permanent residence or U.S. citizenship (and thus can cross the border without worrying about re-entry), made the trip to Lo de Salas to bury their father. When asked about her father's funeral in México, Martha replied:

> Our family members and neighbors in the *rancho* were waiting for my father's body to arrive. You may think this sounds strange, but it almost seemed like they were awaiting a *fiesta*. The *rancho* seemed lively because it was full of people awaiting my father's arrival. It was sad when he arrived, of course, in the manner in which he arrived. But at the same time, all of those people were happy because he was coming home regardless.

Like Don Angel, Don Lino could not vocalize what he wished to be done with his body after his death. However, Martha was convinced that he wanted to return. Not long before his death, Martha played a home video of the annual *fiestas* from Lo de Salas for her father. "Tears were rolling down his face as he watched the video," Martha said. On another occasion at her sister's house, when they asked Don Lino if he wanted to go to bed, he managed to say "*pa' el Rancho.*" He wanted to go to rest in the *rancho* of his birth. Among the prized possessions and recollections of Don Lino his family cherishes are his *sombrero*, his *chirrión* (or whip used on mules or horses), and a proverb denoting the sense of purpose and belonging he saw in his land: "If I lost it over there, that is where I have to find it."

Conclusion

This chapter discussed the sustained and increasingly institutionalized transnational practice of sending the bodies of deceased Mexican migrants from the United States to their hometowns in México, from the perspectives of state actors and migrants and their families. Far from being an apolitical trans-state activity, posthumous repatriation has profound political implications for both México and the United States. In contrast to Waldinger's argument that the assimilatory pressures exerted by U.S. society and government eventually lead to migrant settlement, this chapter suggests that such political forces and constraints have not contained the Mexican diasporic imagination or the attendant transnational practice of repatriating the remains of deceased migrants to be inhumed in their communities of origin. At least for a considerable subset of migrants, who very well may have been settled in the United States for decades, cross-border loyalties live on and often materialize after death. When the institutions of migrant "incorporation" are perceived as discriminatory and punitive in the receiving context, it is no surprise that cross-border identities, loyalties, and orientations persist even among migrants who have become settled and politically engaged in the United States. As Alicia Schmidt Camacho reminds us, many Mexican migrants are "unwilling to relinquish the fantasy of reunion with the lost objects that haunted their residence in the United States: family and [transnational] citizenship" (2008: 301).

With regard to the Mexican state, posthumous repatriation simultaneously represents a crisis and an opportunity. On one hand, it constitutes a potential crisis because posthumous repatriation is a public reminder of the Mexican state's failure to provide a livelihood for its migrant citizens who now return deceased. Or, capitalizing on its recent "heroic migrant narrative" (Smith and Bakker 2008), posthumous repatriation can present an opportunity for the Mexican state to canonize its deceased repatriates like fallen soldiers into its "ghostly national imaginings" (Anderson 2006: 9). As Claudio Lomnitz argues, the political "deployment of death and the dead" and the "nationalization of an ironic intimacy with death is a singularly Mexican strategy" (Lomnitz 2005: 20, 21). In a clear display of necropolitics and an "official language of mourning" (Schmidt Camacho 2008: 308), the Mexican state exerts its sovereignty over its deceased emigrants by institutionalizing their postmortem repatriation.

Borrowing from Lisa Cacho's reflections on posthumous citizenship and necropower, I argue that the increasingly institutionalized practice of repatriating the bodies of deceased Mexican migrants from the United States to México speaks to the utter failure of the U.S. and Mexican governments to "incorporate" these migrants into the respective geo-bodies of their nation-states.[17] From the perspective of the Mexican government, posthumous repatriations can be a transnational "technology of necropower, another means by which the state retains and legitimates its sovereignty through controlling the dead" (Cacho 2012: 110). Conversely, when it comes to the U.S. government, "Because the dead can force us all to reckon with the violences that produced them, the ever-present haunting of these restless ghosts will always be the most salient" reminder of its failure to incorporate Mexican migrants as equal citizens into the body politic (Cacho 2012: 99).

For the scholars of "transnational life" who suggest that transnationalism may die with the first generation of migrants, this chapter suggests that the cross-border movement of the dead, or *transnational afterlife*, is an important corollary. Like other forms of cross-border activities, posthumous repatriation can perpetuate transnational ties among surviving members of the deceased repatriates in the United States and may in turn increase their interest in the public life of their communities of origin, possibly converting an act of socio-cultural transnationalism into a pathway to subsequent political transnation-alism. To put it in the words of Octavio Paz, perhaps Mexicans' "cult in death" is at once a "cult in life" (1997). Or, to borrow from Alicia Schmidt Camacho, in the migration "ritual of departure, the family enacts, in intimate form, the migrant's detachment from the state, a severing of citizenship that is also a death, a death that produces" (2008: 303).

5

Conclusion

TRANSNATIONAL AFTERLIFE

TO END THIS book I followed the lead of a *corrido*. "To sing this *corrido*, I will remove my *sombrero*" the ballad begins. The song is a transnational tribute to a migrant from my ancestral homeland named Arturo Almanza. "He was born in El Tanque de San Juan"—a small ranching village whose families have been bound up in México-U.S. migration for generations—"by the grace of God" the song prophetically states. Actually, Don Arturo was born in California—a U.S. citizen by birth, transnational denizen by choice. "When people ask me where I am from, I always tell them I am from Jerez," he said to me while sitting in the showroom of his successful business in Central California, grinning with pride as I shared that my family hails from the same region. As a young man working for Gallo Winery in California, alongside his late father, all of his co-workers assumed he was born in México and that he was undocumented. "You better fix your son's papers," his co-workers forewarned his father when immigration workplace raids and policing became routine. "They didn't know I was born in the U.S.," he said with a chuckle. The song bears testimony to Don Arturo's transnationality. Financially successful, he visits his family's native village three to four times a year. He funded the remodeling of the community's aging *lienzo charro* (rodeo ring), such a devout *charrería* aficionado he is. He often pays for *el castillo* during the village's annual patron saint *fiesta*—the firework display that resembles a castle and culminates with a burning crown shooting into the dark sky, reminiscent of the migrant who departs but vows to return like the "morning star"—a looming symbol in Don Arturo's life and in his *corrido*.

My favorite verse of the *corrido* comes in its *despedida* (the farewell or ending) because it ominously alludes to transnational temporality and an unfinished diasporic destiny. "With this I bid you farewell, but I have hope that I will fulfill my destiny. We'll see if time is on my side . . ." If there was one haunting lyric that I had to inquire about, this was it. Don Arturo explained that once his parents retired and returned to live in El Tanque de San Juan, after toiling for four decades in the United States, it was his wish to build them the home of their dreams. Don Arturo explained that his father never quite managed to build the home he always wanted. On a short visit they paid their children in California, Don Arturo decided to surprise his parents by having their home in México completely remodeled and expanded. It was the remittance home of their dreams. This was his gift to his parents after a life of hard work in California. Here, Don Arturo's father would live the last years of his life until he passed away in September 2014 and was buried in the region's cemetery in the nearby village of Los Haro, next to the graves of other family members. Don Arturo shared that he will next build the remittance tomb as his final homage to his father (see Lopez 2015).

"I once met the Tomato King," Don Arturo said later in the interview, referring to the late Andrés Bermúdez, who appeared in the previous chapter and who in many ways is the clearest protagonist of the thickening of transnational citizenship traced in this book. "He asked if I could provide the bulls for a *jaripeo* [rodeo] he was organizing shortly after his campaign." When Don Andrés went to pick up the livestock, he complained about the disrepair of the road that leads to Don Arturo's *rancho*. "You're the mayor now," Don Arturo said to his fellow California migrant, "fix it." Shortly thereafter, the migrant-turned-mayor had the road to El Tanque de San Juan paved and repaired. It was the road to the remittance house and the remittance tomb. It was the road where migrant journeys began and ended. It's the road paved with migrant mythologies of transnational citizenship and diasporic dreams of return.

Specters of Belonging ethnographically traced the thickening of transnational citizenship across the political life cycle of Mexican migrants, from the "political baptism," or naturalization in the United States, to repatriation to México after death. It wove together a wide array of sources—from migrant narratives and mythologies, to politics, poetics, and lyricism—to capture how Mexican migrants negotiate transnational citizenship across the span of the migrant political life cycle, from beginning, middle, to end. In doing so, the book illustrated how Mexican migrants *enunciate, enact*, and *embody* transnational citizenship in constant dialectical contestation with the state on either side of the U.S.-México border, what I called diasporic dialectics. In sum, the first substantive chapter examined how Mexican migrants *enunciate* transnational citizenship as they navigate the naturalization process in the United States and grapple with the contradictions of U.S. citizenship and its script of singular political loyalty. The middle chapter analyzed how Mexican migrants *enact* transnational citizenship within the clientelistic orbit of the Mexican state, focusing on a group of U.S.-based returned migrant politicians and transnational activists. Last, the final substantive chapter turned to how Mexican migrants *embody* transnational citizenship by tracing the cross-border practice of repatriating the bodies of deceased Mexican migrants from the United States to their communities of origin in rural México. At every step, the book critically reflected on my accompaniment of Mexican migrants as they navigated and negotiated transnationalism in life and death.

Understood as the "political baptism," naturalization is the moment in migrants' political lives where they most directly confront the expectation of singular citizenship and exclusive political loyalty demanded of them by the United States. The chapter "Enunciations of Transnational Citizenship" marked naturalization as the beginning of the migrant political life cycle insofar as this is the precise moment where migrants contest state scripts of singular loyalty and subjectivity and vocalize alternative cross-border visions of political membership and belonging. While the U.S. government turns a blind eye to dual nationality, Mexican migrants' very transnationality is continuously treated as a marker of foreignness, "disloyalty," and as grounds for exclusion. Drawing on a political ethnography of the naturalization process and the citizenship classroom, this chapter captured Mexican migrants' *mythologies of citizenship* as they collectively exposed the central contradictions of U.S. citizenship and constitutionalism and contested the "strictures of national belonging" (Schmidt Camacho 2008: 59). Rather than conceiving of naturalization as the "divorce from one nation-state and marriage to another nation-state" (Plascencia 2012: 161), this chapter exposed the citizenship process as one rife with institutional racism and discrimination in the eyes of Mexican migrants. Far from "graduating from alienage," naturalization does not *denaturalize* Mexican migrants' "ascribed alienness" in everyday social interactions or in political-institutional processes, including the citizenship-acquisition experience itself (148). As Plascencia argues, recently naturalized Mexican migrants "retain their perceived alienness after becoming citizens," which explains why they "[harbor] fidelities to their country of origin . . . even after taking the oath" (151). The bureaucratic arbitrariness and institutional discrimination that Mexican migrants perceive throughout the naturalization process infuse their mythologies of citizenship and inform their alternative enunciations of transnational political membership and belonging. To borrow from the poetics of Ramón López Velarde, the political ethnography of the citizenship process presented earlier in the book captured Mexican migrants' narratives of naturalization and "the subtle cries of their mythologies" of transnational citizenship.

Moving from these enunciations of bi-national membership in the United States, the book then turned to cross-border ethnography to capture the *enactments of transnational citizenship* of U.S.-based returned migrant politicians and activists within the clientelistic orbit of the Mexican state. Under conditions of political cartelization, whereby Mexican political parties are congealing into a realigned bloc, this chapter argued that Mexican migrants are a critical cross-border constituency that can enter into "socio-electoral" coalitions to challenge the hegemonic party system in México (Trejo 2014). Most of these returned migrant politicians emerged from the cross-border activist networks of hometown associations in the United States and thus are rooted in the transnational "public sphere," understood as "those [transnational] institutional spaces in society where individuals who are affected by collective decisions and societal norms have an opportunity to engage in public dialogue as a means to affect these" decisions (Rocco 2014: 29). However, just as migrants enacting transnational citizenship in an autocratic system must have a dual political strategy—whereby they play by the electoral rules of the game while at the same time contesting them (Trejo 2014)— these cross-border activists must also understand transnational civil society as a site for "regulation and control to maintain the status quo, and also a site for contesting the structure of privilege and domination that characterize it" (Rocco 2014: 101). Indeed, Mexican migrants' enactments of transnational citizenship can only come to fruition if they can resist the corruption, co-optation, coercion, and control of clientelistic party politics in México. While this chapter identified the political pitfalls and contradictions of transnational citizenship, it also showed how the diasporic dialectics of Mexican migrants—that is, their simultaneous contestation and claims making within the sending and home state—can further deepen democratic citizenship on both sides of the U.S.-México border.[1]

Chapter 4 closed the migrant political life cycle with a transnational ethnography of the cross-border practice of repatriating the bodies of deceased Mexican migrants from the United States to their communities of origin in rural México. These embodiments of transnational citizenship are also part of the diasporic dialectics of Mexican migrants—indicative of both their poetics of belonging and their agonistic politics of transnational membership. As Balkan reminds us, "Death in the diaspora also raises existential questions about the meaning of home . . . the act of burial serves as a means to assert belonging, attachment, and . . . loyalty to a particular group, nation, or place" (2015a: 121). On the Mexican side of these diasporic dialectics, posthumous repatriations are driven largely by migrants' ethno-territorial attachments to their communities of origin, as "corporeal assertions of belonging deploy the body as an anchor" (Balkan 2015a: 129). On the U.S. side, a return to México after death is indicative of the host country's failure to "integrate" these migrants as equals. "Experiences with racism, discrimination, or xenophobia generate a feeling of perpetual foreignness, which follows individuals to the grave. Repatriation here might be read as an act of defiance that signals a rejection of a political community that excludes" (Balkan 2015a: 131). By capturing migrants' mythologies of mortality and return, that chapter read the posthumous "poetics of corporality" (Fregoso 2009) of deceased repatriates like "necrographic maps" (Torres 2005: 159), to understand Mexican migrants' cultural politics of mourning and the making of a posthumous transnational tradition. If Mexicans' "cult in death" is also a "cult in life," as the poetics of Octavio Paz remind us (Paz 1997), then the concept of transnational life must necessarily be extended to account for its conceptual corollary: *transnational afterlife*. As Balkan concludes, "By studying the social practices that link the dead to the living, we are better positioned to see how the boundaries of political communities are meaningful in both life and death" (2015a: 132).

In a literary essay on the work of Mexican poet Ramón López Velarde— the celebrated bard born in the now heavily migrant-sending municipality of Jerez, Zacatecas—Octavio Paz describes the recurring theme of the hometown as "a magnetic field" to which the author returns "time and time again, without ever returning fully" (López Velarde 2009: 25). Like in the poetics of López Velarde, the "magnetic field" is an apt allegory for understanding the role of the homeland in contemporary Mexican migrants' transnational lives and identities. By tracing the thickening of transnational citizenship at different stages of the migrant political life cycle, *Specters of Belonging* added to our understanding of migrant cross-border affiliations, allegiances, and attachments. In doing so, this book challenged the linear logic of neo-assimilationists, who contend that the United States continues to "integrate" migrants as it did during previous eras of mass migration—successfully securing singular political loyalties from them (see Waldinger 2007a, 2007b, 2015)—by pointing to the institutional racism that impedes the process of migrant "incorporation". It also challenged the continuous circularity of the transnationalism perspective, which depicts migrants as "doubly ambivalent" about their sense of belonging to their country of settlement and of origin (Smith and Bakker 2008), construing them as being "neither here nor there" (see Zavella 2011). Following Schmidt Camacho, this study depicts Mexican migrants as "'people from here and there' . . . [defying] the unitary logic of citizenship and the state imperative to police its territory" (2008: 2). Indeed, this book showed that Mexican migrants are tenaciously transnational, defying the border in life and death. To conclude with the poetics of Paz, for many Mexican migrants, only death "can provide the sense of totality that is perpetually denied to us by [transnational] time" (López Velarde 2009: 48).

As I was writing the final lines for this book, I received word from Antonio that one of his employees at the *taquería*—a single father of three from his home state of Jalisco—had become deathly ill with an aggressive terminal cancer. I didn't get to know Chuy well—as his co-workers and *paisanos* at the *taquería* affectionately called him—but I fondly remembered him from the countless times that he dutifully emerged from the kitchen to serve me steaming bowls of *pozole*. I learned from Antonio that the forty-one-year-old Chuy was undocumented, arriving at a young age to the United States, fathering three U.S.-born children and raising them on his own, at times working double shifts to make ends meet. Antonio said Chuy was such a devoted single parent that he received recognitions from his children's local public schools. Shortly before he passed, Antonio and I visited Chuy at a hospice in Santa Cruz, finding him in a deep sleep, reduced to a frail cadaver of a man. I was hoping to speak to Chuy one last time but, choosing not to disturb his sleep, I stood quietly by his side, departing without shaking the hand that fed me on so many occasions. Once outside, I asked Antonio whether Chuy had expressed a desire to be repatriated to México posthumously. Nobly, "Chuy said he would like to have his body donated to cancer research in hopes of finding a cure for other patients stricken with the disease and, if possible, have his remains subsequently returned to Jalisco." In that, Chuy is like the many other migrant spirits that inhabit these pages—an undocumented Mexican migrant who came to the United States, worked tirelessly to raise a family, and even in death looked for ways to contribute to society, always seeking to return home at the end of the journey, even when both states shunned them along the way. Surrounded by his children, co-workers, *paisanos*, and loved ones, Chuy passed away on September 20, 2015. It is to the memory of Chuy and the millions of Mexican migrants who left their imprint and wander the transnational space between the United States and México that this book is dedicated. Chuy would have never been able to read this book even if it were translated into Spanish, for he was an unlettered, illiterate, Mexican migrant who toiled anonymously in the United States for years. Nevertheless, this is my way of paying homage to my *paisanos*—the deported and the departed—on either side of the border. To conclude in the words of Máximo Pérez Torres—a self-taught migrant peasant poet from Jerez, Zacatecas—in a poem reflecting on his mortality and transnational afterlife:

> *Once I am dead and buried in this soil,*
> *I will continue composing verses to the dead.*
> *Their specters will be my muse . . .*

Epilogue

PHANTOM PAISANOS

IN HIS SEMI-AUTOBIOGRAPHICAL *Orange County: A Personal History*, Gustavo Arellano describes a surrealist dream of return migration to his ancestral village of El Cargadero, deep in the heart of north-central México. "A couple of months before finishing this book," Arellano writes, "I experienced the most vivid dream: I won a contest in which the main prize was the ability to fly" (2008: 25). After crisscrossing disparate geographies, from South East Asia to Eastern Europe, Gustavo decided to descend on El Cargadero, arriving in the late afternoon, when "the sun bathes everything in a soft, radiant glow." Gustavo's dream depicts the village quite accurately, verging on the utopian before taking a surrealist turn: "El Cargadero sits on the slope of a mountain, so rays either enveloped houses or cast them in shadows." Hovering above, Gustavo tried to eavesdrop on conversations, "but all I heard was the laughs of contentment," he writes. Once he landed on terra firma, "Streetlights flickered on, lending a beautiful shine to the village," and people greeted him warmly.

But when he asked for directions to his grandfather's house, the dream suddenly took on a ghostly quality. "[M]eloncholy seeped in as I continued around El Cargadero," Gustavo recalls.

> The paved roads turned to dirt, and cars transformed into horses that neighed nervously. Houses grew cracks before my eyes. People vanished one by one . . . I walked for what felt like hours, but the sunset never turned to night. I trekked through valleys, next to rivers, up mountains, even to the large reservoir on the outskirts of El Cargadero, looking for my *abuelito*'s house, but no luck. (26, 27)

Gustavo encountered his father in his dream and asked anxiously, "Hey Dad—where's my grandfather's house?" "*Ya no está,*" Gustavo's father replied, shaking his head. "There is nothing left."

At that point, Gustavo awakened from his dystopian dream, unable to fall back asleep, too much weighing on his mind—"the sadness of existence, the reality of knowing that the sights, feelings, and happiness I'd just experienced were never going to return . . . A feeling of unpardonable guilt seeped in . . . " As his ancestral village surreally metamorphosed into a ghost town before his eyes, Gustavo concludes: "El Cargadero is a cipher, a memorial to the tragedy that is modern México and the indomitable wanderlust of the human soul" (27).

Gustavo's spectral dream is a reminder that the saga of Mexican migration can be retold as a ghost tale. Following the migrant political life cycle, if migration leaves in its wake ghost towns throughout rural México, migrant mythologies of return drive haunting homecomings. As Alicia Schmidt Camacho reminds us, "The border crossing implies a psychic wounding for migrants and invests their nostalgic desires for return with political significance" (2008: 299). It is with one such final story of posthumous return migration that I close.

As I visited the local archives in Jerez, Zacatecas, to update the death data on the *fieles difuntos,* the dearly departed who faithfully arrive year after year from the United States, I encountered what at first sight seemed like a double tragedy. A married couple of near centenarians from the outer reaches of the Jerez diaspora (Kansas) passed away only a few months apart from each other and each was subsequently repatriated, seemingly knowing that, in the end, there is no place like home. With only a few days left before my impending return to the United States, and having unsuccessfully exhausted any possible leads to identify the family of the deceased repatriates, I decided to search for and visit the tomb of the elderly migrants for myself, feeling a strange need to pay my respect to people I never met but who nevertheless felt like intimately familiar *paisano* phantoms. I visited the local *camposanto,* where my own ancestors were laid to rest, and found my way to the section of the cemetery with the most recent tombs. A couple of *panteoneros* worked on fresh graves, cooling down with tall cans of Tecate beer on this particularly sun-baked December morning. The lyrics of *El Viejo Roble*—a timeless song in which withering oak trees personify the mortality of aging elders in the hometown—chillingly flowed from the speakers of their small portable radio as they toiled on the crypts. Suddenly, as if guided by the haunting lyrics, I stumbled upon the tomb of the deceased couple, finding them just as I had imagined, reunited in a humble grave in the hard, dry earth. Together. At home. In peace. At last.

Notes

1. *Municipios* are administrative jurisdictions within states, that, as Rouse (1991) reminds us, "are difficult to gloss with any precision" for " 'Municipality' is misleading because of its urban associations, while . . . 'county' runs the risk of suggesting something too large and too powerful" (for a masterful example of subnational comparative analysis of municipal and submunicipal political dynamics involving state violence and rural intra-regional migration in southern México see Trejo 2012). With the above caveat in mind, I use the terms municipal/submunicipal and the Spanish-language *municipio* interchangeably throughout. Much of Gómez's cross-border campaign took place in migrant-sending villages at the submunicipal level, or what Jonathan Fox calls the "invisible fourth level" of the Mexican state (2007). For an analysis of migrants' cross-border struggles to democratize and hold municipal and submunicipal authorities accountable in rural México see Bada (2014).

2. The *New York Times* profiled the *municipio* of Genaro Codina years after my visit, noting the region's depopulation as a result of sustained out migration to the United States (Cave 2013). Instantly, journalist Gustavo Arellano issued a scathing indictment of the mainstream media's ad hoc coverage of these matters. For fine journalistic accounts of Mexican migration, see Arellano's semi-autobiographical *Orange County: A Personal History* (2008) and the earlier freelance investigative reporting by Sam Quinones (2001; 2008). Quinones' third book (2015) is another gripping addition to the journalistic accounts of Mexican migration, providing a sobering tale of the role of migrant village and cross-border kin networks in the distribution of *chiva* (heroin) in the United States.

3. A similar (albeit racially different) politics of recognition of the researcher occurred during Smith and Bakker's ethnography of transnational citizenship (2008).

4. For critical accounts of the "Drug War" in the English language, see Paley (2014) and Aviña (2016).

5. I thank Norma Klahn for her prescient recommendation of López Velarde's *El Retorno Maléfico*. For more on the "spectral quality" of rural México's political history see Aviña (2014).

6. The reference is to López Velarde's *Suave Patria*, which won him the posthumous appropriation by the Mexican state as the country's "national poet."

7. In early August 2011, Lupe Gómez was featured on the front cover of the *Orange County Weekly*, which ran a full-length article on the transnational triangulation of his activism, calling him a "triple player" (see Gerber 2011). For academic accounts on Gómez and other similarly situated cross-border migrant leaders see Smith and Bakker (2008); Iskander (2010); Délano (2011); and Moctezuma (2011).

8. For an analysis of gender dynamics within this Mexican home-state federation see García-Acevedo (2003). See also Viramontes (2008).

9. In developing this concept I triangulate between Jonathan Fox's work on the "thickening" of civil society in rural México (2007), his conceptual mapping of México's migrant civil society (2006; 2009), and his theorization on the conceptual boundaries of transnational citizenship (2005). While the conceptual framing of thickening invokes its binary concept of "thinning"—and while most empirical, survey-based analyses of transnationalism show that cross-border ties decline by the second generation (see, for example, Waldinger 2015)—these studies rely on narrow metrics of transnational "behavior" (i.e., "how often do you send money home" or "how often do you call home" or "dominant language" acquisition) that cannot fully capture or unearth the dimensions of transnationalism revealed in this study. Moreover, even Waldinger (2015), the preeminent skeptic of transnationalism, sees the migration process as dialectical. Albeit, in his framing, the dialectic is between the categories of "emigrant" and "immigrant," with the latter ultimately eclipsing the former as migrants undergo a process of "territorial capture" (2015: 44)—a concept that I contest in my formulation of diasporic dialectics and the thickening of transnational citizenship across the arch of the migrant political life cycle.

10. For critical analyses of deaths at the border and the neoliberal disposability of migrant labor and life see Inda (2007); De Genova (2009); Márquez (2012); and De León (2015).

11. For a discussion of a "global security state" with planetary police powers see De Genova (2010b). For an analysis of the gendered effects of the "national security state" see Sampaio (2015).

12. For a more contemporaneous Marxist analysis that situates the migrant rights movement in the United States within the ongoing global struggle between transnational capital and transnational labor see Robinson (2006). In the context of the "homeland security state," De Genova describes the migrant rights mobilizations of the mid-2000s as the "revolt of the denizens" (2007; see Zepeda-Millán for the definitive account of this migrant "insurgency" and its transnational inflections 2014; 2017). For further anthropological research on the Aguililla-Redwood City transnational migrant network, with a focus on questions of citizenship, see Castañeda (2006).

13. *Corridos* are nonfiction ballads in the Mexican oral tradition. "[T]he *corrido*" wrote Américo Paredes, "tells a story simply and swiftly" (1958: xi).

14. For an empirical analysis on whether migrants "remit democracy" see Pérez-Armendáriz and Crow (2010).

15. Here, I take a structural cue from Adam Morton's Gramscian historical sociology of postrevolutionary Mexican state formation (2011: 5).

16. For more on Los Angeles' *charro* lore see Quinones (2004) and Barraclough (2012). For a discussion of *charrería* as a form of nation-building in the context of diaspora see Nájera-Ramírez (2002). After a long and legendary stint, Rancho El Farallón closed when its owner, renowned Mexican migrant impresario Emilio Franco, was murdered in his home in what was reportedly an attempted armed burglary gone wrong but for some bore all the signs of a gangland murder in Mexican Los Angeles (Quinones 2011).

17. For a discussion of the ethics and polemics of "intimate ethnography" in political science research see Campbell (2015). As Rocco (2014) reminds us, the task of ethnography is to "listen and not just hear what the people we study say." Ethnographic narratives are not merely "data that we are collecting; the individuals who share their stories with us are collaborators and not subjects, and the best ethnographies help us to feel and understand the struggles, fears, joys, and pain of the people who trust us enough to share a part of who they are."

18. I thank Don Herminio Rodríguez, member of PMZ, for initially providing me with this metaphor to explain Mexican migrant political transnationalism in the drafting of this document.

19. For an exhaustive history of the transnational trials of the Flores Magón brothers and the death and posthumous return of Ricardo Flores Magón to México see Lomnitz (2016). Related to the metaphor deployed above, Lomnitz argues that the context of diaspora provided revolutionary exiles with a "protective field where ideological coherence could be reconstituted and projected once again onto the national landscape" (2016: 39; all translations mine).

20. While this study focuses on a unique subset of migrants who have attained a measure of political and economic stability in the United States (e.g., legal permanent residents/naturalized citizens), many of my informants were once undocumented and experiences of racism continued to haunt their civic lives across the stages of the migrant political life cycle.

21. Migrant transnational activists "re-crossing" the border to engage politically in the United States is what Smith and Bakker refer to as the "second face of transnational citizenship" (2008).

22. For an empirical analysis of the staying effect of political transnationalism across the "civic lives" of Mexican migrants in the United States see Wals (2010).

23. For a similar "three vignettes" approach to set up the discussion and analysis of Mexican migration see Bakker (2015).

24. For a discussion of the dialectics of migration politics and migrant social movements in the United States see Gonzales (2016). Raul Delgado Wise and Humberto

Márquez Covarrubias remind us that there is a dialectical tension between transnationalism "from above"—which responds to the interests of U.S. capital—and transnationalism "from below," embodied in the "practices of migrants and their organizations" (2006: 46).

25. In the context of transnational politics, a historical example of counter-revolutionary diasporic dialectics can be found in the U.S.-funded efforts of right-wing Cuban exiles to oust the revolutionary Castro regime (see García Bedolla 2009).

26. For a "political sociology of emigration" from the Los Altos de Jalisco region see FitzGerald (2010).

27. For a history of Mexican food in the United States, interlaced with stories of migration, see Arellano (2012).

28. For a theorization of the "exclusionary inclusion" of U.S. citizenship in relation to Latino migrants in the United States see Rocco (2014).

29. In the early twentieth century, Lomnitz argues that when Mexican revolutionaries were exiled in the United States, they were reduced to anonymous shadows: "phantoms in the Mexican barrio" (2016: 47).

30. For historical and ethnographic studies of Mexican migrants' experiences with naturalization see, respectively, Menchaca (2011) and Plascencia (2012). See also my earlier writings on Mexican migrants' narratives of naturalization (Félix 2008; 2013).

31. For an analysis of the political impact of Spanish-language ballots on Latino voters see Hopkins (2011).

32. As Jonathan Fox reminds us, home-state migrant federations can become appendages of, or subordinate to, their respective state governments in México (2006: 45).

33. For more on the Institute of Mexicans Abroad see González Gutiérrez (2009) and Délano (2011).

34. For a report on the migrant rights mobilizations in San José from the perspective of an "embedded journalist" see Vital (2010).

35. For an analysis of gender quotas in México's mixed-member electoral system see Hinojosa (2008).

36. For a discussion of Andrés Bermúdez, the *Zacatecano* migrant who was the political protagonist and symbol behind these state-level reforms, see Smith and Bakker (2005; 2008); Quinones (2008); and Moctezuma (2011).

37. For a critique of transnational citizenship as complicit in migrants' home government neoliberal projects see Rodriguez (2013).

38. On Mexican migrant gardeners in Los Angeles see Ramírez and Hondagneu-Sotelo (2009).

39. For more on this migrant "nostalgia market" see Lestage (2008). On the Mexican state's institutionalization of posthumous repatriations see Félix (2011). For an analysis of these repatriations among indigenous Mexican migrants see (García Ortega and Celestino Solis 2015).

40. For more on indigenous migrant "transnational moral communities" see Steigenga and Williams (2009).

41. On México's "ironic intimacy" with death see Lomnitz (2005).

42. Without eliding intra-ethnic differences or the "class transformation" of rural-to-urban migrations (Rouse 1992), I extend Fox's argument about the subalternity of indigenous Mexican migrants to their mestizo (nonindigenous) co-nationals. As Fox states regarding indigenous Mexican migrants, "Many . . . work in ethnically segmented seasonal agricultural wage labor, both in México and the US—bringing class and culturally based oppression together in forms that some would consider classically subaltern" (2006). Citing Gramsci, Schmidt Camacho reminds us that "subaltern history is necessarily 'fragmentary and episodic'" (quoted in Schmidt Camacho 2008: 7). "Fragmentary and episodic" is precisely the approach I take in tracing transnationalism across the different stages of the migrant political life cycle, which I treat as diachronic and dialectical. Ethnography is an ideal method for this, as "migrant testimonials belong to a submerged history of migrant struggle, one that has yet to dispel the primacy of the nation over other forms of political community" (Schmidt Camacho 2008: 16).

43. Tomlinson and Lipsitz (2013) provide two metaphors to understand accompaniment that are appropriate here: "(1) accompaniment as participating with and augmenting a community of travelers on a road; (2) accompaniment as participating with others to create music" (2013: 9). The point, of course, is to underscore the "inescapably and quintessentially *social* nature of scholarship and citizenship" (10).

CHAPTER 2

1. For a discussion of the rise of the "national security state" and its surveillance powers see Sampaio (2015).

2. On the gendered and racial struggles of migrant farmworkers in one of the regions where I conducted citizenship education work see Blackwell (2010).

3. In a slightly different theoretical formulation, the political scientist Reuel Rogers refers to this as migrants' ever-present "exit" option (2006). To borrow from anthropologist Pat Zavella, discrimination in the United States explains why Mexican migrants maintain their transnational cultural memory and their cross-border "peripheral vision" (2011).

4. In a broader sense, Waldinger refers to migrants having to learn and abide by the receiving society's "national code" (2015: 46).

5. For a reflection on the meaning and contradictions of becoming a U.S. citizen under Trump see Namwali Serpell's account of naturalization (2017).

6. The repatriations of the 1930s included the U.S.-born children of Mexican migrants, who were rendered the political orphans of the diaspora. Some of these children, who were essentially orphaned by the state, would later attempt re-entry into the United States as child laborers (Rosas 2014).

7. This historical section is not intended to be a comprehensive review of naturalization law but rather a reminder of how citizenship and immigration reforms have created negative political incentives for racialized migrants in the United States, from the Naturalization Act of 1790—which defined "American citizenship in relation to the property of whiteness" (Sampaio 2015)—to the "birther" movement of today, which seeks to strip citizenship from the U.S.-born children of undocumented women (Plascencia 2012; see also Chavez 2017). Sampaio (2015) provides an exhaustive legal analysis of historical citizenship and immigration acts that have raised "interlocking questions about membership, belonging, status, restriction, and removal," including, but not limited to, the Naturalization Act of 1790; Alien and Sedition Act of 1798; Chinese Exclusion Act of 1882; Quota Act of 1921; National Origins Act of 1924; Alien Registration Act of 1940; McCarren-Walter Act of 1952, etc. For a useful timeline of immigration policy—including the Naturalization Act of 1790; Naturalization Act of 1795; Naturalization Act of 1802; and the Naturalization Act of 1906—see the appendix in Friedmann Marquardt et al. (2011). Schmidt Camacho captures the "exclusionary inclusion" of U.S. citizenship vis-à-vis Mexican migrants, stating: "Liberal reforms had a paradoxical effect in the domain of immigration law: although the Immigration and National Services Act (Hart-Cellar) of 1965 removed racial and national quotas in favor of numerical limits, it placed such a low cap on the number of Mexican migrants who could enter . . . that it guaranteed the continued growth of undocumented migration" (2008: 165). However, the "law did offer Mexicans in the United States incentives to naturalize . . . offering new provisions for family reunification" (Schmidt Camacho 2008: 165). This citizenship contradiction would continue with the Immigration Reform and Control Act (IRCA) of 1986. As Schmidt Camacho states: "Following its passage, Mexicans naturalized and registered as voters . . . But the legislation also codified security provisions and penalties that ultimately corroded the capacity of new migrants and Latina/o citizens to secure full civil rights" (2008: 201). Zepeda-Millán captures the double-edged nature of IRCA well. On the one hand, IRCA "sought to deter unauthorized immigrants from coming to the United States by increasing border enforcement and . . . making it illegal for employers to hire undocumented immigrants" (2017: 27). On the other hand, IRCA "legalized three million recent migrants" and "mandated state resources for new and existing immigrant-serving organizations" (2017: 34).

8. In the context of migrant naturalization, contiguity of the home country is often correlated with low citizenship rates. For example, Barreto, Ramírez, and Woods state that "the median number of years of residence between the date of legal permanent residence and date of naturalization for immigrants from North America tends to be about 11 years, but only seven years for European immigrants" (2005: 795). In their case study on Dominican migrants' disinclination to naturalize, Hyde et al. (2013) mention proximity to the home country as one known factor in low naturalization rates but also point to "the salience of unfriendly US procedures in keeping

US naturalization rates comparatively low" (2013: 321). However, as this chapter argues, an antimigrant political context often mobilizes Latino legal permanent residents to naturalize. As Zepeda-Millán states, antimigrant legislation creates "an opportunity for immigrant rights activists to organize a politically complacent segment of their constituency—legal permanent residents" (2017: 194).

9. Relatedly, Ramírez identifies a "reactive mobilization" in response to antimigrant political campaigns (2013). Building on Ramírez's concepts of "reactive" and "proactive" mobilization, where the former is an immediate response to an anti-immigrant policy shock and the latter is the long-term "civic infrastructure" necessary to sustain migrant mobilization, I argue that reactive naturalization is proactive in the sense that migrants who seek citizenship in antimigrant times will be more likely to remain politically engaged throughout their "civic lives." This political engagement in the United States is not inconsistent but rather synergistic with transnational participation in the home country. In an earlier collaborative study, we found that among naturalized Latinos, experiencing discrimination in the United States was positively correlated with transnational engagement across several measures (see Ramírez and Félix 2011). Flipping the causal arrow in the other direction, in an empirical analysis of Dominican transnationalism and U.S. civic engagement, Pantoja finds that "belonging to an association concerned with events in the Dominican Republic and participation in the politics of the Dominican Republic exert a powerful positive influence on US political participation" (2005: 137).

10. Plascencia describes naturalization as migrants "graduating from alienage" (2012: 161).

11. While some observers might argue that the U.S. federal government has invested considerable resources into naturalization assistance, these efforts do little to change the "disconnected institutional configuration" that has long characterized the U.S. approach to citizenship promotion (Bloemraad 2006) or the unchecked discretionary powers immigration officials wield in the process (Plascencia 2012). Even a cursory review of the USCIS webpage reveals a rather sanitized version of the naturalization process, compared to the stories seared in Mexican migrants' mythologies of the process. As Hyde et al. (2013) suggest, "a concerted public policy to encourage naturalization would, at a minimum, have to lower costs; make processes more user-friendly . . . and possibly remove vestiges, such as the oath, of former attitudes, which equated naturalization with renunciation of other national affiliations" (334).

12. Patricia Zavella discusses the emergence of a nativist and antimigrant political context (2011, chap. 1).

13. For a discussion of "electorally armed" naturalized migrants as "political brokers" for "people without papers" see Zepeda-Millán (2017).

14. The names of all participants in this chapter were changed for purposes of anonymity.

15. In this regard José Alfredo is like the migrants in Rouse's ethnographic study decades earlier, who held onto a desire and plans to return to small-scale agriculture in their rural hometown. In the case of Michoacán migrants in the Bay Area, Rouse states: "Some Aguilillans have settled in Redwood City for long periods but few abandon the *municipio* forever" (1991). To return to the point about nationalist restrictions on land ownership in México, in the case of José Alfredo, the irony is that parts of his home state (Guanajuato) have been turned into havens for U.S. Anglo tourists and retirees.

16. For further discussion of mixed-status families see Zavella (2011, chap. 4).

17. AB 60, the California legislation that allowed undocumented migrants to obtain a driver license in the state, was implemented in January 2015.

18. This is what transnational feminists refer to as migrant women's double or triple shift (see Blackwell 2010).

19. For a discussion of immigration officers' discretionary powers see Plascencia (2012). Both Plascencia's and my initial research was conducted prior to the implementation of the new naturalization test, which would ostensibly make its administration less arbitrary. However, my ongoing role as citizenship class facilitator reveals that immigration officials still exercise a great amount of discretionary power in determining who passes and who does not. While there has been little research on the matter, Ramírez does note a steady increase in naturalization rejection rates on the part of USCIS leading up to the redesigned test (Ramírez 2013).

20. The first time I served as a naturalization test interpreter was for another senior migrant from Michoacán—one of my brother's citizenship class students in Los Angeles—in what was a surprisingly smooth and successful interview, years earlier.

21. Hyde et al. found similar statements in their ethnography of Dominican migrants and naturalization. One young woman in their study stated: "What does it mean to be American? I don't know . . . when you live in the United States, you are constantly taught that you are not from this country, but you are from the country were you[r] parents were born . . . I will always say that I am Dominican, maybe I will change and say Dominican American, but always Dominican" (2013: 328).

22. For a critical review of the "civic bigamy" argument see Fox and Bada (2011).

23. As Rogers (2006) reminds us, the racialization experience of Anglophone Afro-Caribbean migrants in the United States lies somewhere between the Black and Latino experience, which he captures in the phrase: "ethnicity, exception or exit."

CHAPTER 3

1. Personal communication with author (May 2009).

2. Letter furnished to author by member of the Political Action Front (May 2009).

3. As the following section will argue, the political ideologies of México's parties have become increasingly colluded. Nominally, México's political parties can be roughly categorized as follows. The three major parties are the right-wing, socially

conservative PAN (National Action Party); the left-leaning PRD (Party of the Democratic Revolution); and the once-dominant centrist PRI (Revolutionary Institutional Party). México's smaller parties include the leftist Labor Party (PT) and the social-democratic Movimiento Ciudadano (formerly Convergencia). In the lead up to México's 2018 presidential election, Movimiento Ciudadano allied with the right-wing PAN, and PT aligned itself with the new force on the left: Morena.

4. Independent candidates are now allowed to contend in presidential elections. As of this writing, the only independent presidential hopeful in the 2018 election to make a serious effort to take U.S.-based migrants into account is María de Jesús Patricio Martínez (Marichuy), an indigenous woman backed by the Zapatista movement EZLN.

5. In a similar vein, Robert C. Smith reminds us that diasporic institutionalization in Mexican political life is one of several forms of "inclusion and control" (2008).

6. For an analysis of PRI decline in Mexican municipal elections see Hiskey and Canache (2005).

7. Historical exceptions include cross-border political campaigns in support of the Partido Liberal Mexicano (PLM) during the revolutionary period.

8. For a discussion of gender quotas in Mexican electoral and party politics see Hinojosa (2008).

9. For a discussion of how the Mexican government has construed migrants as potential micro-investors see Smith and Bakker (2008) and Fox and Bada (2008).

10. For more on this migrant-backed agro-developmental project see Moctezuma (2003).

11. The Dominican migrant experience is another case of cross-border political participation and diasporic dialectics. While Dominican parties like the PRD, PLD, and PRSC established branches in Dominican communities in the Northeast United States, Dominican migrants were "making significant inroads into the school boards and political advisory boards in New York City and Massachusetts" (Pantoja 2005: 128). "All of these political gains occurred" in the United States, Pantoja concludes, "while intense transnational ties were being forged and formalized" (2005: 128).

12. The reference is to Ramón López Velarde's poem *Viaje al Terruño*.

13. For a discussion of efforts to develop institutions for migrant affairs at the national level see González Gutiérrez (2009).

14. For a history of youth activism in México City during the "long" 1960s see Pensado (2013).

15. For a discussion of the iron law of *encierro, destierro o entierro* (jail, exile, or death) during the heyday of PRI hegemony see Bezdek (1995).

16. An eleven-point "PRD Migrant Candidate Platform" was provided to the author by Arango on May 25, 2009.

17. The Mexican government began issuing voter identification cards in select consulates in the United States in the lead up to the 2016 election cycle.

18. Here, Levitt's distinction between organizations that are "horizontally transnational" and "vertically transnational" is instructive. Levitt identifies organizations as "horizontally transnational" when "there are ties between comparable, local-level chapters, such as . . . local-level political groups, in the sending and receiving countries." Organizations are "vertically transnational" when "these horizontal ties form part of a hierarchically integrated organizational system—that is when the ties that horizontally connect local, municipal, and national levels of a political party are also part of a vertically coordinated transnational ladder" (2001: 133). Of course, in a political system as notoriously corrupt and clientelistic as México's, this raises the ever-present danger of domestication in the context of diasporic engagement.

19. For an analysis of the cross-border and multiethnic "labor transnationalism" of Filipino migrants that de-centers citizenship see Rodriguez (2013).

20. As mentioned in the previous chapter, AB 60, the California legislation that allows undocumented migrants to obtain a driver license, was finally implemented beginning January 2015.

21. Gómez's alternate was a woman from the municipality of Jerez.

22. México has a mixed proportional representation and single-member-district electoral system. On México's mixed-member electoral system and the political representation of women see Hinojosa (2008).

23. One strategy of vote buying known as *voto carrusel* involves party operatives delivering premarked ballots to voters prior to entering the polling place. Upon exiting, the voter must return an unmarked ballot to the party operative, ensuring that the vote cast was the premarked ballot. Members of Gómez's campaign staff reported incidents of electoral fraud in multiple municipalities throughout the campaign. In Valparaíso, for example, there were reports of truckloads of cement and other goods destined for buying votes for the PRD. Reportedly, when Gómez's campaign staff filed a report with the municipal police, they were complicit, arguing that by order of the mayor's office they were to suspend any investigation into the matter. In Villanueva, opposition party operatives targeted registered PAN voters, offering cash in exchange for their voter ID cards, which were to be returned after election day (author's field notes).

24. For more on this "dual electoral strategy" pursued by opposition or "movement" parties in electoral autocracies see Trejo (2014).

CHAPTER 4

1. Smith and Bakker define transnational ethnography as "an ethnography of *places* and their *interconnections* rather than a place-focused ethnography of single locales" (2005: 131). As part of a broader project that involves interviews with the families of deceased repatriates on both sides of the border, this study constitutes a transnational ethnography of migrant mourning.

2. I take the term "myth of return" from a chapter by Michael Jones-Correa (1998).

3. On the difference between public and private transnational practices see Itzigsohn and Saucedo (2002).

4. See Omar Valerio-Jiménez (2002) for a discussion of how these local attachments and identities were historically constituted contra the central Mexican government. Padilla (2008) shows us how regional mythologies are central to the localized identities and resistance of peasant communities in rural México.

5. On the enduring legacy of Chalino Sánchez in the Mexican diaspora long after his murder see Arellano (2017).

6. However, in their collaborative ethnography, De Genova and Ramos-Zayas find that Mexican migrant women in Chicago who were undocumented were more likely to endure abusive relationships than U.S. citizen Puerto Rican women who had greater access to legal resources and support (2003).

7. The information for this section is from the author's interview at the Mexican consulate in Los Angeles (March 2007).

8. Information for this section is from author's interview at the Zacatecas international airport (June 2008).

9. Anzaldúa (1987) is more visceral when it comes to the gender politics of this mythology when she states, "There's an ancient Indian tradition of burning the umbilical cord of an infant girl under the house so she will never stray from it and her domestic role."

10. Now Secretariat of the Zacatecan Migrant, headed initially by none other than Rigoberto Castañeda.

11. This section header is taken from a chapter by Alexandra Délano (see Délano 2006).

12. On the personal and political trajectory of Andrés Bermúdez see Quinones (2008); Smith and Bakker (2005; 2008); and Moctezuma (2011).

13. Author interview with Mayor Serafín Bermúdez, Jerez, Zacatecas, May 2007.

14. This is not to suggest that migrant networks are internally consistent. For a discussion of strained internal dynamics and problems of collective action within "transnational communities" in the Mexican context and beyond see Nichols (2006); Bakker (2007); Menjívar (2000); Guarnizo and Diaz (1999).

15. For an account of the migration history between El Cargadero and California see Gustavo Arellano's semi-autobiographical *Orange County: A Personal History* (2008).

16. All names in this section are pseudonyms. Don Angel was repatriated to El Tesorero but inhumed in *rancho* Los Haro, where the region's cemetery is located.

17. See Cacho (2012).

CHAPTER 5

1. For an empirical analysis of when migrant efforts to hold the Mexican local state accountable succeed and fail see Burgess (2016).

References

Acuña, Rodolfo. 2008. *Corridors of Migration: The Odyssey of Mexican Laborers, 1600-1933*. Tucson: University of Arizona Press.

Alvarez, Robert. 1987. "A Profile of the Citizenship Process among Hispanics in the United States." *International Migration Review* 21 (2): 327–347.

Anderson, Benedict. 1998. *The Spectre of Comparisons: Nationalism, Southeast Asia and the World*. London: Verso.

———. 2006. *Imagined Communities: Reflections on the Origin and Spread of Nationalism*. Rev. ed. London: Verso.

Anderson, Leslie E. 2009. "The Problem of Single Party Predominance in an Unconsolidated Democracy: The Example of Argentina." *Perspectives on Politics* 7 (4): 767–784.

Andreas, Peter. 2009. *Border Games: Policing the U.S.-Mexico Divide*. Ithaca, NY: Cornell University Press.

Anzaldúa, Gloria. 1987. *Borderlands/La Frontera: The New Mestiza*. San Francisco: Aunt Lute Books.

Arellano, Gustavo. 2008. *Orange County: A Personal History*. New York: Scribner.

———. 2012. *Taco USA: How Mexican Food Conquered America*. New York: Scribner.

———. 2017. "Twenty-Five Years After His Murder, Chalino Sánchez Remains As Influential As Ever." *OC Weekly*, June 1.

Arredondo, Gabriela. 2008. *Mexican Chicago: Race, Identity, and Nation, 1916-39*. Urbana: University of Illinois Press.

Aviña, Alexander. 2014. *Specters of Revolution: Peasant Guerrillas in the Cold War Mexican Countryside*. New York: Oxford University Press.

———. 2016. "Mexico's Long Dirty War: The Origins of Mexico's Drug Wars Can be Found in the Mexican State's Decades-long Attack on Popular Movements Advocating for Social and Economic Justice." *NACLA* 48 (2): 144–149.

Ayón, David. 2012. "The Legal Side of Mexican Immigration." Washington, DC: Woodrow Wilson International Center for Scholars.

Bada, Xóchitl. 2014. *Mexican Hometown Associations in Chicagoacán: From Local to Transnational Civic Engagement*. New Brunswick, NJ: Rutgers University Press.

Bakker, Matt. 2007. "El Discurso de las Remesas Como Impulsoras del Desarrollo y la Agencia Colectiva del Migrante Colectivo." *Migración y Desarrollo* 9 (2): 45–72.

———. 2015. *Migrating into Financial Markets: How Remittances Became a Development Tool*. Berkeley: University of California Press.

Bakker, Matt, and Michael Peter Smith. 2003. "*El Rey del Tomate*: Migrant Political Transnationalism and Democratization in Mexico." *Migraciones Internacionales* 4: 59–83.

Balkan, Osman. 2015a. "Burial and Belonging." *Studies in Ethnicity and Nationalism* 15 (1): 120–134.

———. 2015b. "Until Death Do Us Depart: The Necropolitical Work of Turkish Funeral Funds in Germany." In *Muslims in the UK and Europe*, ed. Yasir Suleiman, 19–28. Cambdrige: Cambridge University Press.

———. 2016. "Between Civil Society and the State: Bureaucratic Competence and Cultural Mediation among Muslim Undertakers in Berlin." *Jounral of Intercultural Studies* 37 (2): 147–161.

Barraclough, Laura R. 2012. "Contested Cowboys: Ethnic Mexican Charros and the Struggle for Suburban Public Space in 1970s Los Angeles." *Aztlán* 37 (2): 95–124.

Barreto, Matt A. 2007. "¡Sí Se Puede! Latino Candidates and the Mobilization of Latino Voters." *American Political Science Review* 101 (3): 425–443.

Barreto, Matt A., Ricardo Ramírez, and Nathan D. Woods. 2005. "Are Naturalized Voters Driving the California Electorate? Measuring the Effect of IRCA Citizens on Latino Voting." *Social Science Quarterly* 86 (4): 792–811.

Bezdek, Robert. 1995. "Democratic Changes in an Authoritarian System: Navismo and Opposition Development in San Luis Postosí." In *Opposition Government in Mexico*, ed. Victoria Elizabeth Rodríguez and Peter M. Ward, 33–50. Albuquerque: University of New Mexico Press.

Blackwell, Maylei. 2010. "Líderes Campesinas: Nepantla Strategies and Grassroots Organizing at the Intersection of Gender and Globalization." *Aztlán* 35 (1): 13–48.

Bloemraad, Irene. 2006. *Becoming a Citizen: Incorporating Immigrants and Refugees in the United States and Canada*. Berkeley: University of California Press.

Burgess, Katrina. 2016. "Organized Migrants and Accountability from Afar." *Latin American Research Review* 51 (2): 150–173.

Cabrera, Luis. 2010. *The Practice of Global Citizenship*. Cambridge: Cambridge University Press.

Cacho, Lisa. 2012. *Social Death: Racialized Rightlessness and the Criminalization of the Unprotected*. New York: New York University Press.

Cain, Bruce, and Brendan Doherty. 2006. "The Impact of Dual Nationality on Political Participation." In *Transforming Politics, Transforming America: The Political and Civic Incorporation of Immigrants in the United States*, ed. Taeku Lee, S. Karthick Ramakrishnan and Ricardo Ramírez, 89–105. Charlottesville: University of Virginia Press.

Calderón, Felipe. 2006. *El Hijo Desobediente: Notas en Campaña*. Mexico: Editora Aguilar.

Campbell, Andrea Louise. 2015. "Family Story as Political Science: Reflections on Writing *Trapped in America's Safety Net*." *Perspectives on Politics* 13 (4): 1043–1052.

Carbado, Devon. 2005. "Racial Naturalization." *American Quarterly* 57 (3): 633–658.

Castañeda, Alejandra. 2006. *The Politics of Citizenship of Mexican Migrants*. El Paso, Texas: LFB Scholarly.

Cave, Damien. 2013. "In Mexican Villages, Few Are Left to Dream of U.S." *New York Times*, April 2, A1.

Chavez, Leo. 2017. *Anchor Babies and the Challenge of Birthright Citizenship*. Stanford: Stanford University Press.

Ciccariello-Maher, George. 2017. *Decolonizing Dialectics*. Durham, NC: Duke University Press.

Citrin, Jack, Amy Lerman, Michael Murakami, and Kathryn Pearson. 2007. "Testing Huntington: Is Hispanic Immigration a Threat to American Identity?" *Perspectives on Politics* 5 (2): 31–48.

Cohen, Jeffrey. 2004. *The Culture of Migration in Southern Mexico*. Austin: University of Texas Press.

Daulatzai, Sohail. 2012. *Black Star, Crescent Moon: The Muslim International and Black Freedom Beyond America*. Minneapolis: University of Minnesota Press.

Dear, Michael. 2013. *Why Walls Won't Work: Repairing the US-Mexico Divide*. New York: Oxford University Press.

De Genova, Nicholas. 2002. "Migrant 'Illegality' and Deportability in Everyday Life." *Annual Review of Anthropology* 31: 419–447.

———. 2004. "The Legal Production of Mexican/Migrant 'Illegality.'" *Latino Studies* 2 (2): 160–185.

———. 2005. *Working the Boundaries: Race, Space, and "Illegality" in Mexican Chicago*. Durham, NC: Duke University Press.

———. 2007. "The Production of Culprits: From Deportability to Detainability in the Aftermath of 'Homeland Security.'" *Citizenship Studies* 11 (5): 421–448.

———. 2008. "'American' Abjection: 'Chicanos,' Gangs, and Mexican/Migrant Transnationality in Chicago." *Aztlán* 33 (2): 141–174.

———. 2009. "Sovereign Power and the 'Bare Life' of Elvira Arellano." *Feminist Media Studies* 9 (2): 245–250.

———. 2010a. "The Queer Politics of Migration: Reflections on 'Illegality' and Incorrigibility." *Studies in Social Justice* 4 (2): 101–126.

———. 2010b. "Antiterrorism, Race, and the New Frontier: American Exceptionalism, Imperial Multiculturalism, and the Global Security State." *Identities* 17 (6): 613–640.

———. 2010c. "The Deportation Regime: Sovereignty, Space, and the Freedom of Movement." In *The Deportation Regime: Sovereignty, Space, and the Freedom of Movement*, ed. Nicholas De Genova and Nathalie Peutz, 33–65. Durham, NC: Duke University Press.

De Genova, Nicholas, and Ana Y. Ramos-Zayas. 2003. *Latino Crossings: Mexicans, Puerto Ricans, and the Politics of Race and Citizenship*. New York: Routledge.

de la Garza, Rodolfo, Angelo Falcon, and F. Chris Garcia. 1996. "Will the Real Americans Please Stand Up: Anglo and Mexican-American Support of Core American Political Values." *American Journal of Political Science* 40 (2): 335–351.

De León, Jason. 2015. *The Land of Open Graves: Living and Dying on the Migrant Trail*. Berkeley: University of California Press.

Délano, Alexandra. 2006. "De la 'no intervención' a la institucionalización: La evolución de las relaciones Estado-Diáspora en el caso mexicano." In *Relaciones Estado-Diáspora: La perspectiva de América Latina y el Caribe, Tomo II*, ed. Carlos González Gutiérrez, 145–189. México: Miguel Ángel Purrúa.

———. 2010. "Immigrant Integration vs. Transnational Ties? The Role of the Sending State." *Migration Politics* 77 (1): 237–268.

———. 2011. *Mexico and its Diaspora in the United States: Policies of Emigration Since 1848*. Cambridge: Cambridge University Press.

Delgado Wise, Raul, and Humberto Márquez Covarrubias. 2006. "Migración, Políticas Públicas y Desarrollo en México: Problemáticas y Desafíos." In *Relaciones Estado-Diáspora: La Perspectiva de América Latina y el Caribe, Tomo II*, ed. Carlos González Gutiérrez, 45–66. México: Miguel Ángel Purrúa.

DeSipio, Louis. 1996. "Making Citizens or Good Citizens? Naturalization as a Predictor of Organizational and Electoral Behavior Among Latino Immigrants." *Hispanic Journal of Behavioral Sciences* 18: 194–213.

———. 2006. "Transnational Politics and Civic Engagement: Do Home-Country Political Ties Limit Latino Immigrant Pursuit of U.S. Civic Engagement and Citizenship?" In *Transforming Politics, Transforming America: The Political and Civic Incorporation of Immigrants in the United States*, ed. Taeku Lee, S. Karthick Ramakrishnan, and Ricardo Ramírez, 106–126. Charlottesville: University of Virginia Press.

DeSipio, Louis, and Adrian Pantoja. 2007. "Puerto Rican Exceptionalism? A Comparative Analysis of Transnational Ties Among Puerto Rican, Mexican, Salvadoran and Dominican Migrants." In *Latino Politics: Identity, Mobilization and Representation*, ed. Rodolfo Espino, David Leal, and Kenneth Meier, 104–120. Charlottesville: University of Virginia Press.

Duquette-Rury, Lauren. 2014. "Collective Remittances and Transnational Coproduction: The 3x1 Program for Migrants and Household Access to Public Goods in Mexico." *Studies in Comparative International Development* 49 (1): 112–139.

Félix, Adrián. 2008. "New Americans or Diasporic Nationalists? Mexican Migrant Responses to Naturalization and Implications for Political Participation." *American Quarterly* 60 (3): 601–624.

———. 2011. "Posthumous Transnationalism: Postmortem Repatriation from the United States to Mexico." *Latin America Research Review* 46 (3): 157–179.

———. 2013. "Dreams of Citizenship, Naturalization Nightmare: New Naturalization Norms Needed." University of California Berkeley: Center for Latino Policy Research.

Fitzgerald, David. 2000. *Negotiating Extra-Territorial Citizenship: Mexican Migration and the Transnational Politics of Community*. La Jolla: Center for Comparative Immigration Studies, University of California, San Diego.

———. 2010. *A Nation of Emigrants: How Mexico Manages its Migration*. Berkeley: University of California Press.

Fox, Jonathan. 1994. "The Difficult Transition from Clientelism to Citizenship: Lessons from Mexico." *World Politics* 46 (2): 151–184.

———. 2005. "Unpacking 'Transnational Citizenship.'" *Annual Review of Political Science* 8: 171–201.

———. 2005. "Repensar lo Rural Ante la Globalización: La Sociedad Civil Migrante." *Migración y Desarrollo* 5 (2): 35–58.

———. 2006. "Reframing Mexican Migration as a Multi-Ethnic Process." *Latino Studies* 4 (1): 39–61.

———. 2007. *Accountability Politics: Power and Voice in Rural Mexico*. Oxford: Oxford University Press.

Fox, Jonathan, and Xochitl Bada. 2008. "Migrant Organization and Hometown Impacts in Rural Mexico." *Journal of Agrarian Change* 8 (2): 435–461.

———. 2011. "Migrant Civic Engagement." In *Rallying for Immigrant Rights: The Fight For Inclusion in 21st Century America*, ed. Kim Voss and Irene Bloemraad, 142–160. Berkeley: University of California Press.

Fregoso, Rosa-Linda. 2009. "Witnessing and the Poetics of Corporality." *KALFOU* 1 (1): 8–20.

Fregoso, Rosa-Linda, and Cynthia Bejarano. 2010. "Introduction: A Cartography of Feminicide in the Américas." In *Terrorizing Women: Feminicide in the Américas*, ed. Rosa-Linda Fregoso and Cynthia Bejarano, 1–42. Durham, NC: Duke University Press.

Friedmann Marquardt, Marie, Timothy Steigenga, Philip Williams, and Manuel Vásquez. 2011. *Living "Illegal": The Human Face of Unauthorized Immigration*. New York: The New Press.

Garcia-Acevedo, Maria Rosa. 2003. "Politics Across Borders: Mexico's Policies Toward Mexicans in the United States." *Journal of the Southwest* 45 (4): 533–555.

García Bedolla, Lisa. 2009. *Latino Politics*. Cambridge: Polity Press.

García-Ortega, Martha, and Eustaquio Celestino-Solís. "El Otro Viaje: Muerte y Retorno Entre Los Migrantes Nahuas de México." *LiminaR: Estudios Sociales y Humanísticos* 13 (1): 41–55.

Gerber, Marisa. 2011. "Lupe Gomez is a Triple Player." *OC Weekly*, August, 4, front cover.

Goldring, Luin. 1996. "Gendered Memory: Constructions of Rurality Among Mexican Transnational Migrants." In *Creating the Countryside: The Politics of Rural and Environmental Discourse*, ed. E. Melanie DuPuis and Peter Vandergeest, 303–329. Philadelphia: Temple University Press.

———. 2002. "The Mexican State and Transmigrant Organizations: Negotiating the Boundaries of Membership and Participation." *Latin American Research Review* 37 (3): 55–99.

Gonzales, Alfonso. 2009. "The 2006 Mega Marchas in Greater Los Angeles: The Counter-Hegemonic Moment and the Future of El Migrante Struggle." *Latino Studies* 7 (1):30–59.

———. 2013. *Reform Without Justice: Latino Migrant Politics and the Homeland Security State*. New York: Oxford University Press.

———. 2016. "Neoliberalism, the Homeland Security State, and the Authoritarian Turn." *Latino Studies* 14 (1): 80–98.

González, Gilbert. 1999. *Mexican Consuls and Labor Organizing: Imperial Politics in the American Southwest*. Austin: University of Texas Press.

González Gutiérrez, Carlos. 2009. "The Institute of Mexicans Abroad: Dialogues, Diasporas, and Empowerment." In *Closing the Distance: How Governments Strengthen Ties with their Diasporas*, ed. Dovelyn Rannveig Mendoza, 87–98. Washington, DC: Migration Policy Institute.

Gordon, Susan. 2007. "Integrating Immigrants: Morality and Loyalty in U.S. Naturalization Practice." *Citizenship Studies* 11 (4): 367–382.

Guarnizo, Luis Eduardo, and Luz Marina Diaz. 1999. "Transnational Migration: A View From Colombia." *Ethnic and Racial Studies* 22 (2): 397–421.

Guidry, John A., and Mark Q. Sawyer. 2003. "Contentious Pluralism: The Public Sphere and Democracy." *Perspectives on Politics* 1 (2): 273–289.

Gutiérrez, David G. 1995. *Walls and Mirrors: Mexican Americans, Mexican Immigrants, and the Politics of Ethnicity*. Berkeley: University of California Press.

Hardy-Fanta, Carol. 1993. *Latina Politics, Latino Politics: Gender, Culture, and Political Participation in Boston*. Philadelphia: Temple University Press.

Hayes-Bautista, David et al. 2002. "An Anomaly within the Latino Epidemiological Paradox: The Latino Adolescent Male Mortality Peak." *Archives of Pediatrics and Adolescent Medicine* 156 (2): 480–484.

Hinojosa, Magda. 2008. "*¿Más Mujeres?* Mexico's Mixed-Member Electoral System." In *Women and Legislative Representation: Electoral Systems, Political Parties, and Sex Quotas*, ed. Manon Tremblay, 177–189. New York: Palgrave Macmillan.

Hiskey, Jonathan and Damarys Canache. 2005. "The Demise of One-Party Politics in Mexican Municipal Elections." *British Journal of Political Science* 35 (2): 257–284.

Hondagneu-Sotelo, Pierrette. 1994. *Gendered Transitions: Mexican Experiences of Immigration*. Berkeley: University of California Press.

Hopkins, Daniel. 2011. "Translating into Votes: The Electoral Impacts of Spanish-language Ballots." *American Journal of Political Science* 55 (4): 813–829.

Htun, Mala, and Juan Pablo Ossa. 2013. "Political Inclusion of Marginalized Groups: Indigenous Reservations and Gender Parity in Bolivia." *Politics, Groups, and Identities* 1 (1): 4–25.

Hyde, Alan, Ray A. Mateo, and Bridgit Cusato-Rosa. 2013. "Why Don't They Naturalize? Voices from the Dominican Community." *Latino Studies* 11 (3): 313–340.

Inda, Jonathan X. 2007. "The Value of Immigrant Life." In *Women and Migration in the U.S.-Mexico Borderlands: A Reader*, ed. Denise A. Segura and Patricia Zavella, 134–160. Durham, NC: Duke University Press.

Iskander, Natasha. 2010. *Creative State: Forty Years of Migration and Development Policy in Morocco and Mexico.* Ithaca NY: Cornell University Press.

Itzigsohn, Jose, and Siliva Saucedo. 2002. "Immigrant Incorporation and Sociocultural Transnationalism." *International Migration Review* 36 (3): 766–98.

Johnston, Paul. 2004. "The Blossoming of Transnational Citizenship: A California Town Defends Indigenous Immigrants." In *Indigenous Mexican Migrants in the United States*, ed. Jonathan Fox and Gaspar Rivera-Salgado, 385–399. La Jolla, California: Center for US-Mexican Studies.

Jones-Correa, Michael. 1998. *Between Two Nations: The Political Predicament of Latinos in New York City.* Ithaca, NY: Cornell University Press.

———. 2001. "Under Two Flags: Dual Nationality in Latin America and Its Consequences on Naturalization in the United States." *International Migration Review* 35 (4): 997–1029.

Katz, Richard, and Peter Mair. 2009. "The Cartel Party Thesis: A Restatement." *Perspectives on Politics* 7 (4): 753–766.

Keck, Margaret E., and Kathryn Sikkink. 1998. *Activists Beyond Borders: Advocacy Networks in International Politics.* Ithaca, NY: Cornell University Press.

Kun, Josh. 2005. *Audiotopia: Music, Race, and America.* Berkeley: University of California Press.

Laguerre, Michel S. 1999. "State, Diaspora, and Transnational Politics: Haiti Reconceptualised." *Millennium: Journal of International Studies* 28 (3): 633–651.

Lestage, Françoise. 2008. "Apuntes Relativos a la Repatriación de los Cuerpos de los Mexicanos Fallecidos en Estados Unidos." *Migraciones Internacionales* 4 (4): 209–220.

Levitt, Peggy. 2001. *The Transnational Villagers.* Berkeley: University of California Press.

Lomnitz, Claudio. 2005. *Death and the Idea of Mexico.* New York: Zone Books.

———. 2016. *El Regreso del Camarada Ricardo Flores Magón.* México, D.F.: Ediciones Era.

López, Sarah Lynn. 2015. *The Remittance Landscape: Spaces of Migration in Rural Mexico and Urban USA.* Chicago: University of Chicago Press.

López Velarde, Ramón. 2009. *La Suave Patria y Otros Poemas.* México, D.F.: Fondo de Cultura Económica.

Mampilly, Zachariah C. 2011. *Rebel Rulers: Insurgent Governance and Civilian Life During War.* Ithaca, NY: Cornell University Press.

Márquez, John D. 2012. "Latinos as the 'Living Dead': Raciality, Expendability, and Border Militarization." *Latino Studies* 10 (4): 473–498.

Martínez-Saldaña, Jesús, and Raul Ross Pineda. 2002. "Suffrage for Mexicans Residing Abroad." In *Cross-Border Dialogues: U.S.-Mexico Social Movement Networking*, ed. David Brooks and Jonathan Fox, 275–292. La Jolla, California: Center for US-Mexican Studies.

McCann, James A., Wayne A. Cornelius, and David L. Leal. 2006. "Mexico's 2006 *Voto Remoto* and the Potential for Transnational Civic Engagement among Mexican Expatriates." Presented at the Annual Meeting of the American Political Science Association, Philadelphia.

Menchaca, Martha. 2011. *Naturalizing Mexican Immigrants: A Texas History.* Austin: University of Texas Press.

———. 2016. *The Politics of Dependency: US Reliance on Mexican Oil and Farm Labor.* Austin: University of Texas Press.

Menjívar, Cecilia. 2000. *Fragmented Ties: Salvadoran Immigrant Networks in America.* Berkeley: University of California Press.

Michelson, Melissa, and Amalia Pallares. 2001. "The Politicization of Chicago Mexican Americans: Naturalization, the Vote, and Perceptions of Discrimination." *Aztlán* 26 (2): 63–85.

Mines, Richard. 1981. "Developing a Community Tradition of Migration to the United States: A Field Study of Rural Zacatecas, Mexico, and California Settlement Areas." La Jolla: Program in United States-Mexican Studies, University of California, San Diego.

Moctezuma Longoria, Miguel. 2003. "The Migrant Club El Remolino: A Bi-national Community Experience." In *Confronting Globalization: Economic Integration and Popular Resistance in Mexico*, ed. Timothy Wise, Hilda Salazar, and Laura Carlsen, 195–210. West Hartford, CT: Kumarian Press.

———. 2011. *La Transnacionalidad de los sujetos: Dimensiones, Metodologías y Prácticas Convergentes de los Migrantes Mexicanos en Estados Unidos.* Zacatecas: Universidad Autónoma de Zacatecas.

Molina, Natalia. 2010. "'In A Race All Their Own': The Quest to Make Mexicans Ineligible for U.S. Citizenship." *Pacific Historical Review* 79 (2): 167–201.

Moran-Taylor, Michelle, and Cecilia Menjívar. 2005. "Unpacking Longings to Return: Guatemalans and Salvadorans in Phoenix, Arizona." *International Migration* 43 (4): 91–119.

Morton, Adam D. *Revolution and State in Modern Mexico: The Political Economy of Uneven Development.* New York: Rowman and Littlefield.

Nájera-Ramírez, Olga. 2002. "Haciendo Patria: The Charreada and the Formation of a Mexican Transnational Identity." In *Transnational Latina/o Communities: Politics, Processes, and Cultures*, ed. Carlos Vélez-Ibáñez and Anna Sampaio, 167–180. Lanham, MD: Rowman and Littlefield.

Nichols, Sandra. 2006. *Santos, duraznos y vino: Migrantes mexicanos y la transformación de Los Haro, Zacatecas, y Napa, California.* Zacatecas: Universidad Autónoma de Zacatecas.

Ong, Paul, and Joanna Lee. 2007. "Defensive Naturalization and Anti-Immigrant Sentiment: Chinese Immigrants in Three Primate Metropolises." Paper presented at Immigration and Politics Workshop. University of California, Los Angeles.

Özler, İlgü Ş. 2009. "Out of the Plaza and into the Office: Social Movement Leaders in the PRD." *Mexican Studies/Estudios Mexicanos* 25 (1): 125–154.

Padilla, Tanalís. 2008. *Rural Resistance in the Land of Zapata: The Jaramillista Movement and the Myth of the Pax Priísta, 1940-1962*. Durham NC: Duke University Press.

Paley, Dawn. 2014. *Drug War Capitalism*. Oakland, CA: AK Press.

Pantoja, Adrian. 2005. "Transnational Ties and Immigrant Political Incorporation: The Case of Dominicans in Washington Heights, New York." *International Migration* 43 (4): 123–146.

Pantoja, Adrian, and Sarah Gershon. 2006. "Political Orientations and Naturalization among Latino and Latina Immigrants." *Social Science Quarterly* 87 (5): 247–263.

Pantoja, Adrian, Ricardo Ramírez, and Gary M. Segura. 2001. "Citizens by Choice, Voters by Necessity: Patterns of Political Mobilization by Naturalized Latinos." *Political Research Quarterly* 54 (4): 729–750.

Pantoja, Adrian, and Gary Segura. 2003. "Fear and Loathing in California: Contextual Threat and Political Sophistication Among Latino Voters." *Political Behavior* 25 (3): 265–286.

Paredes, Américo. 1958. *With His Pistol in His Hand: A Border Ballad and Its Hero*. Austin: University of Texas Press.

Pastor, Manuel. and Carol Wise. 2005. "The Lost Sexenio: Vicente Fox and the New Politics of Economic Reform in Mexico." *Latin American Politics & Society* 47 (4): 135–160.

Paz, Octavio. 1997. *El laberinto de la soledad y otras obras*. New York: Penguin Books.

Pensado, Jaime. 2013. *Rebel Mexico: Student Unrest and Authoritarian Political Culture during the Long Sixties*. Palo Alto, CA: Stanford University Press.

Pérez-Armendáriz, Clarisa, and David Crow. 2010. "Do Migrants Remit Democracy? International Migration, Political Beliefs, and Behavior in Mexico." *Comparative Political Studies* 43 (1): 119–148.

Plascencia, Luis. 2012. *Disenchanting Citizenship: Mexican Migrants and the Boundaries of Belonging*. New Brunswick, NJ: Rutgers University Press.

Portes, Alejandro, and Rubén Rumbaut. 1996. *Immigrant America: A Portrait*. Berkeley: University of California Press.

Portes, Alejandro, Cristina Escobar, and Renelinda Arana. 2009. "Divided or Convergent Loyalties? The Political Incorporation Process of Latin American Immigrants in the United States." *International Journal of Comparative Sociology* 50 (2): 103–136.

Quinones, Sam. 2001. *True Tales of Another Mexico: The Lynch Mob, the Popsicle Kings, Chalino, and the Bronx*. Albuquerque: University of New Mexico Press.

———. 2004. "Riding on Ropes and Dreams." *Los Angeles Times*, September 4, col. 1.

———. 2008. *Antonio's Gun and Delfino's Dream: True Tales of Mexican Migration*. Albuquerque: University of New Mexico Press.

———. 2011. "A Southland Tragedia." *Los Angeles Times*, July 20, col. 1.

———. 2015. *Dreamland: The True Tale of America's Opiate Epidemic.* New York: Bloomsbury Press.

Ramírez, Ricardo. 2013. *Mobilizing Opportunities: The Evolving Latino Electorate and the Future of American Politics.* Charlottesville: University of Virginia Press.

Ramírez, Ricardo, and Adrián Félix. 2011. "Transnational Stakeholders: Latin American Migrant Transnationalism and Civic Engagement in the United States." *Harvard Journal of Hispanic Policy* 23: 59–82.

Ramírez, Hernán, and Pierrette Hondagneu-Sotelo. 2009. "Mexican Immigrant Gardeners: Entrepreneurs or Exploited Workers?" *Social Problems* 56 (1): 70–88.

Robinson, William I. 2006. "'Aqui estamos y no nos vamos!' Global Capital and Immigrant Rights." *Race & Class* 48 (2): 77–91.

Rocco, Raymond. 2014. *Transforming Citizenship: Democracy, Membership, and Belonging in Latino Communities.* East Lansing: Michigan State University Press.

Rodriguez, Robyn. 2013. "Beyond Citizenship: Emergent Forms of Political Subjectivity Amongst Migrants." *Identities* 20 (6): 738–754.

Rogers, Reuel. 2006. *Afro-Caribbean Immigrants and the Politics of Incorporation: Ethnicity, Exception, or Exit.* Cambridge: Cambridge University Press.

Rosas, Ana E. 2014. *Abrazando el Espíritu: Bracero Families Confront the US-Mexico Border.* Berkeley: University of California Press.

Rosas, Gilberto. 2006. "The Thickening Borderlands: Diffused Exceptionality and 'Immigrant' Social Struggles during the 'War on Terror.'" *Cultural Dynamics* 18 (3): 335–349.

Rouse, Roger. 1991. "Mexican Migration and the Social Space of Postmodernism." *Diaspora* 1 (1): 8–23.

———. 1992. "Making Sense of Settlement: Class Transformation, Cultural Struggle and Transnationalism among Mexican Migrants in the United States." *Annals of the New York Academy of Sciences* 645: 25–52.

———. 1995. "Questions of Identity: Personhood and collectivity in transnational migration to the United States." *Critique of Anthropology* 15 (4): 351–380.

Ruiz Alonso, Ileana Beatriz, Milton Jovanni Sarria, and Arturo Severo Vázquez. 2007. "Migration and Political Participation." In *Mayan Journeys: The New Migration from Yucatán to the United States*, ed. Wayne Cornelius, David Fitzgerald, and Pedro Lewin Fischer, 233–247. La Jolla: Center for Comparative Immigration Studies, University of California, San Diego.

Sampaio, Anna. 2015. *Terrorizing Latina/o Immigrants: Race, Gender, and Immigration Politics in the Age of Security.* Philadelphia: Temple University Press.

Sánchez, George J. 1984. "'Go After the Women': Americanization and the Mexican Immigrant Woman, 1915-1929." Stanford Center for Chicano Research.

———. 1993. *Becoming Mexican American: Ethnicity, Culture, and Identity in Chicano Los Angeles, 1900–1945.* New York: Oxford University Press.

Schmidt Camacho, Alicia. 2008. *Migrant Imaginaries: Latino Cultural Politics in the U.S-Mexico Borderlands.* New York: New York University Press.

Serpell, Namwali. 2017. "Becoming an American Citizen in the Age of Trump." *Los Angeles Times*, September 21.

Shipper, Apichai W. 2008. *Fighting for Foreigners: Immigration and Its Impact on Japanese Democracy*. Ithaca: Cornell University Press.

Smith, Michael Peter, and Matt Bakker. 2005. "The Transnational Politics of the Tomato King: Meaning and Impact." *Global Networks* 5 (2): 129–146.

———. 2008. *Citizenship Across Borders: The Political Transnationalism of* El Migrante. Ithaca, NY: Cornell University Press.

Smith, Robert C. 2006. *Mexican New York: Transnational Lives of New Immigrants*. Berkeley: University of California Press.

———. 2008. "Contradictions of Diasporic Institutionalization in Mexican Politics: The 2006 Migrant Vote and Other Forms of Inclusion and Control." *Ethnic and Racial Studies* 31 (4): 708–741.

Snyder, Richard. 2001. "Scaling Down: The Subnational Comparative Method." *Studies in Comparative International Development*, 36 (1): 93–110.

Stamper Balistreri, Kelly and Jennifer Van Hook. 2004. "The More Things Change the More They Stay the Same: Mexican Naturalization before and after Welfare Reform." *International Migration Review* 38 (1): 113–130.

Staton, Jeffrey K., Robert Jackson, and Damarys Canache. 2007. "Dual Nationality Among Latinos: What Are the Implications for Political Connectedness?" *Journal of Politics* 69 (2): 470–482.

Steigenga, Timothy, and Philip Williams. 2009. "Transnationalism and Collective Action among Guatemalan and Mexican Immigrants in Two Florida Communities." In *A Place to Be: Brazilian, Guatemalan, and Mexican Immigrants in Florida's New Destinations*, ed. Philip Williams, Timothy Steigenga, and Manuel Vásquez, 103–127. New Brunswick, NJ: Rutgers University Press.

Tomlinson, Barbara, and George Lipsitz. 2013. "American Studies as Accompaniment." *American Quarterly* 65 (1): 1–30.

Torres, Gabriela. 2005. "Bloody Deeds/Hechos Sangrientos: Reading Guatemala's Record of Political Violence in Cadaver Reports." In *When States Kill: Latin America, the U.S., and Technologies of Terror*, ed. Cecilia Menjívar and Néstor Rodríguez, 143–169. Austin: University of Texas Press.

Trejo, Guillermo. 2012. *Popular Movements in Autocracies: Religion, Repression, and Indigenous Collective Action in Mexico*. Cambridge: Cambridge University Press.

———. 2014. "The Ballot and the Street: An Electoral Theory of Social Protest in Autocracies." *Perspectives on Politics* 12 (2): 332–352.

Valerio-Jiménez, Omar S. 2002. "Neglected Citizens and Willing Traders: The Villas del Norte (Tamaulipas) in Mexico's Northern Borderlands, 1749-1846." *Mexican Studies/Estudios Mexicanos* 18 (2): 251–296.

Verba, Sidney, Kay Lehman Schlozman, and Henry E. Brady. 1995. *Voice and Equality: Civic Volunteerism in American Politics*. Cambridge, MA: Harvard University Press.

Viramontes, Celia. 2008. "Civic Engagement Across Borders: Mexicans in Southern California." In *Civic Hopes and Political Realities: Immigrants, Community Organizations, and Political Engagement*, ed. Karthick Ramakrishnan and Irene Bloemraad, 351–381. New York: Russell Sage Foundation.

Vital, Rosario. "Coming Out and Making History: Latino Immigrant Civic Participation in San Jose." Washington, DC: Woodrow Wilson International Center for Scholars.

Waldinger, Roger. 2003. "Foreigners Transformed: International Migration and the Remaking of a Divided People." *Diaspora* 12 (2): 247–272.

———. 2007a. "Transforming Foreigners into Americans." In *The New Americans: A Guide to Immigration Since 1965*, ed. Mary C. Waters and Reed Ueda, 137–148. Cambridge, MA: Harvard University Press.

———. 2007b. "The Bounded Community: Turning Foreigners into Americans in Twenty-first Century L.A." *Ethnic and Racial Studies* 30 (3): 341–374.

———. 2008. "Between 'Here' and 'There': Immigrant Cross-border Activities and Loyalties." *International Migration Review* 42 (1): 3–29.

———. 2009. "Connectivity and Collectivity: Immigrant Involvement in Homeland Politics." Presented at the Politics of Race, Ethnicity and Immigration Colloquium, Berkeley, California.

———. 2015. *The Cross-Border Connection: Immigrants, Emigrants, and Their Homelands*. Cambridge: Harvard University Press.

Waldinger, Roger and David Fitzgerald. 2004. "Transnationalism in Question." *American Journal of Sociology* 109 (5): 1177–1195.

Wals, Sergio C. 2010. "Does What Happens in Los Mochis Stay in Los Mochis? Explaining Postmigration Political Behavior." *Political Research Quarterly* 20 (10): 1–12.

Waslin, Michele. 2005. "Latino Naturalization and the Federal Government's Response." Unpublished manuscript. National Council of La Raza.

Wong, Janelle. 2006. *Democracy's Promise: Immigrants & American Civic Institutions*. Ann Arbor: University of Michigan Press.

Zavella, Patricia. 2011. *I'm Neither Here Nor There: Mexicans' Quotidian Struggles with Migration and Poverty*. Durham, NC: Duke University Press.

Zepeda-Millán, Chris. 2014. "Weapons of the (Not So) Weak: Immigrant Mass Mobilization in the US South." *Critical Sociology* 1–19.

———. 2017. *Latino Mass Mobilization: Immigration, Racialization, and Activism*. Cambridge: Cambridge University Press.

Index